ARTIFICIAL INTELLIGENCE IN CONTRACT FORMATION

This book explores how artificial intelligence is reshaping the foundations of contract formation under English contract law.

As AI systems take on critical roles in forming agreements, traditional legal principles rooted in human decision-making are being challenged. The book introduces the concept of the 'meeting of the algorithms' as a modern alternative to the conventional 'meeting of the minds', emphasising how AI-driven contracts differ from human-based ones.

Focusing on algorithmic contracting where both parties operate AI systems – particularly those based on machine learning – the book challenges the adequacy of traditional legal doctrines and terminology. It provides a structured analysis of the legal, conceptual and doctrinal challenges raised by contracts formed without human intervention at the point of agreement.

The book proposes a new legal framework that accommodates algorithmic systems as communication and decision-making tools. It redefines consent, examines the attribution of knowledge and intention, and identifies the legal moment of formation in automated contracting environments. It shows how AI-driven contracting is forcing contract law to evolve without relying on fictional agency constructs or debates around legal personhood.

*Artificial Intelligence in Contract Formation* will appeal to researchers of contract law, technology law and private law theory, as well as legal practitioners interested in AI governance and legal innovation. It contributes to ongoing debates on AI and law, and offers a roadmap for integrating algorithmic transactions into the mainstream of contract doctrine.

# Artificial Intelligence in Contract Formation

*Algorithmic Contracting and Doctrinal Challenges in English Law*

María L Mena-Durán

•HART•
OXFORD • LONDON • NEW YORK • NEW DELHI • SYDNEY

HART PUBLISHING
Bloomsbury Publishing Plc
Kemp House, Chawley Park, Cumnor Hill, Oxford, OX2 9PH, UK
1385 Broadway, New York, NY 10018, USA
Bloomsbury Publishing Ireland Limited, 29 Earlsfort Terrace, Dublin 2, D02 AY28, Ireland

HART PUBLISHING, the Hart/Stag logo, BLOOMSBURY and the Diana logo are trademarks of Bloomsbury Publishing Plc
First published in Great Britain 2026

1



A catalogue record for this book is available from the British Library.

A catalogue record for this book is available from the Library of Congress.

ISBN: HB: 978-1-50999-272-0
ePDF: 978-1-50999-274-4
ePub: 978-1-50999-273-7

Typeset by Lumina Datamatics Ltd

For product safety related questions contact productsafety@bloomsbury.com

To find out more about our authors and books visit www.hartpublishing.co.uk. Here you will find extracts, author information, details of forthcoming events and the option to sign up for our newsletters.

*To my husband, Juan: thank you for your patience, your constant encouragement, and for challenging me to step beyond what felt safe. This book carries your imprint in ways you may not even see.*

*To my children, María and Nico: you give me direction. You make me want to exceed my own limits and live the values I hope to pass on to you.*

## CONTENTS

# TABLE OF CASES

# TABLE OF STATUTES AND STATUTORY INSTRUMENTS

## United Kingdom



## European Union Legislation

## Spain



## United Nations Documents



## United States of America

# 1

# Algorithmic Contracts – What is New that Makes it Different Now?

## I. Introduction

'[W]hat is new and different about algorithmic contracts is [that,] in the process of forming an algorithmic contract, computer programs step into decision-making roles previously performed by humans.'[1] As such, algorithmic contracts can be understood as an 'innovative contractual technology'.[2] They are not, however, 'an exceptional technology';[3] rather their novelty lies in the relocation of formation/relevant choices from the human actor to the deployed system, which warrants closer doctrinal analysis.

Contract formation doctrine assumes that assent is manifested through human acts and that both the relevant knowledge and the timing of agreement can be attributed to an identifiable person. Algorithmic contracting unsettles those assumptions because the legally operative steps – deciding whether to contract, generating terms, communicating an offer, and matching acceptance – may be produced and executed at system level without a contemporaneous human choice. The central pressure point is therefore the requirement of agreement: when, if at all, can system generated communications count as a party's objective manifestation of assent, and at what moment should the contract be treated as formed?

This book argues that orthodox formation concepts can still do the work, but only if the analysis makes explicit which human commitments anchor the system's outputs. The relevant 'meeting' is the convergence of two decision-and-communication processes that are attributable to their respective operators, so

[1] LH Scholz, 'Algorithms and Contract Law' in W Barfield (ed), *The Cambridge Handbook of The Law of Algorithms* (Cambridge University Press, 2020) 141, 141.

[2] The term 'innovative contractual technology' is borrowed from Kevin E Davis' work 'Contracts as Technology' in which he analyses the concept of innovation both from the perspective of contractual documents and contract law. See KE Davis, 'Contracts as Technology' (1950) 88 *New York University Law Review* 83, 83–127.

[3] Carla L Reyes refers to the term 'exceptional technology' in the sense given by Calo 'as a technology that, when introduced into mainstream society, "requires a systematic change to the law or legal institutions in order to reproduce, or if necessary, displace an existing balance of values"'. See R Calo in CL Reyes, 'A Unified Theory of Code-Connected Contracts' (2021) 46 *Journal of Corporation Law* 981, 998.

that consent is located in: (i) the operator's structured delegation of contracting choices to the system; and (ii) the objective meaning of the system's outward communications.

The method is a functional deconstruction of the system's dual role – decision-making and communication – each with internal and external phases. That framework is then used to locate formation, attribute knowledge, and test whether system-level convergence can be translated into a defensible account of a 'meeting of the minds'.

Algorithmic contracts first emerged within the domain of high-frequency trading (HFT),[4] where automated systems execute transactions at speed and scale. Their significance, however, is not confined to finance. Comparable forms of automated contracting now operate across a range of industries and transaction types, which brings the inquiry squarely into general contract law. The question is not whether automation can be accommodated in principle, but how contract doctrine should identify formation, enforceability, and accountability when contracting steps are delegated to systems across diverse sectors.

It is a fact that '[t]echnology, as always, is deployed before society had the opportunity to come to terms with it'.[5] Equally true is that '[l]aw sails as tankers: steadily and with difficulty in changing direction'.[6] For some time now, it has been observed that '[c]omputers are programmed to trade without human oversight, to respond to market information in real-time and to enter into transactions when certain pre-set conditions are met'.[7] However, the current landscape demands a closer examination of how algorithmic contracts are integrated into the framework of contract law. This exploration is crucial as society experiences a rapid increase in exposure to artificial intelligence (AI). Indeed, '[a]lgorithmic agents, just like any other technology, are [already] embedded in the existing economic, social, and political conditions'.[8] Concurrently, commercial practices are evolving into a landscape where data accumulation and sharing on data markets drive increased efficiency of algorithmic recommendations while simultaneously reducing the costs of personalisation.[9]

When Lauren Scholz published *Algorithmic Contracts* in 2017, the use of algorithms for contracting purposes was not a novel practice.[10] Rather, her

[4] High-frequency trading is a subspecies of algorithmic trading characterised by the speed with which market data is analysed. See D Busch, 'MiFID II: Regulating High Frequency Trading, Other Forms of Algorithmic Trading and Direct Electronic Market Access' (2016) 10 *Law and Financial Markets Review* 72, 74.

[5] B Bodo et al, 'Tackling the Algorithmic Control Crisis: The Technical, Legal, and Ethical Challenges of Research into Algorithmic Agents' (2017) 19 *Yale Journal of Law & Technology* 133, 136.

[6] F de Elizalde, Algorithms and Law (2022) 37 *Prometheus* 385, 385.

[7] E Mik, 'The Resilience of Contract Law in Light of Technological Change' M Furmston (ed), *The Future of the Law of Contract* (Routledge, 2020) 112, 115.

[8] Bodo et al (n 5) 136.

[9] ibid.

[10] LH Scholz, 'Algorithmic Contracts' (2017) *Stanford Technology Law Review* 128, 128–69.

contribution was to name and systematise an existing mode of contracting already visible in domains such as high-frequency trading and algorithmically assisted dynamic pricing.[11] Scholz's intervention also sits within a longer line of commentary on 'intelligent' contracting technologies. As early as 1996, Curtis Karnow predicted that intelligent technology would soon 'allow some commercial transactions to take place without any need for human traders to review, or even be aware of, particular transactions'.[12] In 1999, Jean-Francois Lerouge similarly described 'electronic agents' as intelligent software capable of searching for alternatives and proposing transactions responsive to a user's demand.[13]

In general, '[a]lgorithmic contracts are contracts in which one or more parties use an algorithm to determine whether to be bound or how to be bound'.[14] In a broader context, '"algorithmic decision-making" refers to the use of algorithmically generated knowledge systems to execute or inform decisions'.[15] The distinctive feature, for present purposes, is that parties may delegate to a system both the pre-contract evaluation that would ordinarily precede assent and, in some settings, the selection or adjustment of contractual terms in light of data the system processes. The literature describes such systems in different ways – often as 'artificial agents' or[16] 'software agents'[17] – to capture the fact that they can operate both before and during formation.[18] This delegation can generate doctrinal friction because, as Teubner observes, '[i]n the field of contract law, legal doctrine firmly maintains that only natural persons are in a position to make legally binding declarations'.[19]

[11] See above n 4; Scholz (n 10) 143 (dynamic pricing based on algorithmic suggestion).

[12] Karnow in IR Kerr, 'Ensuring the Success of Contract Formation in Agent-Mediated Electronic Commerce' (2001) 1 *Electronic Commerce Research* 183, 184.

[13] J-F Lerouge, 'The Use of Electronic Agents Questioned Under Contractual Law: Suggested Solutions on a European and American Level' (1999) 18 *John Marshall Journal of Computer & Information Law* 403, 405.

[14] Scholz (n 10) 134.

[15] K Yeung and M Lodge, 'Algorithmic Regulation: An Introduction' in K Yeung and M Lodge (eds), *Algorithmic Regulation* (Oxford University Press, 2019) 5.

[16] See, eg, Scholz (n 10) 135; S Chopra and LF White, 'Artificial Agents and the Contracting Problem: A Solution Via an Agency Analysis' (2009) 2009 *University of Illinois Journal of Law, Technology & Policy* 363, 363.

[17] See, eg, G Teubner, 'Digitale Rechtssubjekte? Zum Privatrechtlichen Status Autonomer Softwareagenten / Digital Personhood? The Status of Autonomous Software Agents in Private Law' (2018) 2018 *Ancilla Iuris* 35, 35–78; G Sartor, 'Cognitive Automata and the Law: Electronic Contracting and the Intentionality of Software Agents' (2009) 17 *Artificial Intelligence and Law* 253, 253–290.

[18] These systems are also described as 'intelligent autonomous contracting agents', 'artificially intelligent entities', 'robo assistants', or 'digital assistants'. See G Sartor, *Contracts Without Agreement, or Agreement by Artefacts?* (Academy of Sciences in Göttingen ed, Universitätsverlag Göttingen, 2020) 41, 41–6; Scholz (n 10) 133; P Treleaven, J Barnett and A Koshiyama, 'Algorithms: Law and Regulation' (2019) 52(2) *Computer* 32, 35; C Busch et al, *EU Consumer Law and Automated-Making (ADM): Is EU Consumer Ready for ADM?* (ELI Project on Guiding Principles and Model Rules on Algorithmic Contracts, 2023).

[19] Teubner (n 17) 38.

It may appear that a juncture has been reached at which a new theory is required, since 'commerce is, so to speak, largely conducted by means of a "conversation conducted entirely by machines"'.[20] Put differently, 'computers are no longer merely executing detailed pre-written instructions but are capable of arriving to dynamic solutions to problems based on patterns in data that humans might not be able to perceive'.[21] If so, the giving of consent through algorithmic systems may differ in both timing and content from familiar accounts of assent. The better starting point, however, is not theoretical rupture but doctrinal continuity: contract law has repeatedly adapted to changes in trading practices and communication media, and the task is to identify how existing formation concepts should be applied – carefully and purposively – when decision-making and communication are delegated to systems.[22]

The question that follows is 'why now?' The immediate answer is that algorithmic contracting is moving from bounded, specialist environments to mainstream commercial practice, while the systems involved increasingly rely on AI techniques that can generate outputs in ways that are not fully specified in advance. In that setting, it would be '"contrary to market expectation and potentially disruptive" if an agreement could not be reached in this way'.[23] Recent policy and legislative developments across major jurisdictions reflect the same sense of urgency: AI systems are now treated as a general-purpose technology whose deployment raises cross-sector questions of responsibility, transparency, and governance.[24] That regulatory attention does not resolve the private-law issues, but it signals that AI-enabled decision-making is no longer peripheral. It is therefore timely to ask how contract law should treat system-mediated assent and the moment of formation.

The remainder of this chapter clarifies the term 'algorithmic contracts', narrows the scope of the inquiry, and illustrates the phenomenon through selected use cases before turning to the reasons why English law offers a particularly revealing test case for the formation issues this book addresses.

[20] R Brownsword, 'Smart Transactional Technologies, Legal Disruption, and the Case of Network Contracts' in LA DiMatteo, M Cannarsa and C Poncibò (eds), *The Cambridge Handbook of Smart Contracts, Blockchain Technology and Digital Platforms* (Cambridge University Press 2020) 313, 313.

[21] Y Bathaee, 'The Artificial Intelligence Black Box and the Failure of Intent and Causation' (2018) 31 *Harvard Journal of Law & Technology* 889, 891.

[22] LA Di Matteo, 'Artificial Intelligence: The Promise of Disruption' in LA Di Matteo, C Poncibò and M Cannarsa (eds), *The Cambridge Handbook of Artificial Intelligence: Global Perspectives on Law and Ethics* (Cambridge University Press, 2022) 3, 10.

[23] Although framed in the context of smart contracts, the same point applies to algorithmic contracting today. See Law Commission, *Smart Legal Contracts: Advice to Government* (Law Com No 401, 2021).

[24] See *Artificial Intelligence (Regulation) Bill* [HL] (UK Parliament, Session 2024–26) (Private Member's Bill introduced in the House of Lords), proposing, inter alia, the establishment of an 'AI Authority'. For the EU, see Regulation (EU) 2024/1689 of the European Parliament and of the Council of 13 June 2024 laying down harmonised rules on artificial intelligence (Artificial Intelligence Act), [2024] OJ L2024/1689.

# II. Algorithmic Contracts

## A. Conceptualising Algorithmic Contracts

This study adopts the term 'algorithmic contracts' to describe agreements in which a contracting party deploys an algorithmic system to make formation-relevant choices – whether to contract and, if so, on what terms – and to communicate the results of those choices. In this sense, algorithmic contracts are those 'in which one or more parties use an algorithm to determine whether to be bound or how to be bound'.[25] The definition is concerned with contract formation, not merely with the automation of performance or the ex post completion of terms. The focus is therefore on systems that shape the path to agreement by evaluating inputs, selecting contractual responses, and communicating outcomes on a party's behalf.

The legal status of a party to a contract is acquired not only 'by giving one's assent to an agreement (…) but by undertaking an obligation or doing some other thing requested by the promisor as the price of acquiring the right to the obligation'.[26] The key is to determine under what conditions a party uses an algorithm to assent to or to assume the obligation, and whether the relationship between the party and the algorithm can be appropriately defined with the verb 'use'.

Scholz expands upon her definition and differentiates between two categories of algorithmic contracts. The distinction lies in whether the parties utilise the algorithm as a negotiator before contract formation, determining which terms to propose or agree upon, or, alternatively, if both parties consent to employ an algorithm after contract formation to act as a supplementary mechanism, filling in gaps within the agreement.[27] But she also distinguishes between what she refers to as 'mere tools' and 'artificial agents'.[28] In addition to classifying algorithms according to the roles that the algorithms perform within the contractual process, Scholz introduces a distinction between 'black-box' and 'clear-box' algorithms: 'black-box' algorithms are those whose inner workings or decision-making processes are complex or opaque, making it difficult to understand how they arrive at specific conclusions or decisions; in contrast, 'clear-box' algorithms are characterised by their transparency and explainability, allowing users to more easily understand and track their decision-making processes. This distinction reflects the potential importance of the explainability and transparency of algorithmic operations in the context of contractual agreements, although the degree of importance remains

[25] Scholz (n 10) 133.
[26] J Cartwright, *Contract Law* (Hart Publishing, 2016) 238.
[27] Scholz (n 10) 128.
[28] ibid 135.

a controversial question.[29] Nevertheless, '[w]hile it might indeed be difficult to explain what patterns in the data are being caught by the model of a machine learning algorithm, (…) the general principles and operational logics of these systems are very-well known. That's why they are used in the first place.'[30]

Mere tools and gap fillers do not pose a threat for contract law,[31] nor do interventions subsequent to the formation of the contract. Indeed, '[e]x post gap filling is a central function of contract law'.[32] However, '[w]hen algorithms act as negotiators, more interpretative work is required to show the fit with contract law'.[33]

Building on the taxonomy outlined by Scholz, although categorising all of them as mere tools,[34] Vincent Ooi distinguishes between passive and active 'contract forming mechanisms'.[35] From a passive perspective, the systems function as a communication device that merely transmits the message from the user without being altered in any way.[36] On the other hand, the active role implies entrusting the software with the power to decide on the contractual clauses, relegating the role of the human behind the system to the definition of the rules or objectives that will guide the software throughout the contracting process.[37] This study adopts terminology that avoids anthropomorphic framing – such as 'intelligent agent' – and uses 'algorithmic system' to describe these mechanisms without implying legal personality or independent capacity.[38]

Against that background, the study narrows 'algorithmic contracts' to a specific subset: contracts in which both parties deploy AI-based algorithmic systems as part of their decision-making and communication processes at formation.[39] This bilateral focus is adopted as the primary case because it makes the formation

[29] Eliza Mik takes a contrasting viewpoint, suggesting that the absence of explicability is not important for contract law. See E Mik, 'AI in Negotiating and Entering into Contracts' in LA Di Matteo, C Poncibò and M Cannarsa (eds), *The Cambridge Handbook of Artificial Intelligence* (Cambridge University Press, 2022)45, 56. See also E Mik, 'Much Ado About Artificial Intelligence or: The Automation of Contract Formation' (2023) 30 *International Journal of Law and Information Technology* 484, 504–5.

[30] T Bucher, *If…Then: Algorithmic Power and Politics* (Oxford University Press, 2018) 57.

[31] Scholz (n 10) 136.

[32] From a different perspective and for a deeper analysis of the usage of algorithms for post-contract formation, see AJ Casey and A Niblett, 'Self-Driving Contracts' (2017) 43 *The Journal of Corporation Law* 1, 1–33.

[33] Scholz (n 10) 136.

[34] Ooi sees these mechanisms as mere tools, in contrast with other views of as 'agents'. In this sense, his theory is built on the objective theory of contract. For a comprehensive examination of his contribution, see ch 6, section II.B.

[35] V Ooi, 'Contracts Formed by Software: An Approach Form the Law of Mistake' (2022) 2 *Journal of Business Law* 97, 2.

[36] ibid 3–4.

[37] ibid 4–5.

[38] For a comprehensive exploration of anthropocentrism, see Mik, 'Much Ado About Artificial Intelligence or: The Automation of Contract Formation' (n 29) 493.

[39] In this regard see the work of Nicholas Liu who distinguishes between offeror-side, offeree-side, and pure algorithmic contract meaning that both parties operate through algorithmic systems. N Liu, 'The "Contracting Problem" Revisited: Explaining the Formation of Algorithmic Contracts under the Common Law' in Z Slakoper, and I Tot (eds), *Digital Technologies and the Law of Obligations* (Routledge, 2022) 133, 134.

question most explicit. Agreement is reached through the interaction of two deployed systems rather than through contemporaneous human choice at the point of exchange, and the analysis must therefore specify the conditions under which system-level convergence can be treated as contractual agreement. The resulting framework is capable of extension to less complex settings – including unilateral deployment – once the doctrinal treatment of system-mediated assent is clarified.[40]

Secondly, the distinctive feature of algorithmic contracts – the active participation of algorithmic systems in the decision-making process – is worth emphasising. The involvement of algorithms in automating prior decision-making is what sets them apart from traditional contracts. It also differentiates them from contracts with interventions that occur afterwards, such as in self-driving contracts.[41] It accentuates the difference between algorithmic contracts and earlier technologies used in contracting, such as telephone or email, as these technologies primarily facilitate communication, whereas algorithmic contracts actively contribute to decision-making prior to the finalisation of the agreement. Algorithmic contracts are both a 'predictive and a communication technology'.[42]

Finally, a distinction must be made between algorithmic systems based on artificial intelligence and those that are not. This analysis will focus only on the former, while acknowledging the controversial nature of the term 'artificial intelligence'. There is an important difference between algorithmic systems that rely on advanced learning and decision-making capabilities, and those that operate without such advanced cognitive attributes. The distinction between traditional if-then software coding, and machine learning (ML) is essential in understanding their operational differences. Traditional if-then coding relies on explicit rules, represented as algorithms, where specific conditions trigger predefined actions or decisions. These algorithms execute these rules based on the data inputs and follow a deterministic approach, executing instructions based on explicit programming. In contrast, ML algorithms diverge from this deterministic model by learning from data. Instead of relying solely on predefined rules, ML algorithms adapt and evolve by recognising patterns within the data, enabling systems to make decisions based on learned experiences rather than rigid if-then rules. This flexibility allows ML systems to handle uncertainties or new scenarios more dynamically

[40] This bilateral focus does not deny that additional issues may arise where only one party deploys an algorithmic system at formation. Such cases may raise: (i) questions of timing and communication analogous to those addressed by the postal rule in technologically mediated contracting; (ii) concerns about informational asymmetry and bargaining power between an automated and a non-automated party; and (iii) questions of notice where the non-operating party is unaware that it is interacting with an algorithmic system. The last category may often admit of relatively straightforward responses through established doctrine and regulatory disclosure frameworks, and does not, without more, require a distinct account of formation.

[41] Casey and Niblett (n 32) 1–33.

[42] AJ Casey and A Niblett, 'The Death of Rules and Standards' (2017) 92 *Indiana Law Journal* 1401, 1403.

than traditional algorithmic coding. The former is known as symbolic or old-fashioned AI, the latter as non-symbolic AI.[43] 'Coding is logic. Machine learning is statistical.'[44]

The preference for these systems based on artificial intelligence in defining algorithmic contracts stems from their ability to incorporate machine learning, allowing them to navigate novel situations without explicit programming, providing a genuine rationale and significance to the concept of algorithmic contracts. In contrast, older or symbolic AI, which lies behind so-called expert systems,[45] resembles mere enhancements in the manner of traditional vending machines or parking ticket dispensers, whose challenges have already been effectively resolved through contract law.[46]

The purpose of these definitional and scope choices is not to carve out a novel field, but to isolate the setting in which the doctrinal questions about assent and the moment of formation are most acute. Once the conditions for treating system-mediated communications as manifestations of assent are made explicit in the primary case, the analysis can then be adapted to neighbouring scenarios in which automation is partial, transparent, unilateral, or constrained.

## B. Semantic Choice: The 'Operator' of an Algorithmic System

The integration of artificial intelligence into contracting has introduced a fragmented and often inconsistent terminology, much of it borrowed from computer science and regulatory discourse. In the literature, the relationship between the contracting party and the algorithmic system is variously described using terms such as 'user', 'operator', 'controller', or 'deployer', each carrying different connotations and normative implications. A degree of semantic discipline is therefore required.

For the purposes of this study, neither 'deployer' nor 'resource' is adopted.[47] The former tends to describe the technical developer rather than the contracting party, while the latter often functions as a substitute for anthropomorphic labels such as 'agent'.[48] Both deviate from the contractual relationship that is central to the present analysis.

[43] J Linarelli, 'Artificial Intelligence and Contracts Formation: Back to Contract as Bargain?' (2023) *Emerging Issues at the Intersection of Commercial Law and Technologies* 5 ssrn.com/abstract=4363410 accessed May 2024.

[44] ibid 4.

[45] J Turner, *Robot Rules: Regulating Artificial Intelligence* (Palgrave Macmillan, 2019) 18.

[46] See ch 3, section III for an analysis of the implications of automatisation for contract law.

[47] Some accounts describe the relevant human party as a 'deployer' and refer to the AI system itself as a 'resource'. See Mik, 'Much Ado About Artificial Intelligence or: The Automation of Contract Formation' (n 29) 501–05.

[48] See ch 2, section III for an analysis of all related figures/terms. Mik also specifies that he prefers the use of the term 'resource' due to the different meanings of the word 'agent' in the field of technology and law, which may lead to further confusion. See ibid.

The choice between 'user', 'operator', and 'controller' is more consequential. Some make use of the term 'user' when referring to the passive role of the system, meaning when it is used as a communication tool, while choosing 'operator' when referring to the active role or decision-maker.[49] The distinction between these roles is, however, somewhat artificial because, in algorithmic contracts, these functions coexist. There are no instances of algorithmic contracts where the algorithmic system solely acts as a communication tool without contributing to decision-making, or vice versa, as both elements are integral to the nature of an algorithmic contract. Another perspective involves regarding the operator as the primary beneficiary, with the user being the one engaging with the system.[50] In a contracting context, however, that usage risks confusion because the party 'using' the interface may simply be the counterparty to the contract.

From the semantic point of view, the distinction between the words 'operator' and 'user' is blurred. Each term has its own subtle connotations. The term 'operator' implies a more hands-on role in managing the system's operations, whereas 'user' typically suggests someone who interacts with the system to accomplish specific tasks without direct involvement in its management or technical aspects. Within an algorithmic contract, the individual or entity involved is responsible for executing various tasks. These tasks encompass setting contract parameters, determining criteria, assigning weights, and selecting the data used to generate the intended output.[51] All these tasks suggest more involvement than simple interaction and therefore the use of the term 'operator' seems more appropriate than 'user'. Other scholars have also questioned the appropriateness of the latter term, given that there is a greater level of immersion or fusion between people and new technologies.[52]

The alternative term 'controller' is also rejected.[53] In the context of machine-learning systems, a central difficulty is precisely the limited ability of the party to predict or reconstruct the path by which a particular output is generated: 'the user might not have the capacity or the permission to exercise effective control over the algorithm's choice'.[54] From a different angle, the patterns the algorithms employ which lead to a particular solution might be entirely beyond the operator's ability to comprehend,[55] and therefore to control. Describing a party as a

[49] Ooi (n 35) 99–100.

[50] Mik (n 7) 117.

[51] M Milossi, E Alexandropoulou and KE Psannis, 'AI Ethics: Algorithmic Determinism or Self-Determination? The GDPR Approach' (2021) 9 *IEEE Journals & Magazine* 58455, 58458 ieeexplore.ieee.org/stamp/stamp.jsp?tp=&arnumber=9400809 accessed 2 May 2024.

[52] P-P Verbeek, 'Subject to Technology: On Autonomic Computing and Human Autonomy' in M Hildebrandt and A Rouvroy (eds), *Law, Human Agency and Autonomic Computing: The Philosophy of Law Meets the Philosophy of Technology* (Taylor & Francis Group, 2011)27, 28.

[53] The term controller is used, for example, by Allen and Widdison. See T Allen and R Widdison, 'Can Computers Make Contracts?' (1996) 9 *Harvard Journal of Law & Technology* 25, 39.

[54] MS Gal, 'Algorithmic Challenges to Autonomous Choice' (2018) 1 *Michigan Technology Law Review* 59, 63.

[55] Bathaee (n 21) 891.

'controller' risks obscuring that lack of direct control and introducing conceptual confusion.

Accordingly, this study adopts the term 'operator' to refer to the party on whose behalf an algorithmic system is deployed in contract formation.[56] The operator is the party that sets the system's objectives and parameters and bears responsibility for its use in the contractual process, without implying either effective control over individual outcomes or the attribution of legal personality to the system itself.

# III. Algorithmic Contracts in Action

Section III situates the analysis in practice by identifying settings in which systems generate the operative communications and choices on which formation turns. The purpose is not to catalogue technological applications, but to isolate recurring legal features – how offers are generated, how acceptances are registered, how terms are selected, and how outputs are attributed to an operator – so that the later doctrinal analysis has clear points of reference.

## A. Looking Back to the Origins of Algorithmic Contracts: High Frequency Trading

'[I]n the context of high frequency trading, automated offer and acceptance happens all the time.'[57] HFT, a subset of algorithmic trading, involves the use of proprietary algorithms to place, adjust, and execute orders at speed, often within milliseconds.[58] As Scholz notes, at each moment the algorithm either offers a price based on its programming and market conditions or decides whether to accept an offer on the same basis.[59] Transactions executed in this way are treated as legally effective trades, and therefore provide a clear instance of algorithmic contracting in practice.

The prominence of HFT has also drawn attention to the risks associated with automation at scale, particularly in episodes of extreme volatility such as the 'flash

[56] 'Operator' is also used in the *Principles of AI in Contracting*, where it is defined as 'the party using the electronic agent for automated contracting in which that party is involved'. C Wendehorst, 'Discussion Draft: Principles for AI in Contracting (Version 2.1)' (2024) 13 *Journal of European Consumer and Market Law* 43, 49.

[57] Law Commission (n 23) 47.

[58] R Merli, I Massa and MC Lucchetti, 'High Frequency Trading: Technology, Regulation and Ethical Issues' in A Chochól, and J Szakiel (eds), *Achievements and Challenges of Commodity Science in the Age of Globalization* (Polish Society of Commodity Science, 2014) 179, 179.

[59] Scholz (n 10) 140. Also, Schmidt-Kessen, Eenmaa and Mitre analyse this use case in relation to contract automation and more specifically to algorithmic contracts. See MJ Schmidt-Kessen, H Eenmaa and M Mitre, 'Machines That Make and Keep Promises - Lessons for Contract Automation from Algorithmic Trading on Financial Markets' (2022) 46 *Computer Law & Security Review* 105717, 105717.

crash' of 6 May 2010 and its subsequent regulatory and enforcement aftermath.[60] For present purposes, the key point is not the market-abuse analysis, but that the legal and regulatory response proceeds on the assumption that system-generated bids and acceptances are contractually operative and attributable to the party deploying the system, even where outcomes diverge from the operator's expectations.

## B. From Dynamic Pricing to Non-Disclosure Agreements

Dynamic pricing serves as an example of an algorithmic contract primarily due to its utilisation of algorithms to ascertain the appropriate pricing. In this context, it could be perceived as the most basic manifestation of one of the functionalities inherent in contemporary algorithmic contracts. The scrutiny of this technique has predominantly revolved around its fairness, with legal contract perspectives framing it in terms of incomplete contracts.[61] Indeed, despite its simplicity, dynamic pricing represents an algorithmic contract wherein one party opts to delegate the determination of pricing solely to the algorithm's discretion. This delegation may operate on both the selling and the buying side of the transaction. In e-commerce settings in particular, such arrangements raise familiar concerns about information asymmetry and consumer protection, but they also provide a clear illustration of system-generated terms functioning as elements of an offer.

At the other end of the spectrum, algorithmic systems are increasingly used in the negotiation of preliminary commercial instruments, including non-disclosure agreements (NDAs) and related transaction documents. Reports of system-to-system negotiation and the development of AI-enabled negotiation tools indicate a move from automated term selection to automated exchange of legally operative

[60] The 'flash crash' that occurred on Thursday, 6 May 2010, resulted in one of the most significant intraday declines in the history of the Dow Jones Industrial Average. This sudden drop amounted to 998.5 points, equivalent to over 9% of the index's value, causing a staggering loss of approximately $1 trillion. Remarkably, the majority of this decline occurred in just four and a half minutes. However, after a temporary market suspension, prices swiftly rebounded. The name 'flash crash' was coined due to the rapid plummet and subsequent recovery in prices. The cause of this flash crash was attributed by some to algorithmic finance, where orders are executed through entirely automated computer algorithms, operating without direct human intervention. In April 2015, UK trader Navinder Singh Sarao was arrested in connection with alleged market manipulation ('spoofing') said to have contributed to the episode, and was charged in parallel criminal and civil proceedings in the US. C Borch, 'High-Frequency Trading, Algorithmic Finance and the Flash Crash: Reflections on Eventalization' (2016) 45 *Economy and Society* 350, 351. This case holds significance for two primary reasons: firstly, it drew considerable attention from both the media and academia towards this particular form of contracting; and secondly, it was not scrutinised from the standpoint of contract law regarding a potential misalignment between the intentions or objectives of the system operator and the resultant outcome. Instead, it was treated as a fraud case, resulting in the imposition of a prison sentence on the perpetrator. Furthermore, examining them from a regulatory standpoint reveals a predominant emphasis on risk mitigation. See See Schmidt-Kessen, Eenmaa and Mitre (n 59) 10–2.

[61] Scholz (n 10) 141–5.

communications.[62] For the purposes of this study, the significance lies in the same formation questions: when a system proposes, revises, and accepts terms, on what basis are those communications attributed to the operator, and at what point should agreement be treated as concluded?

A leading judicial illustration of these issues is *Quoine Pte Ltd v B2C2 Ltd*,[63] a dispute arising from algorithmic trading on a cryptocurrency exchange platform. Following a platform malfunction, trades were executed at prices far removed from prevailing market levels, and the exchange later reversed the transactions. The Singapore Court of Appeal proceeded on the basis that contracts had been formed through automated trading and addressed whether they were voidable for unilateral mistake. It rejected the mistake argument on the facts, but the case is significant for present purposes because it treats system-generated bids and acceptances as legally operative manifestations of assent and examines how knowledge should be attributed where a party acts through an algorithmic system – including by assessing the relevant knowledge over the period from programming and deployment up to contract formation.

More recently, the operation of algorithms in contract formation has been considered in *Moffatt v Air Canada*.[64] In February 2024, the British Columbia Civil Resolution Tribunal awarded damages of approximately C$650 to the claimant after misleading information about fare conditions was communicated through an AI-powered chatbot.[65] Despite Air Canada's argument that it could not be held liable for information provided by a chatbot,[66] the claim succeeded on the basis of negligent misrepresentation. Most significantly for present purposes, the decision proceeds on the assumption that system-mediated communications form part of the contracting interface and may give rise to legally binding consequences attributable to the deploying party.

[62] On 7 November 2023, reports emerged of the formalisation of the first fully negotiated NDA conducted solely between two AI-based systems: an 'artificial intelligence demonstrated the ability to negotiate a contract autonomously with another artificial intelligence without any human involvement'. See R Browne, 'An AI Just Negotiated a Contract for the First Time Ever — and No Human Was Involved' www.cnbc.com/2023/11/07/ai-negotiates-legal-contract-without-humans-involved-for-first-time.html accessed 2 May 2024. Allan and Overy made a significant announcement, unveiling an innovative tool named 'ContractMatrix'. This tool was specifically designed to facilitate the negotiation of M&A terms and conditions as well as confidentiality agreements. C Criddle and S Ring, 'Allen & Overy Rolls out AI Contract Negotiation Tool in Challenge to Legal Industry' (London, 21 December 2023) www.ft.com/content/f1aff4d0-b2c5-4266-aa0a-604ef14894bb accessed 2 May 2024.

[63] *Quoine Pte Ltd v B2C2 Ltd* [2020] SGCA(I) 2.

[64] *Moffatt v Air Canada*, 2024 BCCRT 149 (CanLII).

[65] While the text of the court decision lacks explicit confirmation regarding the classification of the chatbot as AI-powered, as opposed to rule-based chatbots utilising predefined responses triggered by keywords and language identifiers, the characteristics of the incident strongly suggests an AI-powered system. Specifically, 'Air Canada suggests the chatbot is a separate legal entity that is responsible for its own actions'. See *Moffatt v Air Canada* (n 64) at [27]. Furthermore, media reports also support this inference. See Marisa Garcia, 'What Air Canada Lost In "Remarkable" Lying AI Chatbot Case' (19 February 2024) www.forbes.com/sites/marisagarcia/2024/02/19/what-air-canada-lost-in-remarkable-lying-ai-chatbot-case/?sh=143f0411696f accessed 2 May 2024.

[66] *Moffatt v Air Canada* (n 64) at [27].

The examples in this section are chosen because each isolates a different formation pressure point: the generation of contractual terms (dynamic pricing), the exchange of assent through iterative proposals (AI-enabled negotiation), and the attribution of system-generated communications to the deploying party (algorithmic trading in *Quoine* and chatbot contracting in *Moffatt*).

## IV. English Law in the Age of Algorithmic Contracts: A Strategic Choice

This study adopts English contract law as its primary reference point. The choice is not motivated by jurisdictional preference, but by the analytical characteristics of English formation doctrine and its historical capacity to accommodate new modes of contracting without wholesale doctrinal reconstruction.

English law is anchored in an objective theory of contract formation, under which agreement is identified through outward manifestations rather than subjective intention. That feature is particularly significant in algorithmic contracting, where the legally operative acts are generated and communicated by systems rather than by a human decision-maker at the moment of exchange. The question is therefore not whether English law can recognise contracts concluded through automated means – this has long been accepted – but how its formation concepts should be applied where decision-making and communication are delegated to algorithmic systems.[67]

A further reason for focusing on English law lies in its incremental and context-sensitive method of doctrinal development. English contract law has repeatedly responded to technological change by adapting existing categories rather than introducing technology-specific rules.[68] The evolution of formation doctrine in response to postal communications, telex, fax, and electronic contracting illustrates a willingness to treat new media as variations on established problems of timing, attribution, and manifestation, rather than as grounds for conceptual rupture.[69] That tradition makes English law a demanding test case for assessing whether orthodox formation concepts can accommodate AI-enabled contracting.

[67] Law Commission (n 23) 46: 'The process of offer and acceptance itself can be undertaken automatically by computer programs, whether on a DLT or non-DLT system, without the need for human intervention.'

[68] *Brinkibon Ltd v Stahag Stahl* [1983] 2 AC 34 (HL) 42 (Lord Wilberforce).

[69] See *Adams v Lindsell* (1818) 1 B & Ald 681 (postal rule: acceptance effective on posting); *Entores Ltd v Miles Far East Corporation* [1955] 2 QB 327 (CA) (instantaneous communications: contract 'only complete when the acceptance is received'); *Brinkibon Ltd v Stahag Stahl* [1983] 2 AC 34 (HL) (confirming *Entores* approach for telex, while emphasising context); and *Thomas v BPE Solicitors* [2010] EWHC 306 (Ch) (email acceptance analysed by reference to receipt and the parties' intentions/business practice).

English contract law's largely incremental, case-driven mode of development tends to expose points of doctrinal strain with particular clarity.[70] Where automated systems generate offers, acceptances, or representations without contemporaneous human review, English doctrine forces explicit answers to questions about when agreement is formed, to whom knowledge is attributed, and how system outputs are to be characterised within the framework of assent.[71] Those questions cannot be resolved by reference to efficiency or policy alone, but must be addressed within the structure of formation doctrine itself.

The focus on English law does not imply that the issues examined are jurisdiction-specific. On the contrary, the problems raised by algorithmic contracting – system-mediated assent, attribution of knowledge, and the timing of agreement – are common across legal systems. English law is used here as a reference framework because it brings those issues into sharp relief. Where appropriate, comparative references are introduced to test the generality of the analysis and to indicate how the proposed framework may translate beyond the English context.

## V. Significance, Timeliness, and the Pivotal Query in Algorithmic Contracts

Algorithmic contracting raises a focused doctrinal problem for contract formation. Formation doctrine ordinarily proceeds on the premise that legally operative communications are generated through human acts at the point of exchange, so that both the relevant timing of agreement and the knowledge bearing on contractual validity can be attributed to an identifiable person. Where systems generate offers, acceptances, or key contractual terms without contemporaneous human review, those assumptions are placed under strain. The pivotal question is therefore whether, and on what basis, system-generated communications can count as a party's objective manifestation of assent – and, relatedly, when formation should be treated as occurring for the purposes of attribution.

English law has not treated automated contracting as conceptually incapable of producing agreement. The Law Commission has stated that '[t]he process of offer and acceptance itself can be undertaken automatically by computer programs (…) without the need for human intervention.'[72] Yet that position does not itself supply the criteria needed to locate the moment of formation, to attribute knowledge

[70] See *Chartbrook Ltd v Persimmon Homes Ltd* [2009] UKHL 38, [2009] 1 AC 1101, [2] (Lord Hope); *Brinkibon Ltd v Stahag Stahl* [1983] 2 AC 34, 42 (Lord Wilberforce).

[71] The resulting exposure of doctrinal strain is illustrated by cases involving automated or mediated communications, where courts have been required to determine the timing of agreement and the attribution of knowledge: see *Brinkibon Ltd v Stahag Stahl* [1983] 2 AC 34 (HL); *Quoine Pte Ltd v B2C2 Ltd* [2020] SGCA(I) 02, esp [108]–[110].

[72] Law Commission (n 23) 46.

where contracting is mediated by a system. As Scholz stated, '[f]ormation theory gives us reason to doubt that algorithmic contracts are properly formed at law.'[73]

The need for greater precision is illustrated by judicial engagement with algorithmic contracting in practice. In *Quoine Pte Ltd v B2C2 Ltd*, the Singapore Court of Appeal treated contracts formed through automated trading as legally operative, but the analysis exposed the difficulty of identifying both the relevant person to whom knowledge should be attributed and the appropriate time at which attribution should occur.[74] The case therefore confirms that attribution and timing are not merely theoretical concerns, but live issues that arise once contract formation is effected through system-generated communications.

The literature has not yet produced a settled framework capable of addressing these points in a systematic way, particularly where systems rely on machine learning techniques whose specific outputs are not fully specified in advance. The resulting debate is often either overly general – invoking 'autonomous agents' or 'AI contracting' at a high level – or fragmented across adjacent doctrines such as mistake, misrepresentation, consumer protection, and undue influence.[75] Those questions matter, but the focus here is narrower: to articulate a formation account that explains how assent and knowledge attribution should be handled where contracting choices and communications are delegated to algorithmic systems. Existing treatments also tend to draw on case law concerned with deterministic systems, leaving under-analysed the harder question of how formation concepts should operate where determinism is absent.

The technology underpinning algorithmic contracts, big data and artificial intelligence endows them with a dual role: functioning as both predictive and communication technologies.[76] The method adopted in this study is a functional deconstruction of the system's dual role in formation: decision-making and communication. The decision-making function concerns how contractual positions are generated from operator-defined objectives and constraints; the communication function concerns how those positions are conveyed, matched, and acted upon in the external environment. By separating these functions, and

[73] Scholz (n 10) 158.

[74] *Quoine Pte Ltd v B2C2 Ltd* [2020] SGCA(I) 02, [2020] 2 SLR 20, esp [97]–[99]. In *Quoine* 'the judges (…) struggled to identify both a person to whom knowledge could be attributed and a time at which it was appropriate to do so'. See KFK Low and E Mik, 'Lost in Transmission: Unilateral Mistakes in Automated Contracts' (2020) 136 *Law Quarterly Review* 563, 566.

[75] See, eg, Ooi (n 35) 97–117; M Rizzi and N Skead, 'Algorithmic Contracts and the Equitable Doctrine of Undue Influence: Adapting Old Rules to a New Legal Landscape' (2020) 14 *Journal of Equity* 301, 301–26; M Oliver, 'Contracting by Artificial Intelligence: Open Offers, Unilateral Mistakes, and Why Algorithms Are Not Agents' (2021) 2 *Australian National University Journal of Law and Technology* 45, 83–87; Busch et al (n 18); M Lippi et al, 'Consumer Protection Requires Artificial Intelligence' (2019) 1 *Nature Machine Intelligence* 168, 168–69; G Howells, 'Protecting Consumer Protection Values in the Fourth Industrial Revolution' (2020) 43 *Journal of Consumer Policy* 145, 145–75.

[76] This categorisation is borrowed from another application of these technologies, specifically referring to microdirectives. A microdirective is a precise, context-specific command conveyed by a machine to an individual, facilitating exact adherence to the law without the need for further legislative or judicial actions. See Casey and Niblett (n 42) 1401–47.

by distinguishing their operator-facing and counterparty-facing dimensions, the analysis provides a basis for identifying the moment of formation and the proper locus of knowledge attribution. The final step is to test whether system-level convergence can be translated into a defensible account of agreement without resorting to legal personhood or metaphor. In other words, how the 'meeting of the algorithms' can be considered the 'meeting of the minds'.

The scope of this study is deliberately confined. It focuses on a subset of algorithmic contracting in which both parties deploy AI-based algorithmic systems as part of the decision-making and communication processes relevant to contract formation. This bilateral setting is adopted as the primary case because it brings the formation problem into sharpest relief: agreement is reached through the interaction of deployed systems rather than through contemporaneous human choice at the point of exchange. The analysis is anchored in English contract law, used as a reference framework for its objective account of assent and its incremental, case-driven development, with comparative references introduced where they test the generality of the argument.

This book develops an account of contract formation capable of accommodating agreements concluded through AI-based algorithmic systems. Its focus is the requirement of agreement, and in particular the conditions under which system-generated decisions and communications can be attributed to contracting parties as manifestations of consent.

Three issues structure the analysis: the timing of formation in system-mediated exchange; the attribution of knowledge where contracting choices are delegated to a system; and the translation of system-level convergence into a doctrinally defensible account of agreement under the objective approach.

To address these questions, the study adopts a doctrinal methodology. It proceeds through close analysis of case law, law reform materials, and established principles of contract formation, with the aim of clarifying how existing doctrine should be applied where formation-relevant acts are generated and communicated by systems. Because the subject lies at the intersection of law and technology, the doctrinal analysis is informed – where necessary – by a limited engagement with technical concepts drawn from computer science, sufficient to distinguish deterministic systems from systems that rely on machine learning. The purpose is not to import technical classifications into contract law, but to ensure that doctrinal conclusions do not rest on inaccurate assumptions about how these systems operate.

The chapters that follow develop this analysis in stages. The next chapters situate algorithmic contracting within the broader evolution of technologically mediated exchange and review the existing literature. The core chapters then apply the analytical framework to three linked issues: the identification of the moment of formation in system-mediated exchange; the attribution of knowledge where contracting choices are delegated to a system; and the relationship between system-level convergence and the legal requirement of agreement. The concluding chapter draws these strands together and identifies the conditions under which algorithmic contracting can be analysed as consistent with formation doctrine, while indicating the limits of that account.

# 2

# Shaping the Contract Landscape: The Journey from Automation to Autonomy

## I. Introduction

Technological change has always compelled contract law to adapt its doctrines to new modes of exchange. The present period, often described as part of the fourth industrial revolution, is no exception. Among the many innovations of this era, two stand out for their impact on contracting: blockchain and artificial intelligence (AI). Both have reconfigured how agreements are concluded and enforced, raising new questions about the boundaries of automation and the emergence of contractual autonomy. While blockchain technologies prompted the rise of so-called 'smart contracts',[1] AI now pushes further, introducing systems capable of determining contractual terms without direct human oversight. These developments bring to the surface a pressing question for English contract law: how far can doctrines of agreement and consent accommodate contracting practices in which the human role is diminished or displaced?

A proper understanding of algorithmic contracting requires placing it within the longer trajectory of contract automation. Each technological wave has pressed English law to adapt, from mechanised transactions to internet based commerce. What scholars now describe as a 'new season of the contract' reflects not a rupture but a continuation:[2] contracting has evolved from a static record of obligations into a dynamic mechanism capable of facilitating, monitoring, and recording performance.[3] This observation, made by Garside and Blycha in the context of

[1] Blockchain technology began its development back in 1991 when it was first described by Dr Stuart Haber and Dr W Scott Stornetta as a cryptographically protected chain of blocks which could be used to prevent the manipulation of document timestamps. The term smart contract was coined in 1996 by Nick Szabo, although it gained traction when the Ethereum blockchain platform was launched by Vitalik Buterin. See S Haber and W Stornetta, 'How to Time-Stamp a Digital Document' (1991) 3(2) *Journal of Cryptology*; N Szabo, 'Smart Contracts: Building Blocks for Digital Markets' (1996) 1 *First Monday* 1; V Buterin, 'Ethereum White Paper. A Next Generation Smart Contract & Decentralized Application Platform' burnersxxx.files.wordpress.com/2015/01/pdfs-ethereumwhitepaper.pdf.

[2] Expression from the work of S Martinelli and C Rossi Chauvenet, 'From Document to Data: Revolution of Contract through Legal Technologies' in M Ebers, C Poncibò and M Zou (eds), *Contracting and Contract Law in the Age of Artificial Intelligence* (Hart Publishing, 2022) 81.

[3] A Garside and N Blycha, 'A Model for the Integration of Machine Capabilities into Contracts' in JG Allen and P Hunn (eds), *Smart Legal Contracts* (Oxford University Press, 2022) 142–81.

smart legal contracts, is equally pertinent to the formative impact of algorithmic contracts. Seen in this light, algorithmic contracts mark the latest stage in a process by which human intention has gradually been supplemented – and sometimes displaced – by technological systems.

The advent of blockchain technologies marked a turning point in debates on contract automation. Conceived as a decentralised ledger for digital transactions, blockchain soon generated the idea of 'smart contracts': self-executing agreements in which performance is triggered by predefined rules and conditions. These developments quickly drew attention beyond the technology sector. Legal scholarship began to explore the implications of self-executing agreements, including their potential to reduce transaction costs, the challenges of ensuring security and privacy in blockchain-based systems, and the extent to which automated performance might disrupt established doctrines of interpretation and rectification.[4] Crucially, however, smart contracts operate primarily at the level of execution, automating the performance of obligations. Algorithmic contracts, by contrast, intervene at the stage of formation, delegating to machines the determination of whether and on what terms parties are bound. It is this focus on formation that makes them doctrinally distinct, and far more disruptive for English contract law.

Artificial intelligence has quickly emerged as a transformative force in contract automation. Recent years have seen the integration of AI into the contract lifecycle, from drafting and negotiation to analysis and enforcement. Unlike earlier forms of automation, AI's strength lies in its capacity for large-scale data processing, pattern recognition and natural language processing. As Martinelli and Rossi Chauvenet observe '[t]he revolution is the application of data analysis and data management in legal works and contracting practices.'[5] This chapter introduces those developments at a general level, laying the groundwork for later analysis of how algorithmic contracts reshape core doctrines of English contract law.

The influence of technological disruption on contract law cannot be understood solely through recent innovations. As Brownsword has observed, two distinct phases of disruption may be distinguished.[6] The first coincided with the Industrial Revolution, when new forms of mechanisation prompted a redefinition of liability across private law. In contrast, nineteenth-century developments replaced

[4] See, eg, K Werbach and N Cornell, 'Contracts Ex Machina' (2017) 67 *Duke Law Journal* 313; S Green, 'Smart Contracts, Interpretation and Rectification' (2018) 134 *Law Quarterly Review* 234; M Durovic and A Janssen, 'Formation of Smart Contracts under Contract Law' in LA DiMatteo, M Cannarsa and C Poncibò (eds), *The Cambridge Handbook of Smart Contracts, Blockchain Technology and Digital Platforms* (Cambridge University Press, 2019) 61–79. See further A Savelyev, 'Contract Law 2.0: "Smart" Contracts As the Beginning of the End of Classic Contract Law' (2016) 26 *Information & Communications Technology Law* 1; E Schuster, 'Cloud Crypto Land' [2021] *Modern Law Review* 974.

[5] Martinelli and Rossi Chauvenet (n 2) 96.

[6] R Brownsword, 'Smart Transactional Technologies, Legal Disruption, and the Case of Network Contracts' in LA DiMatteo, M Cannarsa and C Poncibò (eds), *The Cambridge Handbook of Smart Contracts, Blockchain Technology and Digital Platforms* (Cambridge University Press, 2020) 313, 315–19.

transactionalist notions of consent with objective tests derived from prevailing business practices. The focus shifted from proving actual intent or agreement to assessing obligations through external manifestations. This marked the beginning of a broader doctrinal bifurcation: while some areas of law remained anchored in traditional principles, others sought to balance technological advance against the risks it created.[7]

The second phase of disruption arose in industrialised societies with the advent of computers and the internet. Here, regulators increasingly viewed technology as a regulatory tool, adopting risk-management strategies and flexible standards in place of prescriptive rules.[8] For contract law, this phase laid the groundwork for digital contracting and electronic commerce, further entrenching the move away from subjective consent towards objective manifestations of agreement.

Separately, Wilkinson and Giuffre have proposed a taxonomy of contracting technologies according to degrees of automation. Their six-level classification runs from complete absence of digitisation (level 0) to fully autonomous systems operating without human intervention (level 5).[9] The focus of their framework, however, lies in the enforcement stage, assessing the digital accessibility of contracts and the mechanisation of performance.[10] While valuable for distinguishing traditional contracts from those relying on automated execution, this approach is less helpful for algorithmic contracts, whose distinctive feature lies in the delegation of decision-making during the formation phase. This emphasis on execution highlights the novelty of algorithmic contracts, which alter the point of formation itself and thereby challenge the foundations of agreement in English law.

Although autonomy and automation are sometimes presented as separate concepts, in technical terms autonomy is best understood as the most advanced form of automation.[11]

Confusion arises when legal or philosophical understandings of 'autonomy' are mapped onto technological classifications. In practice, levels of automation range from minimal, where humans retain full control, to near-complete delegation of decision-making to machines. Systems that gather information, process it and act upon the results are properly described as autonomous. Full autonomy, at the opposite end of the scale, involves tasks delegated to machines without any direct or continuous human control.[12] Whether considered the culmination of automation or a distinct phenomenon, both automation and autonomy challenge contract law

[7] ibid 316–17.

[8] ibid 317–19.

[9] S Wilkinson and J Giuffre, 'Six Levels of Contract Automation: The Evolution of "Smart Legal Contracts"' in JG Allen and P Hunn (eds), *Smart Legal Contracts: Computable Law in Theory and Practice* (Oxford University Press, 2022) 182–204.

[10] ibid 193–94.

[11] E Mik, 'AI as a Legal Person?' in J-A Lee, RM Hilty and K-C C Liu (eds), *Artificial Intelligence and Intellectual Property* (Oxford University Press, 2021) 423.

[12] ibid 423–24.

by displacing human intention and raising questions about how agreements can be formed, interpreted and enforced in machine-driven environments.

Yet the automation of contracting is not a recent phenomenon. Long before the rise of smart contracts, courts and scholars had already grappled with technologies that reduced or displaced human involvement. The vending machine became an early paradigm of automated contracting,[13] while electronic data interchange (EDI) enabled the computer-to-computer exchange of contractual information before the advent of e-commerce.[14] Even prior to the development of autonomous software agents in financial markets, commentators were already asking whether computers could themselves conclude contracts.[15]

The remainder of this chapter proceeds in three stages. It first traces the evolution of automation in contracting, from early mechanised devices to contemporary algorithmic systems. It then considers related phenomena that, while described under different labels, share features with algorithmic contracts and shed light on their operation. Finally, the chapter distinguishes algorithmic contracts from smart contracts, with particular attention to the approach of the Law Commission of England and Wales, before drawing together some concluding observations. As will be shown in later chapters, the most pressing challenge lies in whether English law can preserve the principle of meaningful consent in contracts increasingly formed by autonomous systems.

## II. From Vending Machines to Algorithmic Contracts

The last half-century has seen profound changes in the way parties communicate and transact. Letters and telephone calls have largely given way to email and instant messaging; paper ledgers have been replaced by electronic databases and enterprise systems; and travel bookings that once required an agent are now concluded online. Each of these shifts has carried implications for contract law, which has had to adapt doctrines of formation, communication, and consent to reflect new modes of interaction.[16] Against this background, academic attention to contract automation intensified with the rise of smart contracts, presented as the latest stage in a much longer trajectory of technological innovation.[17] This has ushered in a period of substantial research in the field of contract automation.

The discussion of related technological developments serves two functions in this chapter. It situates algorithmic contracts within a broader landscape of

[13] Szabo (n 1) 1–2.

[14] S Eiselen, 'The Electronic Data Interchange Agreement' (1995) 7 *South African Mercantile Law Journal* 1, 1.

[15] T Allen and R Widdison, 'Can Computers Make Contracts?' (1996) 9 *Harvard Journal of Law and Technology* 25, 25.

[16] Werbach and Cornell (n 4) 108.

[17] See n 4.

automated contracting, highlighting both overlaps and distinctions with neighbouring concepts. It also allows insights drawn from those other contexts to inform the analysis of algorithmic contracts, particularly in identifying the points at which English law must adapt its doctrines of agreement and consent.

The vending machine is often taken as the starting point for modern discussions of automated contracting.[18] By reducing agreements to a sequence of pre-programmed steps, it illustrates how transactions can be concluded with minimal human involvement. Similar logic applies to other machine-based arrangements, such as ticket machines, self-service petrol stations and automated car parks. English case law was forced to adapt established doctrines of offer and acceptance to these contexts. In *Thornton v Shoe Lane Parking Ltd*, the Court of Appeal held that a contract was concluded when the customer activated the machine, not later when the terms printed on the ticket were brought to his attention,[19] while *Re Charge Card Services* raised further questions about how contractual intention should be ascertained in machine-mediated exchanges.[20] These decisions show how even simple mechanisms required the law to reconsider where and how agreements are formed once direct human interaction was displaced.

EDI is widely regarded as a precursor of smart contracts and, by extension, of algorithmic contracting.[21] Identified by Szabo alongside point-of-sale systems, SWIFT, and other financial infrastructures,[22] EDI introduced automated communication between machines without human intervention. This system is defined as '[t]he electronic interchange of machine processable, structured data, which has been formatted according to agreed standards, and which can be transmitted directly between different computer systems with the aid of telecommunication interfaces'.[23] Although sometimes described as a contracting technology,[24] EDI is more accurately a method of communication that operates within a master agreement setting out the legal rules governing its use.[25] In this framework, EDI messages may create binding obligations only because the parties have already consented to treat them as such. EDI constitutes a way for

[18] It was Nick Szabo himself, the father of smart contracts, who introduced vending machines to the field of contract automation analysis, but the history of vending machines goes back to ancient Egypt or, somewhat more recently, to circumventing tobacco censors in 17th-century England. See Szabo (n 1) 3; M Raskin, 'The Law and Legality of Smart Contracts' (2017) 1(2) *The Georgetown Law Technology Review* 305, 315.

[19] *Thornton v Shoe Lane Parking Ltd* [1971] 2 QB 163, 169.

[20] *Re Charge Card Services* [1989] Ch 497, 512.

[21] EDI originated during the Berlin Airlift when US Army Master Sergeant Guilbert devised a radiotelephone, telex, or telephone manifest for supplying Berlin. Subsequently, while employed at DuPont, he modified and formalised this technology into what we now know as EDI in 1965. See P De Filippi and A Wright, *Blockchain and the Law: The Rule of Code* (Harvard University Press, 2018) 72–73.

[22] Szabo (n 1) 2.

[23] Eiselen (n 14) 1.

[24] JM Sklaroff, 'Smart Contracts and the Cost of Inflexibility' (2017) 166 *University of Pennsylvania Law Review* 263, 263.

[25] ibid 288.

the parties to a contract to digitally communicate 'automatically and without human intervention'.[26]

For contract law, EDI raised familiar issues: liability for erroneous transmissions, compliance with agreed standards, security of data, and the timing of contractual communication. These challenges remain instructive for algorithmic contracts. Yet the differences are significant. Whereas EDI facilitated the communication of agreements made by human parties, algorithmic contracts extend automation into the formation stage itself, delegating aspects of contractual decision-making to machines.

Electronic commerce built directly on the foundations of EDI. By the mid-1990s, online transactions between private parties were becoming feasible,[27] and in 1998 the World Trade Organization formally defined e-commerce as the production, distribution and sale of goods and services by electronic means.[28] For contract law, the significance of these developments lay not in the novelty of the goods exchanged but in the questions raised about formation. Courts and legislators had to clarify how the rules of offer and acceptance applied to online environments and whether traditional doctrines could accommodate click-wrap agreements, browse-wrap notices and email-based exchanges. Although these contracts were digital in form, they remained substantively human-dependent, with consent still provided by the contracting parties rather than by machines.

Although e-commerce contracts were novel in form, they remained substantively dependent on human negotiation. Early debates centred on how the rules of offer and acceptance should apply in online settings, but the prevailing view settled that the purchaser makes the offer, which the seller accepts. These agreements were therefore 'electronic' only in their mode of communication; their substance and performance remained human-dependent,[29] not digitally executable.[30] By contrast, algorithmic contracts may be seen as an evolution of e-commerce: here the acts of offer and acceptance can themselves be delegated to algorithms, with

[26] Eiselen (n 14) 3.

[27] It was in 1994 when Phil Brandenberg and Dan Kohn carried out the first e-commerce transaction between ordinary people. See PH Lewis, 'Attention Shoppers: Internet Is Open' *New York Times* (New York, 12 August 1994) search.proquest.com/docview/429852687 accessed 27 August 2025. Some argue that, even earlier, in 1971 a group of MIT and Stanford students were involved in a clandestine cannabis transaction using the earlier version of the Internet, the ARPAnet. M Tafula, 'A Brief History of E-Commerce' *Medium* (22 February 2024) michaeltefula.medium.com/a-brief-history-of-e-commerce-c4692a3b2cd9 accessed 27 August 2025.

[28] WTO, *Work Programme on Electronic Commerce* (1998) WT/L/274, para 4. This replaced an earlier conception in which 'electronic commerce [was] broadly defined as referring to six instruments, namely: "the telephone, the fax, television, electronic payment and money transfer systems, Electronic Data Interchange and the Internet"'. See P Todd, *E-Commerce Law*, 1st edn (Routledge-Cavendish, 2005) 290.

[29] Werbach and Cornell (n 4) 109.

[30] R De Caria, 'The Legal Meaning of Smart Contracts' (2018) 26 *European Review of Private Law* 731, 742.

contractual terms determined by machines rather than their human operators. Algorithmic contracts may or may not be digitally executable.[31]

For contract law, e-commerce primarily raised questions of application rather than of principle. Issues such as cross-border enforceability and consumer protection prompted new legislation, but the doctrinal structure of contract formation remained intact. Within the European Union, the E-Commerce Directive requires Member States to permit contracts to be concluded electronically and to regulate the placing of online orders, yet it leaves the core rules of formation untouched.[32] Judicial recognition of click-wrap and browse-wrap agreements has consolidated their enforceability, and email-based contracting has long been accepted as valid.[33] These developments show that, while e-commerce transformed the medium of communication, it did not alter the essence of contract law.

Ricardian contracts, first proposed by Ian Grigg and Gary Howland in 1996, gained visibility in parallel with the development of smart contracts. They are often described as bridging the gap between legal prose and 'automatically executable contracts',[34] representing a step towards greater computational integration in contracting.[35] Their relationship with smart contracts has been much debated. Grigg suggested that the two perform different parts of the same process, yet they remain distinct: not all Ricardian contracts are smart contracts, and not all smart contracts are Ricardian.[36] The key difference lies in execution. While smart contracts are self-executing and immutable, Ricardian contracts establish the terms of agreement in a digital form that software can subsequently execute under the control of the parties. They therefore occupy an intermediate position. By rendering contractual provisions simultaneously human- and machine-readable, Ricardian contracts paved the way for algorithmic contracts, in which machines

[31] Having introduced the term 'digital' in this context, it is necessary to distinguish algorithmic contracts from the concept of digital contracts introduced by the EU. The EU's notion of 'digital contracts' pertains specifically to transactions involving the sale and acquisition of digital content, digital services, and 'smart goods' within the defined legal framework. See European Commission, 'Digital Contract Rules' commission.europa.eu/business-economy-euro/doing-business-eu/contract-rules/digital-contracts/digital-contract-rules_en accessed 2 May 2024.

[32] See, eg, Directive 2000/31/EC of the European Parliament and of the Council of 8 June 2000 on certain legal aspects of information society services, in particular electronic commerce, in the Internal Market [2000] OJ L178/1 (E-Commerce Directive), art 9(1) (requiring Member States to permit contracts to be concluded electronically) and art 11 (establishing minimum requirements for the placing of orders by technological means).

[33] A Maria Gambino and A Stazi, 'Contract Automation from Telematic Agreements to Smart Contracts Essays' (2021) 7 *The Italian Law Journal* 97, 100.

[34] L Cervone, M Palmirani and F Vitali, 'The Intelligible Contract' (Proceedings of the 53rd Hawaii International Conference on System Sciences 2020) core.ac.uk/download/pdf/286030279.pdf accessed 29 August 2025, 1780–89.

[35] I Grigg, 'The Ricardian Contract' (1996) available at iang.org/papers/ricardian_contract.html accessed 27 August 2025. The Ricardian model has been defined as a single document that is: (a) a contract offered by an issuer to holders, (b) for a valuable right held by holders and managed by the issuer, (c) easily readable by people, (d) readable by programs, (e) digitally signed, (f) containing keys and server information, and (g) linked to a unique identifier.

[36] I Grigg, 'On the Intersection of Ricardian and Smart Contracts' (February 2015) iang.org/papers/intersection_ricardian_smart.html accessed 27 August 2025.

do not merely execute agreements but participate in defining their content at the stage of formation.

Another influential attempt to frame the interface between law and software is Harry Surden's account of 'computable contracts'.[37] Rather than translating prose into code,[38] Surden proposed that contractual terms could be expressed directly as structured data, so that they are both intelligible to human parties and interpretable by machines. This 'data-oriented' model underscored that automation requires contracts to be represented in a format processable by computer systems, not only in natural language.[39]

Surden further distinguished between computable contracts in general and autonomous computable contracts. The latter involves agreements expressed in computable terms where both formation and performance occur automatically, without human intervention – a model that closely anticipates algorithmic contracting.[40] In this sense, computable contracts provide the conceptual foundation for algorithmic contracts: while all algorithmic contracts are computable, not all computable contracts are algorithmic. The broader field of 'computational law', which applies logical and formal methods to legal concepts, is inherently intertwined with the domains of computational contracts and algorithmic contracts.[41]

The idea of 'self-driving contracts' illustrates another step in the attempt to integrate artificial intelligence into contracting. In this model, the parties agree on a desired outcome and rely on machine-assisted analytics to identify the means of achieving it.[42] Unlike algorithmic contracts, however, the determination of the contractual terms takes place after formation, once the parties have already committed to shared objectives.[43] In that respect, self-driving contracts have been described as operating in the execution phase, akin to Scholz's second variety of algorithmic contracts, and as filling contractual gaps where the precise outcome cannot be specified ex ante.[44]

Other labels have also emerged in this field. 'Telematic contracts' are used to describe contracts concluded through electronic means that connect parties at a distance,[45] while 'expert systems' refer to rule-based programs structured on if-then logic. The latter constitute unlike contemporary AI systems, they cannot adapt or self-improve, and thus represent an earlier, more limited stage of technological development.

[37] H Surden, 'Computable Contracts' (2012) 46 *UC Davis Law Review* 629. Surden describes 'data-oriented contracts' as agreements expressed directly in structured data, addressing the limitations of technology in parsing prose and assessing compliance with abstract terms.

[38] ibid 634.

[39] ibid 641.

[40] ibid 694–95, noting the potential for 'autonomous "computer-to-computer" contracting'.

[41] CL Reyes, 'A Unified Theory of Code-Connected Contracts' (2021) 46 *Journal of Corporation Law* 981, 985.

[42] AJ Casey and A Niblett, 'Self-Driving Contracts' (2017) 43 *Journal of Corporation Law* 1, 6.

[43] ibid 2.

[44] LH Scholz, 'Algorithmic Contracts' (2017) 20 *Stanford Technology Law Review* 128.

[45] Gambino and Stazi (n 33) 99.

## III. Algorithmic Contracts and Their Kin

The literature on automated contracting has produced a wide variety of terms – 'intelligent agents', 'electronic agents', 'contracting agents', 'autonomous software agents', and 'digital assistants' – yet all point to the same phenomenon: software empowered to make contractual decisions without direct human oversight. This section surveys those concepts in order to show their commonalities and to situate algorithmic contracts within this broader landscape.

Early discussions of autonomous contracting focused on the emergence of 'intelligent agents' designed to facilitate electronic commerce.[46] Writing in 2001, Ian Kerr analysed 'agent-mediated' contracting and highlighted the doctrinal challenges that such systems posed for contract law, including questions of intention, contractual capacity, and consensus ad idem.[47] These early debates recognised that, once software was able to initiate and conclude transactions without direct human oversight, traditional doctrines would need to address whether an agreement generated by machines could be treated as binding between human principals.

Other scholars adopted related terminology to capture the same phenomenon. Jean-François Lerouge described 'electronic agents' as programs capable of searching for offers and conducting negotiations across digital platforms, while Emily Weitzenboeck used the term 'intelligent agents' to emphasise their autonomy from human supervision.[48] Francisco Andrade and others went further, describing 'contracting agents' not merely as tools for information processing but as entities entrusted with reasoning, decision-making and independent action.[49] These accounts anticipate what we now describe as algorithmic contracts: systems that mark the transition from automation to autonomy by introducing data analysis and decision-making into the contractual process.[50] Despite their terminological differences, they converge on the same insight: once contracting functions are delegated to software, the law must determine how doctrines of consent and agreement apply when decisions are taken by machines rather than by people.

[46] IR Kerr. 'Ensuring the Success of Contracts Formation in Agent-Mediated Electronic Commerce' (2001) 1 *Electronic Commerce Research* 183. Throughout this article, Kerr referred to this innovative software by various names, such as 'intelligent agent technology', 'electronic agents' or simply 'contracting agents'. The important point is that when this article was written in 2001, before the current landscape of algorithmic contracts, Kerr had already foreseen the emergence of software capable of autonomously initiating and concluding transactions. Algorithmic contracts are merely the realisation of what Kerr announced: 'agreements made by agents [that] will be generated by machines, not merely through them'.

[47] ibid 187–90.

[48] J-F Lerouge, 'The Use of Electronic Agents Questioned Under Contractual Law: Suggested Solutions on a European and American Level' (1999) 18 *John Marshall Journal of Computer & Information Law* 403, 405; EM Weitzenboeck, 'Electronic Agents and the Formation of Contracts' (2001) 9 *International Journal of Law and Information Technology* 204, 206–07.

[49] F Andrade et al, 'Contracting Agents: Legal Personality and Representation' (2007) 15 *Artificial Intelligence and Law* 357, 358.

[50] Martinelli and Rossi identify these two elements, data analysis and data management, as driving the revolution brought by artificial intelligence to contractual practices. See Martinelli and Rossi Chauvenet (n 2) 96.

As autonomous software became more widespread, attention shifted from the possibility of agent-mediated contracting to the legal consequences of delegating decision-making to machines. Samir Chopra and Laurence White described these systems as 'artificial agents' and analysed their use in automated trading, where operators did not exercise direct control over the agent's decisions.[51] They framed this as the 'contracting problem': the law must account for agreements concluded by entities that cannot themselves be parties, since they lack legal personality.[52]

Giovanni Sartor likewise examined the implications of what he termed 'cognitive automata' or 'software agents' – programs entrusted to make contractual choices on the basis of their own knowledge, without user review.[53] He identified 'cognitive delegation' as the distinctive feature of these systems: the decision to entrust both the content and conclusion of a contract to another cognition, albeit within pre-set objectives and constraints.[54] This description closely parallels the delegation of formation functions found in algorithmic contracts. In later years, Sartor took up this subject with a more contract-centric approach, labelling these entities 'intelligent autonomous contracting agents',[55] adding yet another term to the lexicon of algorithmic contracts.

Gunther Teubner extended these insights by referring to 'autonomous software agents', emphasising their ability to negotiate and conclude binding agreements on behalf of others.[56] For Teubner, the significance lay in the unpredictable behaviour of self-learning algorithms and the revolutionary implications of entrusting negotiation and execution to non-human systems.[57] His analysis underscores that autonomy in contracting software does not simply replicate existing tools of automation but fundamentally alters the legal landscape by displacing human decision-making at the point of contract formation.[58]

Recent scholarship has introduced further terms to capture contracting by autonomous systems. Vincent Ooi distinguishes between software in a passive role and software in an active role, the latter being capable of determining whether, and on what terms, a contract should be formed.[59] Contracts formed by software fall

[51] S Chopra and L White, 'Artificial Agents and the Contracting Problem: A Solution via an Agency Analysis' [2009] *University of Illinois Journal of Law, Technology & Policy* 363, 363–64.

[52] See ch 4, s II.A.ii (discussing the solutions proposed by Samir Chopra and Laurence White).

[53] G Sartor, 'Cognitive Automata and the Law: Electronic Contracting and the Intentionality of Software Agents' (2009) 17 *Artificial Intelligence and Law* 253, 253–90.

[54] ibid 281–82.

[55] G Sartor, *Contracts Without Agreement, or Agreement by Artefacts?* (Academy of Sciences in Göttingen ed, Universitätsverlag Göttingen, 2020) 41, 41–46.

[56] G Teubner, 'Digitale Rechtssubjekte? Zum Privatrechtlichen Status Autonomer Softwareagenten/Digital Personhood? The Status of Autonomous Software Agents in Private Law' [2018] *Ancilla Iuris* 35, 77.

[57] ibid 45.

[58] See ibid 59–60, describing autonomous software agents as capable of seeking out offers, negotiating with prospective partners, selecting counterparties, exercising discretion in contract finalisation and determining the essential elements of transactions.

[59] V Ooi, 'Contracts Formed by Software: An Approach Form the Law of Mistake' (2022) 2 *Journal of Business Law* 97.

within this active category: agreements in which algorithms autonomously decide to contract and to define the terms on which the parties are bound.

In the financial sector, the term 'robo-investors' has been used to describe algorithms that execute investment decisions without human intervention. Operating on the basis of predefined criteria, data analysis and market conditions, robo-investors highlight how algorithmic systems can autonomously determine binding transactions in fast-moving markets.[60] They exemplify a species of algorithmic contracting in which discretion over whether, how and when to contract is delegated entirely to the machine.

Marco Rizzi and Natalie Skead propose the broader label of 'digitally enhanced contracts', encompassing smart contracts, contracts formed by software, algorithmic contracts, agreements facilitated by electronic agents, and even prospective contracts concluded with artificial general intelligence (AGI).[61] Their analysis illustrates both the breadth of activity now included under this heading and the continuing need to distinguish between automation that operates in the execution of contracts and autonomy that extends into their formation.

Institutional bodies have also contributed to the expanding lexicon. The European Law Institute (ELI) has referred to 'digital assistants' in its principles on automated decision-making for consumer contracts, drawing on the OECD's definition of AI systems as algorithms that generate outputs such as predictions, recommendations or decisions capable of influencing digital environments.[62] Yet the choice of terminology is problematic. It risks confusion with the EU's 'digital contracts' framework and obscures the central element of autonomy that characterises algorithmic contracting.[63]

These varied terms highlight the unsettled vocabulary of the field. Despite differences in emphasis, they all point to the same development: the delegation of contractual formation to software operating without direct human oversight. For the sake of clarity, this book employs the terms 'algorithmic contracts' and 'algorithmic systems'. This reflects Lauren Scholz's influential definition of algorithmic contracts as agreements 'in which one or more parties use an algorithm to determine whether to be bound and how to be bound'.[64] These terms capture the defining feature of autonomy while avoiding the doctrinal ambiguities associated with agency-based terminology. They also provide a foundation for the next section, which distinguishes algorithmic contracts, centred on the automation of formation, from smart contracts, concerned with the automation of execution, so as to clarify the unique doctrinal challenges raised by autonomy in contract formation.

[60] P Treleaven and others, 'Algorithms: Law and Regulation' (2019) 52 *Computer* 32.

[61] M Rizzi and N Skead, 'Algorithmic Contracts and the Equitable Doctrine of Undue Influence: Adapting Old Rules to a New Legal Landscape' (2020) 14 *Journal of Equity* 301, 308.

[62] C Busch et al, 'EU Consumer Law and Automated Decision-Making (ADM): Is EU Consumer Ready for ADM?' (2023) 9, citing OECD, *Recommendation of the Council on Artificial Intelligence* (2019) OECD/LEGAL/0449.

[63] See above note to n 31.

[64] Scholz (n 44) 134.

## IV. Differentiating Smart Contracts from Algorithmic Contracts

Although smart contracts and algorithmic contracts are sometimes conflated,[65] they concern distinct phenomena.[66] Smart contracts automate the performance of obligations, whereas algorithmic contracts delegate aspects of contract formation to autonomous systems. Occasional confusion has arisen because both forms of contracting reduce human involvement,[67] and even early proponents such as Vitalik Buterin described smart contracts as 'autonomous software agents', a label more appropriately associated with algorithmic contracts.[68] The overlap of terminology, and the fine line between automation and autonomy, have contributed to blurred usage in both scholarship and practice.[69]

The distinction, however, is fundamental. Autonomy is characteristic of algorithmic contracts at the stage of formation, while automation without human intervention defines smart contracts at the stage of execution.[70] A further difference lies in their technological foundations: blockchain and distributed ledger technologies underpin smart contracts, while artificial intelligence provides the enabling tools for algorithmic contracts.[71] The following discussion develops these distinctions in greater detail, in order to clarify the specific doctrinal challenges posed by algorithmic contracts.

[65] See, eg, J Linarelli, 'Artificial Intelligence and Contracts Formation: Back to Contract as Bargain?' (2023) *Emerging Issues at the Intersection of Commercial Law and Technologies* papers.ssrn.com/sol3/papers.abstract_id=4363410. Similarly, it contributes to this confusion that expressions such as 'algorithmic contracting' and 'smart contracting' are grouped together as forming part of the same phenomenon. See, eg, C Wendehorst, 'Discussion Draft: Principles for AI in Contracting (Version 2.1)' (2024) 13 *Journal of European Consumer and Market Law* 43, 44.

[66] Scholz (n 44) 148; LH Scholz, 'Algorithms and Contract Law' in W Barfield (ed), *The Cambridge Handbook of The Law of Algorithms* (Cambridge University Press, 2020) 141, 148; J Linarelli, 'Artificial General Intelligence and Contract' (2019) 24 *Revue de droit uniforme* 330, 332; Lord Sales, 'Law and the Digital World' (16 April 2021); C Poncibò, 'Artificial Intelligence as a Communication Tool in Contract Law' (2023) 31 *European Review of Private Law* 239, 240.

[67] In the same vein, referring to smart contracts as 'smart agents' or 'software agents' is controversial. See Stark in M Cannarsa, 'Interpretation of Contracts and Smart Contracts: Smart Interpretation or Interpretation of Smart Contracts?' (2018) 26 *European Review of Private Law* 773, 777.

[68] V Buterin, 'On Public and Private Blockchains' (Ethereum Blog, 7 August 2015) blog.ethereum.org/2015/08/07/on-public-and-private-blockchains/ accessed 30 August 2025.

[69] For the distinction between autonomy and automation, see above section I, text to n 11.

[70] See, eg, MJ Schmidt-Kessen, H Eenmaa and M Mitre, 'Machines That Make and Keep Promises - Lessons for Contract Automation from Algorithmic Trading on Financial Markets' (2022) 46 *Computer Law & Security Review* 105717 /www.sciencedirect.com/science/article/pii/S0267364922000553 accessed 30 August 2025; see also Law Commission, *Smart Legal Contracts: Advice to Government* (Law Com No. 401, 2021) 11 publicinformationonline.com/download/231719 accessed 30 August 2025.

[71] M Ebers, 'Artificial Intelligence, Contracting and Contract Law: An Introduction' in M Ebers, C Poncibò and M Zou (eds), *Contracting and Contract Law in the Age of Artificial Intelligence* (Hart Publishing, 2022) 19–20. The seemingly indissoluble link between blockchain technology and smart contracts is also contested. The Law Commission has expressly stated that it 'no longer consider DLT to be an essential feature of smart legal contracts': 'Law Commission No. 401 Smart Legal Contracts. Advice to Government' (Law Com No. 401, 2021) 39, [2.32]. For a fuller exploration of how smart contracts may exist independently of blockchain, see H Halaburda, 'Economic and Business Dimensions: Blockchain Revolution without the Blockchain?' (2018) 61 *Communications of the ACM* 27, 27.

## A. Smart (Legal) Contracts and Algorithmic Contracts: A Doctrinal Distinction

The idea of the 'smart contract' long predates the debates on algorithmic contracting. In 1994 Nick Szabo described a smart contract as 'a computerized transaction protocol that executes the terms of a contract',[72] later refining this into a conception of contracts expressed in digital form with protocols for performance.[73] His primary concern was the fulfilment of agreements, aiming to make breach costly for the party in default.[74] This early work situated smart contracts squarely in the domain of performance rather than formation.

Smart contracts gained renewed attention with the rise of blockchain technologies. While Szabo envisaged the use of trusted intermediaries, Satoshi Nakamoto's Bitcoin network demonstrated how cryptographic consensus could eliminate them.[75] Building on this, Vitalik Buterin launched Ethereum in 2015 as a blockchain platform with a built-in programming language, enabling smart contracts and decentralised applications.[76] Buterin's reference to a 'Turing-complete' system contributed to later confusion, as it suggested affinities with artificial intelligence even though the underlying technology remains distinct.

The term 'smart contract' has since been used inconsistently – sometimes to denote legally binding agreements, sometimes to describe self-executing code, and sometimes both. The Law Commission's 2021 report clarified the landscape by distinguishing between 'smart contracts' as computer programs that run automatically, and 'smart legal contracts' as legally binding contracts in which some or all obligations are defined in and/or performed by code.[77] This clarification reinforces the difference with algorithmic contracts: while smart legal contracts rely on code to execute obligations, they do not delegate decision-making in formation. That role belongs to algorithmic systems.

Nevertheless, only a subset of smart legal contracts could be said to overlap with algorithmic contracts, which confirms the need for a sharp doctrinal distinction between the two. The Law Commission identified three forms of smart legal contracts: first, natural language contracts with automated performance, in which code merely facilitates execution without defining obligations; second, hybrid contracts, where natural language and code together define the obligations, some

[72] N Szabo, 'Smart Contracts' (1994) Essays on Smart Contracts, Commercial Controls and Security www.fon.hum.uva.nl/rob/Courses/InformationInSpeech/CDROM/Literature/LOTwinterschool2006/szabo.best.vwh.net/smart.contracts.html.

[73] Szabo (n 1).

[74] ibid 1.

[75] S Nakamoto, 'Bitcoin: A Peer-to-Peer Electronic Cash System' (2008) bitcoin.org/bitcoin.pdf accessed 2 May 2024.

[76] Buterin, 'Ethereum White Paper. A Next Generation Smart Contract & Decentralized Application Platform' (2013) burnersxxx.files.wordpress.com/2015/01/pdfs-ethereumwhitepaper.pdf.

[77] Law Commission (n 71) vii.

or all of which are executed automatically; and third, solely code contracts, where all contractual terms are both defined in and executed by code.[78]

It might be argued that algorithmic contracts fall within the second and third categories, where the system is capable of defining obligations in code. Yet algorithmic contracts are best understood as a distinct phenomenon. Unlike smart legal contracts, they involve the delegation of decision-making in formation to autonomous systems. Treating them as a sub-category of smart contracts risks obscuring their distinctive features. A clearer analysis therefore requires considering them separately, so that their implications for doctrines of agreement and consent can be addressed in their own terms.

Smart legal contracts can be distinguished from algorithmic contracts along three dimensions: the function of the system, the phase of the contract lifecycle in which it operates, and the technologies that underpin it.[79]

First, the function of code differs in each case. In smart legal contracts, code may define obligations in part and then execute them, or it may simply execute obligations already defined in natural language.[80] In either scenario, the code does not perform a decision-making process: it translates, but it does not decide.[81] By contrast, algorithmic contracts delegate the determination of contractual obligations to algorithms, which operate autonomously in formation. This distinction is reflected in the Law Commission's definitions. While the Commission refers to code as 'a language used to give instructions to computers',[82] an algorithm is more accurately described as 'a set of mathematical instructions that must be followed in a fixed order' to calculate a solution.[83] Code therefore carries instructions; algorithms generate the outcome.

Second, the difference lies in the moment of the contract lifecycle at which the system operates. Smart legal contracts are associated with execution. They embody Szabo's insight that contractual clauses can be embedded in hardware or software so as to make breaches prohibitively costly.[84] Self-execution has become their defining feature. The Law Commission has likewise emphasised that 'a distinctive feature of smart legal contracts is [that] some or all of the obligations under the

[78] ibid 21–22. Regarding the category of hybrid smart legal contract, the Law Commission explicitly associates it with the Ricardian contracts. See nn 35–36 above.

[79] The term 'system' is used in this context to refer generically both to the simple code and algorithms used in smart contracts, and to the machine learning-based algorithms used in algorithmic contracts.

[80] In the context of smart legal contracts, in which the main feature is automated execution, this interpretation is grammatically sound for the phrase 'defined in and/or performed automatically'.

[81] The Law Commission employs the term 'define', which specifically pertains to the contract formation phase, and thus, it can lead to some confusion regarding the extent of the involvement of the code in the provision of consent during the contract formation phase. In certain smart legal contracts, the code, as per the Commission's terminology, specifies the parties' obligations. There is no delegation of the decision-making process in this type of smart legal contract. Law Commission (n 71) [2.3]; see also the definition of 'smart legal contract' (terms 'defined in and/or performed automatically by a computer program') at [2.11]. See further ch 2, text to nn 37–40 (computable contracts).

[82] Law Commission (n 71) v.

[83] ibid

[84] N Szabo, 'Formalizing and Securing Relationships on Public Networks' *First Monday*, (1997) 2(9). http://doi.org/10.5210/fm.v2i9.548.

contract are performed automatically without the need for human intervention'.[85] Algorithmic contracts, by contrast, focus on formation: they outsource decision-making at the point of agreement, using data analysis to customise terms.[86] Debates on algorithmic contracting therefore centre on doctrines of offer and acceptance, the contracting problem, and the objective theory of contract.

Third, the technologies involved are different. Smart contracts rely primarily on blockchain and related cryptographic tools, while algorithmic contracts depend on artificial intelligence.[87] Although blockchain has been treated in much of the literature as an essential feature of smart contracts,[88] the Law Commission has taken a technology-neutral approach, observing that other decentralised ledger technologies may also be employed.[89] Algorithmic contracts, by contrast, depend on machine learning and other AI techniques that enable autonomous decision-making.

In sum, the comparison between smart legal contracts and algorithmic contracts reveals both convergence and divergence. Smart contracts, rooted in blockchain and cryptography, are defined by their capacity to enforce obligations automatically, yet they remain rigid and inflexible, bound to the limits of their code.[90] Algorithmic contracts, enabled by artificial intelligence, operate at the formative stage of agreement, where decision-making is delegated to autonomous systems. Their breadth and adaptability stand in contrast to the immutability of smart

[85] Law Commission (n 71) 12. See also CD Clack, VA Bakshi and L Braine, 'Smart Contract Templates: Foundations, Design Landscape and Research Directions' (2016) *arXiv preprint* arXiv:1608.00771 arxiv.org/abs/1608.00771 accessed 30 August 2025, defining a smart contract as 'an automatable and enforceable agreement. Automatable by computer, although some parts may require human input and control. Enforceable either by legal enforcement of rights and obligations or via tamper-proof execution of computer code'. See further A Savelyev, 'Contract Law 2.0: "Smart" Contracts as the Beginning of the End of Classic Contract Law?' (2017) 26 *Information & Communications Technology Law* 116, 118, describing 'agreements existing in the form of software code implemented on the blockchain platform, which ensures autonomy and self-executive nature of smart contract terms based on predetermined set of factors'. See also S Farrell, H Machin and R Hinchcliffe, 'Lost and Found in Smart Contracts Translation: Considerations in Transitioning to Automation in Legal Architecture' (2017) 25 *Journal of Banking and Finance Law and Practice* 1, observing that 'smart contracts are more than mere automated processes for enabling performance, they also have the means of ensuring the performance'.

[86] Scholz (n 44) 132; Scholz (n 66) 141.

[87] Ebers (n 71) 20.

[88] KEC Levy, 'Book-Smart, Not Street-Smart: Blockchain-Based Smart Contracts and the Social Workings of Law' (2017) 3 *Engaging Science, Technology, and Society* 1, 1–15; Durovic and Janssen (n 4) 61–79; H Eenmaa-Dimitrieva and MJ Schmidt-Kessen, 'Creating Markets in No-Trust Environments: The Law and Economics of Smart Contracts' (2019) 35 *Computer Law & Security Review* 69, 69–88; Savelyev (n 85); Schuster (n 4); S Agnikhotram and A Kouroutakis, 'Doctrinal Challenges for the Legality of Smart Contracts: Lex Cryptographia or a New, "Smart" Way to Contract?' (2019) XIX(2) *Journal of High Technology Law* 300; P Cuccuru, 'Beyond Bitcoin: An Early Overview on Smart Contracts' (2017) 25 *International Journal of Law and Information Technology* 179, 179–95; Caria (n 30) 731–51; P Sirena and FP Patti, 'Smart Contracts and Automation of Private Relationships' in HW Micklitz, O Ofteringer and A Ruzza (eds), *Constitutional Challenges in Algorithmic Society* (Cambridge University Press, 2020) 17, 17; M Raskin, 'The Law and Legality of Smart Contracts' (2017) 1 *Georgetown Law Technology Review* 305; R O'Shields, 'Smart Contracts: Legal Agreements for the Blockchain' (2017) 21 *North Carolina Banking Institute* 177, 177.

[89] Law Commission (n 71) [2.32].

[90] JM Sklaroff, 'Smart Contracts and the Cost of Inflexibility' (2017) 166(1) *University of Pennsylvania Law Review* 263–303.

contracts. When combined, the two models can create powerful instruments in which algorithms determine contractual content and blockchain ensures its execution.[91] This synergy explains why scholarship and even the Law Commission have sometimes blurred the categories under the label of 'computer programs reaching agreement'.[92] But such overlap should not obscure their doctrinal distinctiveness.

The task for legal analysis is to preserve that distinction. Only by doing so can the implications of algorithmic contracts be assessed on their own terms – particularly their impact on doctrines of agreement, consent, and contractual capacity. Smart contracts and algorithmic contracts may work together in practice, but their normative challenges differ. The following section examines how the Law Commission of England and Wales has approached these issues, and how far its analysis of smart legal contracts leaves open questions specific to algorithmic contracting.

## B. Smart Legal Contracts, Algorithmic Contracts, and English Contract Law. The Law Commission Position

The Law Commission's analysis of smart legal contracts makes no explicit reference to algorithmic contracts, yet its discussion of hybrid and solely code agreements inevitably touches upon them. Chapter 3 of the *Advice to Government* addresses the requirement of agreement and identifies novel issues, particularly in relation to types 2 and 3 smart legal contracts.[93] In hybrid contracts, code operates alongside natural language to define certain obligations; in solely code contracts, all obligations are both defined in and executed by code. The Commission highlights two situations in which problems of agreement may arise: where all interaction between the parties occurs through code, without prior negotiation or communication in natural language;[94] and where parties deploy computer programs – such

[91] For a more comprehensive analysis of the potential relationship between these two technologies, see AA Hussain and F Al-Turjman, 'Artificial Intelligence and Blockchain: A Review' (2021) 32 *Transactions on Emerging Telecommunications Technologies* e4268; see also M Zou, 'When AI Meets Smart Contracts: The Regulation of Hyper-Autonomous Contracting Systems?' in M Ebers, C Poncibò and M Zou (eds), *Contracting and Contract Law in the Age of Artificial Intelligence* (Hart Publishing, 2022) 41–58.

[92] Law Commission (n 71) [3.36]–[3.38]. When the Law Commission report takes a closer look at smart legal contracts from the contract formation perspective, and more specifically, in terms of the agreement requirement, it focuses on the absence of natural language use. Nonetheless, the Law Commission extends the scope of the initial definition of smart legal contracts, particularly with regard to types 2 and 3, to explore the issue of 'computer programs reaching agreement'. While the Law Commission previously defined smart legal contracts as having automated execution and being legally binding, it is clear that these 'contracts formed by computer programs' with automated execution do not conform to the traditional definition of smart legal contracts. Instead, they represent a combination of smart legal contracts and algorithmic contracts. Smart contracts that do not incorporate an algorithmic contract cannot reach agreements on their own.

[93] Law Commission (n 71) [3.1]–[3.147].

[94] With respect to scenarios outside the scope of this study, the Law Commission notes that automated communications may amount to invitations to treat or offers, and that a counterparty's direct execution of the relevant act can constitute acceptance under ordinary principles of English contract law. See Law Commission (n 71) 41–42.

as those operating on a distributed ledger – that subsequently interact and execute transactions with one another.[95]

These scenarios are, in substance, instances of algorithmic contracting, although the Commission does not use that terminology. Its analysis of agreement rests on the traditional presumption that intention to create legal relations is present where agreement and consideration coexist,[96] but it concedes that this presumption may not hold when contracts are formed exclusively through machine interaction. Rather than offering a doctrinal solution, the report retreats to caution, suggesting only that 'additional evidence may be required to evidence an agreement in more complex scenarios'.[97]

The Law Commission describes a solely code contract as 'a smart legal contract in which all of the contractual terms are defined in, and performed automatically by, the code of a computer program'.[98] Scholz, by contrast, defines algorithmic contracts as agreements 'in which one or more parties use an algorithm to determine whether to be bound or how to be bound'.[99] The Commission's formulation is imprecise: code and algorithms are not interchangeable. An algorithm is the set of instructions that determines an outcome, while code is the language through which those instructions are communicated to a computer for execution. Only an algorithm can 'define' obligations in the sense of determining contractual content; code merely implements that determination.[100] Solely code contracts therefore presuppose the use of algorithms, but the converse does not hold: not all algorithmic contracts fall within the category of smart legal contracts.

The analysis of agreement is inseparable from that of intention, which under English law must be manifested and is tested objectively.[101] Some of the terminology deployed in relation to agreement in fact overlaps with the language of intent. The Law Commission identifies two scenarios in which difficulties may arise. The first is where the parties state expressly that they do not intend their agreement to be legally binding, relying instead on the performance of the code.[102] The second is where an agreement is concluded on a distributed ledger system without any natural language documents or communications between the parties.[103] In these cases, the Commission suggests that an intention to create legal relations may nonetheless be inferred from the expectations of platform users, and it notes that the courts of England and Wales have enforced agreements based on conduct alone where necessary to give business efficacy to a transaction.[104]

[95] ibid 40.

[96] J Cartwright, *Contract Law* (Hart Publishing, 2016) 156.

[97] Law Commission (n 71) [3.15]–[3.18].

[98] ibid viii.

[99] Scholz (n 44) 134.

[100] See text to nn 80–83.

[101] *RTS Flexible Systems Ltd v Molkerei Alois Müller GmbH & Co KG* [2010] UKSC 14 [45]; *Smith v Hughes* (1871) LR 6 QB 597.

[102] This possibility of contractual self-exclusion is not pursued here, but it is enough to note that English law permits it. Law Commission (n 71) 55–56.

[103] ibid 56.

[104] Law Commission (n 71) [3.72]. See also *The Aramis* [1989] 1 Lloyd's Rep 213, 224, by Bingham LJ; *Glencore Energy UK Ltd v OMV Supply & Trading Ltd* [2018] EWHC 895 (Comm), [2018] 2 All ER (Comm) 876 at [51] by Sir Ross Cranston.

These situations amount, in substance, to algorithmic contracting: agreements formed by the interaction of programs deployed by the parties rather than by natural language exchange. Yet the Commission does not confront the doctrinal implications. Its response is confined to a practical recommendation that parties wishing to create legal relations should record that intention in natural language.[105]

Lauren Scholz had already anticipated that smart contracts would serve as an early use case of algorithmic contracting.[106] The Law Commission's analysis points in the same direction: its notion of solely code smart legal contracts presupposes the operation of algorithms, even if the report does not label them as such. What emerges is a category that is algorithmic in substance but absent in terminology. The Commission acknowledges that such systems create difficulties for agreement and intention, yet it limits its remarks to practical advice for contracting parties and leaves the doctrinal implications unexamined.

## V. From Automation to Autonomy: Concluding Reflections

The trajectory traced in this chapter shows that automation in contracting is neither novel nor confined to the current era. From vending machines to electronic data interchange, and from e-commerce to Ricardian and computable contracts, each stage of technological development has tested the adaptability of English contract law. Smart contracts, grounded in blockchain, extended automation into the domain of self-execution. Algorithmic contracts push further still, introducing autonomy into the formation of agreements themselves.

Distinguishing algorithmic contracts from neighbouring concepts is therefore more than a question of terminology. It is essential to understanding the doctrinal challenges raised when algorithms determine contractual content. While the Law Commission's account of smart legal contracts touches upon this phenomenon, it leaves its implications largely unexamined. Recognising the autonomy of algorithmic systems at the stage of formation clarifies both their novelty and the limits of existing frameworks.

The discussion now turns from the historical trajectory of automation to the technical features that matter for formation. Because doctrinal conclusions are often distorted by loose or anthropomorphic descriptions of AI, the next chapter sets out a minimal technical baseline – sufficient to distinguish deterministic automation from machine-learning systems whose outputs are not fully specified in advance.

[105] Law Commission (n 71) 57.
[106] Scholz (n 44) 145–49.

# 3

# When Technology Meets the Law

## I. Introduction

Contract law has long been shaped by technological disruption. From the mechanisation of production in the Industrial Revolution to the successive waves of communication technologies – postal mail, telegraph, telephone, fax, and eventually the internet – each innovation has prompted legal systems to re-examine how agreements are formed and validated. The present study situates itself within this lineage, with a particular focus on the implications of algorithmic contracting for the doctrinal requirement of agreement. Unlike earlier tools, algorithmic systems, and especially those grounded in artificial intelligence, they do not merely provide new channels of communication but actively participate in the processes of negotiation and formation. In this respect, their impact on contract law recalls prior episodes of technological transformation while at the same time raising qualitatively distinct challenges.[1]

Successive industrial revolutions have consistently altered the trajectory of contract law, and the transformative effects of the present technological revolution were no less predictable. Prior to the First Industrial Revolution, however, contract law occupied only a marginal place within the legal order. William Blackstone's *Commentaries on the Laws of England* famously devoted a mere 28 pages to contractual obligations, in contrast to nearly 400 pages on real property.[2] This imbalance underscored the peripheral role of contracts in a society where economic activity remained largely structured around landholding and status rather than exchange and commerce.

Advances in communication have repeatedly forced contract law to recalibrate its rules of formation. Doctrines originally framed for face-to-face bargaining

[1] JP Barlow, 'A Declaration of the Independence of Cyberspace' www.eff.org/es/cyberspace-independence accessed 2 May 2024; FH Easterbrook, 'Cyberspace and the Law of the Horse' [1996] *University of Chicago Legal Forum* 207, 207–16; L Lessig, 'The Law of the Horse: What Cyberlaw Might Teach' (1999) 113 *Harvard Law Review* 501, 501–49. These debates illustrate how successive technological innovations – from cyberspace to the internet – were framed both as continuous with, and as disruptive of, established legal categories.

[2] W Blackstone, *Commentaries on the Laws of England* (Clarendon Press, 1766) bk II, chs 1–29, 2–441 (property); ch 30, 442–70 (contracts). See also A Burrows, J Cartwright and J Beatson, *Anson's Law of Contract* (Oxford University Press, 2020) 1; G Gilmore, 'From Tort to Contract: Industrialization and the Law' (1977) 86 *Yale Law Journal* 788, 788–97.

proved inadequate once agreements began to be concluded across distance. The emergence of postal contracting in the nineteenth century required new principles to determine when and where agreement was formed, principles later tested again with the arrival of the telephone and telefax, and more recently with email and electronic platforms. Each technological innovation prompted courts and legislators to refine the law, illustrating how seemingly technical changes in communication reshape foundational questions of offer and acceptance.

A decisive shift in the modern law of contract came with the Unfair Contract Terms Act 1977 (UCTA).[3] For the first time, Parliament intervened comprehensively in the allocation of contractual risk by restricting the enforceability of exclusion and limitation clauses. The Act introduced statutory controls to ensure that certain terms – particularly those purporting to exclude liability for negligence or fundamental breach – could not be relied upon unless they satisfied a test of reasonableness. In doing so, UCTA reoriented contract law from a model centred on freedom of contract toward one that placed fairness, equity, and consumer protection at its core. Its enactment marked the emergence of substantive regulation of contract terms, anticipating later European directives on unfair terms and reshaping the balance between private autonomy and public oversight in contractual dealings.[4]

European initiatives on e-commerce trace back to the European Commission's 1993 White Paper *Growth, Competitiveness and Employment*, which identified the digital economy as a priority for market integration.[5] This policy agenda was reinforced at the international level by the 1995 G7 Conference on the Information Society and by the adoption of the UNCITRAL Model Law on Electronic Commerce in 1996.[6] These developments culminated in the EU's Directive 2000/31/EC on electronic commerce, which established a harmonised legal framework for online business activity. Article 9(1) of the Directive requires Member States to ensure that contracts may be validly concluded by electronic means, thereby embedding electronic contracting within European private law and securing its recognition across Member States.[7]

The contemporary challenge is no longer confined to new modes of communication but to the emergence of contracts generated and executed through algorithmic processes. These arrangements form part of a broader technological revolution driven by data analysis and artificial intelligence. John McCarthy, who first coined

[3] Unfair Contract Terms Act 1977, c 50.

[4] See R Brownsword and G Howells, 'When Surfers Start to Shop: Internet Commerce and Contract Law' (1999) 19 *Legal Studies* 287, 292–95.

[5] Commission of the European Communities, *Growth, Competitiveness and Employment: The Challenges and Ways Forward into the 21st Century* (White Paper, COM(93) 700 final).

[6] UNCITRAL, *Model Law on Electronic Commerce with Guide to Enactment* (1996); See also G Pearce and N Platten, 'Promoting the Information Society: The EU Directive on Electronic Commerce' (2000) 6 *European Law Journal* 363, 365–66.

[7] Directive 2000/31/EC of the European Parliament and of the Council on certain legal aspects of information society services, in particular electronic commerce, in the Internal Market [2000] OJ L178/1, art 9(1).

the term 'artificial intelligence' in the mid-1950s, defined it as 'the science and engineering of making intelligent machines, especially intelligent computer programs', stressing that such intelligence need not replicate biologically observable processes.[8] For McCarthy, intelligence denoted 'the computational part of the ability to achieve goals in the world', a quality that may manifest not only in humans but also in animals and machines.[9] These foundational definitions remain instructive: they capture both the functional orientation of AI and its potential autonomy, features that directly inform contemporary debates on algorithmic contracting.

Any assessment of algorithmic contracting must begin with the technological foundations of artificial intelligence. Its defining features – data-driven computation, inference, and varying degrees of autonomy – indicate where friction with established doctrines of contract law is most likely to arise. This chapter examines the interaction between law and technology by tracing three trajectories. It begins with a historical survey of humanity's pursuit of automation, from ancient automata to the rise of machine learning. It then considers how successive innovations, from the postal rule to electronic commerce and smart contracts, have reshaped the law of contract formation. Finally, it clarifies the key concepts of artificial intelligence and algorithmic contracts, highlighting the tensions around determinism, autonomy, and explainability. Taken together, these discussions show how contract law has repeatedly adapted to technological change while underscoring why algorithmic systems raise questions that extend beyond incremental adaptation.

## II. Between Humans and Machines. The History of Humankind's Search for Automation

### A. A Brief History of Automation

Human fascination with creating self-moving and self-thinking artefacts is as old as recorded imagination. From myth to mechanism, the desire to reproduce human functions through technology reveals a continuous thread in the history of civilisation: the pursuit of automation. In Homer's Iliad and Odyssey, the term 'automata' describes devices endowed with self-propelled movement – animated servants forged by the god Hephaestus – seeming to possess an intrinsic vitality akin to living organisms.[10] These mythic automata were more than symbols of divine craftsmanship; they embodied the aspiration to infuse inert matter with agency, to reproduce the attributes of life through artifice. Within these early

[8] J McCarthy, 'What Is Artificial Intelligence?' (November 2007) www-formal.stanford.edu/jmc/whatisai.pdf accessed 2 May 2024, 2.

[9] ibid 3.

[10] D Kalligeropoulos and S Vasileiadou, *The Homeric Automata and Their Implementation* (SA Paipetis ed, Springer Netherlands, 2008) 77, 77–84.

depictions also lay a subtle association between machines and servitude,[11] a theme that would echo through later centuries in the evolving relationship between humans and their mechanical counterparts.[12]

Centuries later, the mathematician and engineer Heron of Alexandria provided the first detailed descriptions of self-operating mechanisms. His treatises, notably *Peri automatopoietikes* (On Automata-Making),[13] described theatrical devices and temple machines powered by air pressure and water.[14] Heron's work marks a turning point from myth to mechanical design, replacing divine animation with reproducible engineering principles. The idea that a device could imitate human action through internal mechanisms was revolutionary, and its legacy endured throughout the medieval and early modern periods.

In the ninth century, the Banu Musa brothers of Baghdad advanced this tradition, presenting programmable machines such as an automatic flute player. Their work demonstrated that mechanical behaviour could not only be automated but also varied through human design – an early glimpse of what we might now call programmability.[15] Similar ingenuity resurfaced in fourteenth-century Europe, where accounts attributed to Albertus Magnus described talking statues or automata capable of responding to questions, blurring the boundary between sacred miracle and mechanical invention.[16]

During the Renaissance, the rediscovery of classical philosophy rekindled reflection on the relationship between humans and their tools. Aristotle's view that instruments were extensions of the master's body inspired early modern thinkers to explore whether such extensions might themselves act autonomously. Writers and artisans alike imagined artificial beings – the Homunculus, the Golem, or mechanical servants – that mirrored the human form while lacking independent will. These creations revealed both admiration for human ingenuity and unease at its implications: a tension that continues to shape contemporary debates about artificial intelligence.[17]

[11] K LaGrandeur, *Artificial Slaves in the Renaissance and the Dangers of Independent Innovation* in S Cave, K Dihal and S Dillon (eds), *AI Narratives: A History of Imaginative Thinking about Intelligent Machines* (Oxford University Press, 2020) 95, 98.

[12] In relation to the so-called 'electronic slave metaphor' and a more in-depth analysis of the recourse to the Roman law of slavery see A Katz and M MacDonald, 'Autonomous Intelligent Agents and the Roman Law of Slavery' in L Edwards, S Burkhard and E Harbinja (eds), *Future Law: Emerging Technology, Regulation and Ethics* (Edinburgh University Press, 2022) 295, 295–312. This comparison is not new, however. See also S Chopra and LF White, 'Artificial Agents and the Contracting Problem: A Solution via an Agency Analysis' [2009] *University of Illinois Journal of Law, Technology & Policy* 363, 377.

[13] S Murphy, 'Heron of Alexandria's on Automation-Making' in G Hollister-Short, and F James (eds), *History of Technology* (Bloomsbury Academic, 1996)1, 1–44.

[14] Notably, one of the most popular machines that Heron invented was the holy water dispenser, considered the most ancient precursor of vending machines. See K Segrave, *Vending Machines: An American Social History*, 1st edn (McFarland & Co, 2002) 290–94.

[15] S Shakerin, 'Engineering Art' (2001) 123 *Mechanical Engineering* 66, 66–69.

[16] M Kang and B Halliburton, 'The Android of Albertus Magnus: A Legend of Artificial Being' in S Cave, K Dihal and S Dillon (eds), *AI Narratives: A History of Imaginative Thinking about Intelligent Machines* (Oxford University Press, 2020) 72, 72–94.

[17] LaGrandeur (n 11) 95–118.

By the eighteenth century, the fascination with lifelike machines reached new sophistication. Wolfgang von Kempelen's 'Mechanical Turk', an elaborate chess-playing automaton exhibited across Europe, captivated audiences who believed they were witnessing a machine capable of independent thought. In truth, a concealed chess master operated the mechanism, but the illusion proved powerful enough to sustain public belief in mechanical intelligence for decades.[18] Equally symbolic were the so-called 'talking dolls' and automaton musicians of the late Enlightenment, which expressed a growing obsession with reproducing not merely motion but *voice*, the quintessential mark of humanity. These devices blurred the distinction between entertainment and experimentation, hinting at deeper questions about what it means for a creation to speak or decide.[19]

A century later, Ada Lovelace offered a radically different perspective on mechanical intelligence. Her insight reframed the limits of automation: creativity required human input, but collaboration between human and machine could yield genuinely novel outcomes.[20] Modern computer scientists would later name this boundary the 'Lovelace Test', a benchmark for judging whether a system can be said to exhibit originality.[21]

Shortly after the end of the First World War, a new term entered the lexicon: 'robot'. Coined by Karel Čapek in his play *R.U.R. (Rossum's Universal Robots)* (1920), the word derived from the Czech *robota*, meaning forced labour, and captured both the promise and the unease of mechanical servitude.[22] His humanoid creations were conceived as workers designed to serve humanity, yet they ultimately rebelled – a narrative that mirrored enduring anxieties about control, dependence, and autonomy. However, although these early robots possessed great physical strength, they lacked the intelligence we associate with modern artificial intelligence.[23]

The conceptual leap from mechanical automation to cognitive systems began in the mid-twentieth century. Alan Turing's seminal work *On Computable Numbers* (1936) established the theoretical foundations of computation, showing that reasoning itself could be expressed as an algorithmic process.[24] His wartime cryptographic work and later reflections on 'learning machines' anticipated the shift from mechan-

[18] E Stephens, 'The Mechanical Turk: A Short History of "Artificial Artificial Intelligence"' (2023) 37 *Cultural Studies* 65, 65–87.

[19] J Park, 'Making the Automaton Speak: Hearing Artificial Voices in the Eighteenth Century' in S Cave, K Dihal and S Dillon (eds), *AI Narratives: A History of Imaginative Thinking about Intelligent Machines* (Oxford University Press, 2020) 119, 119–43.

[20] M Ward, 'Victorian Fictions of Computational Creativity' in S Cave, K Dihal and S Dillon (eds), *AI Narratives: A History of Imaginative Thinking about Intelligent Machines* (Oxford University Press, 2020)144, 144–64.

[21] S Bringsjord, P Bello and D Ferrucci, 'Creativity, the Turing Test, and the (Better) Lovelace Test' (2001) 11 *Minds and Machines* 3, 3–27.

[22] P March-Russell, 'Machines Like Us? Modernism and the Question of the Robot' in S Cave, K Dihal and S Dillon (eds), *AI Narratives: A History of Imaginative Thinking about Intelligent Machines* (Oxford University Press, 2020)165, 165. ibid 165–86.

[23] JF Engelberger, *Robots in Practice* (Kogan Page Ltd, 1980).

[24] AM Turing, 'On Computable Numbers, with an Application to the Entscheidungsproblem' (1937) 42 *Proceedings of the London Mathematical Society* 230, 230–65.

ical replication to adaptive systems.[25] In his 1950 paper 'Computing Machinery and Intelligence', Turing asked the now-canonical question, 'Can machines think?', reframing intelligence as a functional, not biological, property.[26]

A few years later, the 1956 Dartmouth Summer Research Project on Artificial Intelligence, organised by John McCarthy and Marvin Minsky, marked the institutional birth of AI as a scientific field.[27] Its ambition was explicit: to design machines capable of performing tasks that, when done by humans, would require intelligence. Early successes such as the 'Logic Theorist' and later programs like *ELIZA* demonstrated the potential of symbolic reasoning systems but also revealed their limitations: they could process information according to predefined rules yet lacked understanding or adaptability.[28]

The history of artificial intelligence since then has unfolded in alternating cycles of enthusiasm and disillusionment – the so-called 'AI winters.' Periods of rapid progress, fuelled by advances in computing power and funding, were followed by setbacks when expectations outpaced technical feasibility. Still, each generation of research expanded the frontier of what machines could do: from expert systems in the 1980s to neural networks and machine learning in the 1990s. The symbolic culmination of this trajectory was IBM's *Deep Blue* defeating Garry Kasparov in 1997, a milestone that, while rooted in brute computational power, demonstrated how algorithmic processes could now outperform humans in domains once thought to require intuition.[29] But notably, IBM avoided using the term 'artificial intelligence', which was somewhat controversial at that time.[30]

From Hephaestus's golden servants to Turing's abstract machines, the evolution of automation traces a persistent human ambition: to externalise thought, judgement, and agency. Across centuries, this aspiration has oscillated between wonder and apprehension – between the hope that machines might liberate humanity from labour and the fear that they might replicate, or even replace, human decision-making itself. Understanding this long historical continuum is essential for grasping the current transformation driven by artificial intelligence.

[25] B Jack Copeland, *The Essential Turing* (Oxford University Press, 2004) 375.

[26] A Turing, 'Computing Machinery and Intelligence' (1950) 49 *Mind* 433, 434.

[27] See J McCarthy et al, 'A Proposal for the Dartmouth Summer Research Project on Artificial Intelligence: August 31, 1955' (2006) 27 *The AI magazine* 12, 12–14; M Haenlein and A Kaplan, 'A Brief History of Artificial Intelligence: On the Past, Present and Future of Artificial Intelligence' (2019) 61 *California Management Review* 5, 7.

[28] A Newell and H Simon, 'The Logic Theory Machine–A Complex Information Processing System' (1956) 2 *IRE Transactions on Information Theory* 61, 61–79. See also L Gugerty, 'Newell and Simon's Logic Theorist: Historical Background and Impact on Cognitive Modeling' (2006) 50 *Proceedings of the Human Factors and Ergonomics Society Annual Meeting* 880, 880–84; A Newell, H Simon and JC Shaw, 'Report on a General Problem-Solving Program' (International Conference on Information Processing June 1959) exhibits.stanford.edu/feigenbaum/catalog/sy501xd1313 accessed 2 May 2024; J Weizenbaum, 'ELIZA - a Computer Program for the Study of Natural Language Communication Between Man and Machine' (1966) 9 *Communications of the ACM* 36, 36–45; Haenlein and Kaplan (n 27) 8.

[29] J Schaeffer and A Plaat, 'Kasparov versus Deep Blue: The Rematch' (1997) 20 *International Computer Games Association Journal* 95, 95–101.

[30] RE Korf, 'Does Deep Blue Use AI?' (AAAI Press, 1997) 1–2.

Algorithmic systems are not a radical departure from this lineage but its latest expression, distinguished by their capacity to learn, infer, and act with degrees of autonomy that challenge the traditional boundaries between human intention and mechanical execution.

## B. The Fourth Industrial Revolution and the Rise of Machine Learning

The notion of industrial revolution captures moments of profound and rapid transformation, when technological innovation reshapes production, exchange, and social organisation.[31] The turn of the twenty-first century marked the beginning of what is commonly described as the *Fourth Industrial Revolution*. This period is distinguished by the rapid proliferation of cutting-edge technologies, with the internet assuming a central role in driving these transformative changes. To understand its scope, it is instructive to recall the earlier stages of industrial change. The First Industrial Revolution harnessed the power of water and steam to mechanise production; the second employed electricity to enable mass manufacturing; the third introduced electronics and information technology to automate processes,[32] and subsequently, the Internet.[33] The fourth builds upon these foundations, extending automation into interconnected and intelligent networks capable of independent operation. While some commentators view it as a continuation of the digital revolution of the late twentieth century rather than a distinct epoch,[34] its defining feature lies in the transition from automation to autonomy. Systems now not only perform tasks efficiently but also learn, adapt, and make decisions with limited human oversight.

In Industry 3.0, the introduction of computers marked a disruptive departure from previous forms of mechanisation, as computation itself became a productive resource.[35] Yet the transition to the fourth industrial revolution represents an even more radical shift. Computers are no longer isolated tools performing pre-programmed tasks; they are interconnected systems capable of communication, coordination, and increasingly, autonomous decision-making. This progression – from automation to autonomy – is decisive. The distinctive power of Industry 4.0 lies in its networked architecture: digitally connected machines that exchange data,

[31] K Schwab, *The Fourth Industrial Revolution* (Crown Business, 2017) 6.

[32] M Xu, JM David and S Hi Kim, 'The Fourth Industrial Revolution: Opportunities and Challenges' (2018) 9 *International Journal of Financial Research* 90, 90–95.

[33] A Wellstead, T Heikkila and M Wood, 'Fourth Industrial Revolution and Algorithms: New Challenges for Policy Design' in BG Peters and G Fontaine (eds), *Research Handbook of Policy Design* (Edward Elgar Publishing, 2022) 194, 196.

[34] I Moll, 'The Myth of the Fourth Industrial Revolution' (2021) 68 *Theoria* 1, 1–38.

[35] The terms 'Industry 3.0' and 'Industry 4.0' are used interchangeably with the concepts of the Third and Fourth Industrial Revolutions, respectively, with equivalent meanings in the context of industrial and technological advancements.

learn from interaction, and collaborate with minimal human oversight. It is this networked autonomy that underpins the transformative potential of the current technological revolution.

Industry 4.0 does not consist of a single technological breakthrough but of an ecosystem of interrelated innovations promoted by leading firms, integrators, and policymakers.[36] Its defining feature lies in the convergence of digital infrastructures and intelligent systems that operate collectively rather than in isolation. Among the technologies driving this transformation are the Internet of Things, Big Data analytics, and Artificial Intelligence.[37] These rely on complex algorithmic architectures to collect, process, and interpret information, hence their characterisation as '*algorithm-driven technologies*'. Algorithms are not ancillary to this process but constitute the operative logic through which the Fourth Industrial Revolution advances.[38]

A decisive component of this transformation is the rise of machine-learning techniques, particularly deep-learning models. The renewed momentum of artificial intelligence since 2010 stems from the large-scale application of deep neural networks capable of extracting patterns and correlations from massive datasets.[39] Two developments made this possible: first, the exponential increase in computational capacity that allows for the training of highly complex models; and second, the unprecedented availability of data that such systems require to improve and refine their performance.[40] Together, these advances have shifted technological progress from pre-programmed automation to adaptive, data-driven intelligence, marking a qualitative leap in the autonomy of contemporary systems. As in earlier industrial revolutions, such shifts compel the law – and particularly contract law – to re-examine the assumptions that govern agreement, intention, and responsibility when decisions emerge from autonomous processes rather than deliberate human choice.

# III. Contracts in the Digital Age: The Technological Revolution from Paper to Data

## A. The Impact of Digital Technologies on Contract Law

The progressive digitisation of contracting marks a decisive stage in the historical relationship between technology and private law. Digital contracting operates on two interrelated levels: first, the digital content that may constitute the object of

[36] A Martinelli, A Mina and M Moggi, 'The Enabling Technologies of Industry 4.0: Examining the Seeds of the Fourth Industrial Revolution' (2021) 30 *Industrial and Corporate Change* 161, 162.

[37] ibid 163. Artificial Intelligence is better understood not as a technology in itself but a field of knowledge, from which particular techniques – such as machine learning – are implemented in specific technologies. See Moll (n 34) 20.

[38] Wellstead, Heikkila and Wood (n 33) 195.

[39] G Kutyniok, 'The Mathematics of Artificial Intelligence' 1, 1 https://arxiv.org/abs/2203.08890.

[40] ibid.

the contract; and second, the use of digital technologies throughout the contractual lifecycle.[41] This section concentrates on the latter, examining how digital tools mediate contract formation and reshape the conditions under which parties express consent. While many technological developments can be accommodated within existing principles, others – particularly those linked to e-commerce, platform intermediation, smart contracts, and blockchain – introduce elements of automation that challenge traditional doctrines of formation and responsibility.

Traditional paper-based contracting fulfilled legal functions that extended beyond communication. The physical medium itself provided tangible evidence of authenticity, integrity, and consent, satisfying formal requirements such as signature and documentation. By contrast, electronic communications separate message from medium: they convey the same informational content but without material form. This dematerialisation raises questions about reliability and alteration, though it has also prompted the development of digital equivalents – electronic signatures and encryption – that in some respects offer greater security than paper documentation.[42]

The emergence of the World Wide Web in the mid-1990s introduced a new mode of contracting – electronic contracting – requiring the law to revisit traditional formalities of offer, acceptance, and proof.[43] Early uncertainty centred on two issues: whether an electronic communication could satisfy statutory requirements for writing and signature, and whether digital exchanges could produce binding obligations. The Electronic Communications Act 2000 addressed these concerns by adopting a *functional approach*, assessing whether electronic communications fulfilled the same evidentiary and procedural functions as their paper-based counterparts.[44] This pragmatic framework allowed digital documents to substitute for written instruments where they achieved equivalent reliability. Questions of offer, acceptance, and jurisdiction were subsequently refined through case law, illustrating the law's incremental capacity to absorb technological change without abandoning its core principles.[45]

In parallel, the adoption of the UNCITRAL Model Law on Electronic Commerce provided a crucial foundation for legal certainty in digital transactions.[46] Article 5 prohibits discrimination against electronic documents solely on account of their digital form, thereby affirming their equivalence to paper instruments.[47] Complementing this principle, Article 6 establishes that where the law requires

[41] S Grundmann and P Hacker, 'Digital Technology as a Challenge to European Contract Law' (2017) 13 *European Review of Contract Law* 255, 264.

[42] J Werner, 'E-commerce.co.uk - Local Rules in a Global Net' (2000) (6) *International Journal of Communications, Law and Policy* 1, 3.

[43] ibid 1.

[44] Electronic Communications Act 2000, s 7. See also Werner (n 42) 2–3.

[45] ibid 4–8. For a detailed discussion of the evolution from the dispatch to the receipt rule, see ch 5, section III.A.

[46] United Nations Commission on International Trade Law (UNCITRAL), Model Law on Electronic Commerce (1996).

[47] UNCITRAL Model Law (1996) [art 5].

information to be 'in writing', the requirement is satisfied if the electronic record is both accessible and capable of retention for future reference.[48] Together, these provisions codified the functional equivalence approach at the international level, ensuring that digital communications could serve as valid vehicles for contractual consent and evidentiary proof.

The European Union sought to ensure that it did not lag behind in the regulation of electronic commerce. Its most significant intervention came with Directive 2000/31/EC on electronic commerce, which required Member States to establish legal frameworks permitting the formation of contracts by electronic means.[49] Article 9(1) of the Directive codified this obligation, thereby facilitating the legal recognition of e-contracting and promoting confidence in cross-border digital transactions.[50] However, the UK's implementation of Article 9(1) proved notably limited. Despite the Directive's objective of enhancing legal certainty for both consumers and businesses, pre-existing statutory requirements – most prominently those contained in the Consumer Credit Act 1974 – continued to restrict the enforceability of contracts concluded electronically, impeding the full realisation of the Directive's harmonising aims.[51]

Digital platforms have profoundly reshaped the environment in which contracts are created, negotiated, and executed. Often referred to as 'online intermediary platforms' (OIPs),[52] they constitute the digital infrastructure through which supply and demand are coordinated, transactions facilitated, and contractual relationships governed.[53] Within this ecosystem, three contractual layers coexist: between the platform and providers, between the platform and consumers, and between providers and consumers themselves.[54] The platform thus functions not merely as an intermediary but as an active architect of exchange, defining the technological and legal parameters under which parties transact. Through algorithmic matching, dynamic pricing, and standardised terms of service, platforms exercise a structural influence that can blur the boundary between facilitator and contracting party. This centralised control has prompted increasing scrutiny from competition and consumer protection authorities, given the risks of market concentration, information asymmetry, and weakened consent.[55] This structural dominance has prompted increasing scrutiny from competition and consumer protection authorities, given the risks of market concentration,

[48] ibid [art 6].

[49] Directive 2000/31/EC.

[50] Directive 2000/31/EC, [art 9(1)].

[51] M Turner, M Traynor and H Smith, 'E-Commerce Directive – UK Implementation: Electronic Commerce (EC Directive) Regulations 2002 – Worth the Wait?' (2002) 18 *Computer Law & Security Review* 396, 400.

[52] See, eg, C Twigg-Flesner, 'Online Intermediary Platforms and English Contract Law' in PS Davies and T Cheng-Han (eds), *Intermediaries in Commercial Law* (Hart Publishing, 2022)171, 171.

[53] Grundmann and Hacker (n 41) 273.

[54] Twigg-Flesner (n 52) 172.

[55] Grundmann and Hacker (n 41) 273–76.

information asymmetry, and weakened consent.[56] Recent legislative reforms have also reshaped the regulatory landscape for digital platforms. In the UK, the Digital Markets, Competition and Consumers Act 2024 establishes an ex ante framework empowering the Competition and Markets Authority to designate firms with 'strategic market status' and to impose conduct requirements aimed at ensuring fair competition and consumer protection.[57] These reforms parallel, though do not replicate, the European Union's Digital Markets Act and Digital Services Act, which pursue similar objectives within the internal market.[58] Collectively, these instruments mark a decisive turn towards anticipatory regulation, recognising that platform-based contracting demands legal structures capable of safeguarding transparency, fairness, and accountability in increasingly algorithmic market environments.[59]

Smart contracts represent the next stage in the digital evolution of contracting. Unlike the mere digitisation of written agreements, they are self-executing and self-enforcing instruments that automate performance once predefined conditions are met, typically through blockchain technology.[60] The concept was first articulated by Nick Szabo, who envisaged digital protocols capable of securing and verifying contractual obligations without intermediaries.[61] Academic debate following their emergence in the mid-2010s centred on whether such automation could displace traditional legal oversight.[62] Yet, despite early claims of disruption, English law has proven capable of accommodating smart contracts within its existing principles. The Law Commission has confirmed that the common law is 'able to facilitate and support the use of smart legal contracts',[63] and that no legislative intervention is required to ensure their enforceability.[64]

The progressive adaptation of contract law to digital communication and e-commerce has created a legal environment increasingly receptive to technological innovation, including smart contracts. Yet algorithmic contracts stand apart.

[56] For a more in-depth analysis of this topic, see Twigg-Flesner (n 52) 171–92.

[57] Digital Markets, Competition and Consumers Act 2024 (UK).

[58] Regulation (EU) 2022/1925 of the European Parliament and of the Council of 14 September 2022 on contestable and fair markets in the digital sector (Digital Markets Act) [2022] OJ L265/1; Regulation (EU) 2022/2065 of the European Parliament and of the Council of 19 October 2022 on a Single Market for Digital Services (Digital Services Act) [2022] OJ L277/1.

[59] See O Andriychuk, 'The New EU and UK Regimes for Regulating Competition in Digital Markets: We Finally See What's on the Plate–but Do We Know How to Eat It?' (2024) 12 *Journal of Antitrust Enforcement* 195; M Eifert, A Metzger, Heike Schweitzer and G Wagner, 'Taming the Giants: The DMA/DSA Package' (2021) 58 *Common Market Law Review* 987.

[60] For a more comprehensive examination of the genesis and progression of smart contracts, see ch 2, section IV.A.

[61] N Szabo, 'Formalizing and Securing Relationships on Public Networks' (1997) 2, 2 doi.org/10.5210/fm.v2i9.548.

[62] See, eg, M Byrne and A Cunningham in K Werbach and N Cornell, 'Contracts Ex Machina' (2017) 67 *Duke Law Journal* 103. The Law Commission also referred to the manifested intention of the parties to exclude the application of contract law. See Law Commission, *Smart Legal Contracts: Advice to Government* (Law Com No. 401, 2021) 55.

[63] Law Commission No. 401 (n 62) 5.

[64] ibid 73.

Whereas smart contracts merely automate performance through code, algorithmic contracts integrate artificial intelligence into the processes of negotiation and formation themselves. This qualitative shift – from automation to autonomous decision-making – raises novel questions for contract doctrine and underscores the need for closer analysis of how AI-driven systems interact with the requirements of agreement and consent.

## B. The Impact of AI on Contracts

Artificial intelligence marks the latest stage in the technological evolution of contracting, extending automation beyond execution to the very processes of negotiation, drafting, and enforcement. By integrating machine-learning and natural-language-processing techniques into the contract lifecycle, AI systems increasingly participate in activities once confined to human decision-makers. Their adoption promises substantial gains in speed, accuracy, and efficiency, yet also compels a reassessment of how intention and consent are expressed, attributed,[65] and evidenced within the framework of English contract law.

The use of artificial intelligence in the preliminary stages of contracting has transformed how parties identify and assess potential counterparts.[66] Profiling techniques that combine data mining, scoring, and machine-learning methods allow firms to infer personal characteristics, behavioural patterns, and purchasing preferences from vast datasets. While these tools enhance efficiency and targeting, they also generate significant legal concerns. The extensive exchange of data between platforms, brokers, and analytics providers creates asymmetries of information and raises questions of fairness, transparency, and consent.[67] Risks of algorithmic price discrimination and behavioural manipulation blur the line between commercial strategy and undue influence.[68] From the perspective of English law, these developments invite renewed scrutiny of pre-contractual duties and the application of the fairness principle, as the law seeks to balance innovation in contracting with the protection of weaker parties.

During the negotiation phase, machine-learning applications are used to model strategic alternatives and to support decision-making. Systems designed to estimate the 'best alternative to a negotiated agreement' (BATNA) as well as to enhance argumentation support tools and decision support systems.[69] Such tools increasingly replicate aspects of legal reasoning and bargaining strategy, narrowing the space for human discretion. Their use raises questions about the attribution

[65] M Ebers, 'Artificial Intelligence, Contracting and Contract Law: An Introduction' in M Ebers, C Poncibò and M Zou (eds), *Contracting and Contract Law in the Age of Artificial Intelligence* (Hart Publishing, 2022) 19, 19.

[66] ibid 21.

[67] Grundmann and Hacker (n 41) 277.

[68] Ebers (n 65) 22.

[69] ibid 22–23.

of intention and the extent to which algorithmically generated proposals can be regarded as genuine expressions of a party's will.

The drafting phase has likewise evolved from the use of static templates and decision-tree questionnaires to the deployment of adaptive, AI-driven drafting systems.[70] These tools employ natural-language-processing and machine-learning techniques to identify appropriate clauses and supporting documentation based on contextual inputs such as subject matter, performance obligations, and counterparties. By analysing large repositories of contractual data, they can propose formulations that minimise the likelihood of dispute or renegotiation. Such systems increasingly perform functions analogous to junior legal drafting, producing coherent initial versions that can later be refined by human review. The result is a more dynamic and personalised approach to contract creation, reflecting the growing integration of algorithmic reasoning into professional legal practice.[71]

The development of AI-based decision-making in contracting can be broadly divided into two generations. First-generation systems were designed to assist users through recommendation functions, providing analysis or ranked options while leaving the final decision to human operators. By contrast, second-generation algorithms possess the capacity to make determinations autonomously, often executing predefined criteria or optimising outcomes without direct human intervention.[72] This transition from assisted to automated decision-making marks a decisive step towards algorithmic contracting in the strict sense. This latter category has become the principal focus of contemporary legal analysis, as algorithmic outputs may directly influence – and, in some instances, determine – the process through which contractual consent is formed and expressed.

While the primary concern here lies with the role of artificial intelligence in contract formation, it is important to note that AI applications extend well beyond this stage. In practice, AI systems are widely employed to support the performance and management of contracts. They facilitate transaction execution in areas such as electronic payment systems and supply chain logistics,[73] automate document extraction and tracking, and assist in risk assessment and compliance monitoring. AI tools also contribute to due diligence by analysing extensive datasets in mergers, acquisitions, and investment processes,[74] and are increasingly used to generate

[70] S Martinelli and C Rossi Chauvenet, 'From Document to Data: Revolution of Contract through Legal Technologies' in M Ebers, C Poncibò and M Zou (eds), *Contracting and Contract Law in the Age of Artificial Intelligence* (Hart Publishing, 2022) 81, 83.

[71] Grundmann and Hacker (n 41) 279–80. See also B Werthmann, 'Legal Drafting and Automation' in LA Di Matteo and others (eds), *The Cambridge Handbook of Lawyering in the Digital Age* (Cambridge University Press, 2021).

[72] M Gal, 'Algorithmic Challenges to Autonomous Choice' (2018) 1 *Michigan Technology Law Review* 59, 60.

[73] Ebers (n 65) 23.

[74] ibid.

and manage confidentiality agreements.[75] In the post-contractual phase, artificial intelligence has also become an important instrument for dispute resolution and litigation support. AI systems assist in managing customer complaints, facilitating online dispute resolution, and predicting potential outcomes of judicial proceedings through the analysis of past case data.[76] These tools enhance efficiency and consistency in adjudication and settlement processes, yet their increasing role in evaluating evidence and anticipating judicial reasoning raises questions about transparency and accountability in decision-making.

Contracts have evolved from static documents to dynamic data structures – 'set[s] of fluid information that can be organised and managed by technology for the efficient (and peaceful) relationship of the parties'.[77] Artificial intelligence now permeates the entire contractual lifecycle. While many applications fall within the operational domain of legal technology – such as contract-management systems and drafting tools – others, most notably algorithmic selection of counterparties and automated decision-making during formation, directly engage core doctrines of agreement. These developments bring the mechanics of consent to the foreground. To assess how algorithmic systems interact with agreement in English law, the next section clarifies the technical vocabulary – algorithms, data, learning, determinism, and explainability – on which the legal analysis must rest.

# IV. The Technical Context: A Terminological Clean-Up

## A. AI Terminology: Why Cleaning Up Matters

Artificial intelligence permeates an exceptionally wide range of disciplines, from the sciences to the humanities and the fields that bridge them, such as psychology and cognitive science.[78] This ubiquity has fostered an inconsistent and sometimes misleading use of AI-related terminology. The problem stems from several factors: the interdisciplinary nature of AI, its rapid technical evolution, the absence of

[75] For a more comprehensive analysis of this use case, see C Elia, 'Automation of Non-Disclosure Agreements: A Roadmap for a Legal Department to Gain Advantage Using AI (Artificial Intelligence)' (2019) 12 *International In-House Counsel Journal* 1, 1–6.

[76] Ebers (n 65) 23. For a more comprehensive analysis of these use cases, see: M Medvedeva, M Wieling and M Vols, 'Rethinking the Field of Automatic Prediction of Court Decisions' (2023) 31 *Artificial Intelligence and Law* 195, 195–212; D Carneiro et al, 'Online Dispute Resolution: An Artificial Intelligence Perspective' (2014) 41 *Artificial Intelligence Review* 211, 211–40; DM Katz, 'Quantitative Legal Prediction -or- How I Learned to Stop Worrying and Start Preparing for the Data-Driven Future of the Legal Services Industry' (2013) 62 *Emory Law Journal* 909, 909–66.

[77] Martinelli and Rossi Chauvenet (n 70) 83.

[78] L Portinale, 'Mapping Artificial Intelligence: Perspectives from Computer Sciences' in M Ebers, C Poncibò and M Zou (eds), *Contracting and Contract Law in the Age of Artificial Intelligence* (Hart Publishing, 2022) 3, 3–4. Russell and Norvig refer specifically to the disciplines contributing to the development of AI, namely: philosophy, mathematics, economics, neuroscience, psychology, computer engineering, control theory and cybernetics, and linguistics. See S Russell and P Norvig, *Artificial Intelligence: A Modern Approach*, 4th edn (Pearson, 2020) 23–35.

terminological standardisation, and the popularisation of complex concepts in non-technical discourse. Such imprecision can obscure the underlying mechanisms by which AI systems operate and lead to analytical error when those systems are examined through a legal lens. Greater conceptual clarity and contextual precision are therefore essential. In particular, legal analysis must remain grounded in the specific technical realities of AI – its data-driven inference, optimisation processes, and human-defined objectives – rather than in anthropomorphic metaphors. As one scholar aptly observed, '[e]xpressions of AI anxiety tend to abstract AI out of the context of its existence and use, ignoring the human beings and the social institutions and social arrangements that give AI its capacity to do or mean anything'.[79]

The field of artificial intelligence has borrowed extensively from other disciplines, often importing terminology that carries distinct conceptual weight in its original domain. The notion of 'autonomy', traditionally rooted in philosophy,[80] has been adapted to describe computational entities capable of acting without direct human instruction. Yet the analogy is imperfect. As one commentator observes, 'autonomy in computational entities is very different from autonomy in humans, although for AI anxiety the former is often conflated with the latter'.[81] Human autonomy entails the capacity to make decisions, choices, and take actions, and this is inherently tied to the concepts of freedom and morality. It is only individuals with autonomy who can be expected to adhere to rules and laws. In contrast, autonomy in AI systems refers to the capacity to perform tasks or make inferences within parameters defined by human designers. It is a functional independence, not a moral one. Behind this confusion lies a deeper conceptual misunderstanding: a false equivalence between 'agency' in its legal sense and human agency in the philosophical sense. Early discussions of AI personhood, such as those by Lawrence Solum and Curtis Karnow, illustrate how extending the language of agency and personhood to machines risks obscuring the fundamentally instrumental nature of AI systems.[82] The widespread metaphorical use of terms such as 'autonomy' or 'agents' perpetuates confusion by suggesting that machines can have machine-independent behaviour.[83] In reality, what appears as autonomy in algorithmic processes is the execution of goals, rules, and optimisations set by humans. In the context of algorithmic contracts, control and intention therefore remain

[79] DG Johnson and M Verdicchio, 'AI Anxiety' (2017) 68 *Journal of the Association for Information Science and Technology* 2267, 2268.

[80] See, eg, M-A Williams, 'Autonomy: Life and Being' (International Conference on Knowledge Science, Engineering and Management, Belfast, 2010) link.springer.com/book/10.1007/978-3-642-15280-1 137–47. J Collier, 'What Is Autonomy?' (2002) 12 *International Journal of Computing Anticipatory Systems* 212, 212–21.

[81] Johnson and Verdicchio (n 79) 2268.

[82] See LB Solum, 'Legal Personhood for Artificial Intelligences' (1992) 70 *North Carolina Law Review* 1231, 1231–87; CEA Karnow, 'The Encrypted Self: Fleshing out the Rights of Electronic Personalities' (1994) 13 *The John Marshall Journal of Computer & Information Law* 1, 1–16.

[83] Johnson and Verdicchio (n 79) 2268–69.

human: as one scholar notes, 'in fact what is erased is not so much the human, but how humans make judgements and decisions'.[84]

It is therefore essential to refine the terminology used in discussions of algorithmic contracts, as much of the conceptual confusion surrounding their legal character arises from inaccurate or metaphorical language. Statements such as 'a non-deterministic algorithm has "a mind of its own" – given the same inputs, the output may vary'[85] are misleading. The expression 'mind', even when used rhetorically, introduces an anthropomorphic distortion.[86] Non-determinism in computation simply denotes that an algorithm's outputs may differ across runs because of probabilistic elements in its design – random initialisation, data sampling, or hardware variation – not because of any independent volition. The persistence of metaphors drawn from human cognition contributes to this misunderstanding. Since its inception, artificial intelligence has relied on analogies between the human brain and the computer;[87] the term *neural network* itself reflects this lineage, referring to architectures that imitate, only superficially, the structure of biological neurons. Such analogies risk reinforcing a human-centred view of intelligence that obscures the functional nature of AI systems.[88] In legal analysis, where the attribution of consent and intention is central, conceptual precision demands that these systems be treated as engineered mechanisms of optimisation rather than as cognitive agents.

## B. Understanding the Fundamentals of AI

### *i. What is artificial intelligence?*

Artificial intelligence encompasses a wide family of computational techniques designed to perform tasks that would ordinarily require human judgement. At its core, an AI system is a machine-based architecture capable of inferring, from the data it receives and the objectives defined by its designers, how to produce outputs such as classifications, predictions, or decisions that influence a given

[84] M Indira Ganesh, 'The Ironies of Autonomy' (2020) 7 *Humanities and Social Sciences Communications* 1, 1–10.

[85] J Tan Ming En, 'Non-Deterministic Artificial Intelligence Systems and the Future of the Law on Unilateral Mistakes in Singapore' (2022) 34 *The Singapore Academy of Law Journal* 91, 93.

[86] PD König et al, 'Essence of AI: What Is AI?' in LA DiMatteo, C Poncibò and M Cannarsa (eds), *The Cambridge Handbook of Artificial Intelligence: Global Perspectives on Law and Ethics* (Cambridge University Press, 2022) 18, 23.

[87] A Campolo and K Crawford, 'Enchanted Determinism: Power without Responsibility in Artificial Intelligence' (2020) 6 *Engaging Science, Technology, and Society* 1, 2.

[88] For a more comprehensive analysis of this human-centric vision, see section 3.1 'Human-Centric Definitions' in J Turner, *Robot Rules: Regulating Artificial Intelligence* (Palgrave Macmillan, 2019) 9–13. This ongoing debate has been extensively covered in the literature. For instance, Bellia advocated for a shift away from human-centric attributions of intelligence, see AJ Bellia, 'Contracting with Electronic Agents' (2001) 50 *Emory Law Journal* 1047, 1051.

environment.[89] From a functional perspective, every AI system can be understood through three elements: a goal (the task it is programmed to achieve), a performance measure (the criterion by which success is evaluated), and experience or data (the information from which the system learns or improves).[90] This triad captures the logic of optimisation that defines modern AI.

The term *artificial intelligence* itself was first introduced in the 'Proposal for the Dartmouth Summer Research Project on Artificial Intelligence', which marked the formal beginning of AI as a scientific discipline.[91] Yet, despite this early milestone, the field still lacks a standardised definition. For John McCarthy – one of the founders of the discipline – artificial intelligence is 'the science and engineering of making intelligent machines, especially intelligent computer programs. It is related to the similar task of using computers to understand human intelligence, but AI does not have to confine itself to methods that are biologically observable.'[92] While this definition remains historically significant, it provides limited conceptual clarity: it reflects the early ambition to replicate aspects of human intelligence without specifying the mechanisms through which computational inference and optimisation actually occur. In contemporary terms, the behaviour of AI systems is not autonomous in a human sense but emerges from mathematical functions that adjust internal parameters – so-called *weights* – to minimise error relative to a target outcome.[93] Through this process, AI systems approximate reasoning by iteratively refining patterns across large datasets.[94] Understanding these mechanisms is essential for legal analysis: it reveals where human intention enters the design process and how responsibility can be traced when algorithmic outputs influence the formation of contractual consent.

The very notion of 'intelligence' adds further complexity to defining artificial intelligence. The field evolves so rapidly that what once appeared intelligent soon becomes routine automation.[95] Contemporary definitions therefore emphasise functionality rather than imitation of human cognition. Both the OECD and the European Union now characterise AI as a *machine-based system* that, for explicit

[89] 'AI-Principles Overview - OECD.AI' oecd.ai/en/principles accessed 2 May 2024.

[90] On the classic T–P–E triad – task (T), performance measure (P), and experience (E) – see TM Mitchell, *Machine Learning* (McGraw–Hill, 1997) 2 ('A computer program is said to learn from experience E … with respect to some class of tasks T and performance measure P').

[91] J McCarthy et al, 'A Proposal for the Dartmouth Summer Research Project on Artificial Intelligence: August 31, 1955' (2006) 27 *Haenlein* 12, 12–14.

[92] J McCarthy, 'What Is Artificial Intelligence?' (November 2007) 2 www-formal.stanford.edu/jmc/whatisai.pdf accessed 2 May 2024.

[93] On the mathematical basis of AI behaviour and the adjustment of internal parameters or 'weights', see Russell and Norvig (n 78) ch 20; RS Sutton and AG Barto, *Reinforcement Learning: An Introduction*, 2nd edn (MIT Press, 2018) ch 1.

[94] On the iterative refinement of patterns across large datasets, see I Goodfellow, Y Bengio and A Courville, *Deep Learning* (MIT Press, 2016) chs 6 and 8.

[95] A Kaplan and M Haenlein, 'Siri, Siri, in My Hand: Who's the Fairest in the Land? On the Interpretations, Illustrations, and Implications of Artificial Intelligence' (2019) 62 *Business Horizons* 15, 17. For example, some authors consider that symbolic AI and expert systems are no longer forms of artificial intelligence. See, eg, Turner (n 88) 18.

or implicit objectives, *infers* from input data how to generate *outputs* – predictions, recommendations, or decisions – that can influence physical or virtual environments, while operating with varying levels of *autonomy* and *adaptiveness* after deployment.[96] This functional focus reflects the defining mechanisms of AI: the capacity to learn from data, extract patterns, and iteratively improve performance.[97] For legal analysis, this dynamic conception of intelligence is crucial. It directs attention away from anthropomorphic comparisons and towards the operational processes – data inference, optimisation, and feedback loops – that determine how AI systems affect contractual formation and consent.

In November 2023, Lord Holmes of Richmond introduced a Private Members' Bill in the House of Lords to make provision for the regulation of artificial intelligence.[98] The Bill proposed a working definition of AI as

> technology enabling the programming or training of a device or software (a) to perceive environments through the use of data; (b) interpret data using automated processing designed to approximate cognitive abilities; and (c) make recommendations, predictions, or decisions with a view to achieving a specific objective.[99]

It also explicitly included generative AI, defined as 'deep or large language models able to generate text and other content based on the data on which they were trained'.[100] Although this initiative did not progress beyond its initial steps,[101] it illustrates the direction of the current UK debate: a move towards a functional and capability-based definition rather than a purely anthropomorphic or technology-specific one. Its emphasis on perception, interpretation, and decision-making aligns conceptually with international standards, yet it remains legally significant in the English context, where regulation must interact with doctrines of responsibility, consent, and agency grounded in common law rather than codified administrative oversight.

Although the term 'artificial' is relatively straightforward – denoting something synthetic rather than natural – the main challenge lies in the word 'intelligence', a term encompassing a broad spectrum of capacities and interpretations.[102] From a functionality perspective, intelligence may be understood as the automation of 'non-cognitive computational techniques that employ heuristics or proxies

[96] 'AI-Principles Overview - OECD.AI' oecd.ai/en/principles accessed 2 May 2024; Art 3(1) AI Act.

[97] Kaplan and Haenlein (n 95) 19.

[98] Artificial Intelligence (Regulation) Bill [HL], Private Members' Bill (Starting in the House of Lords) 2023–24.

[99] Art 7 Artificial Intelligence (Regulation) Bill [HL].

[100] ibid.

[101] The Bill was dropped with the dissolution of Parliament in May 2024 and did not complete its passage in that session. In March 2025, it was reintroduced in the House of Lords under the session 2024–26 *as Artificial Intelligence (Regulation) Bill [HL]. Artificial Intelligence (Regulation) Bill [HL]* (Private Members' Bill, House of Lords, 2023–24 Session) bills.parliament.uk/bills/3519 accessed 17 October 2025; reintroduced as *Artificial Intelligence (Regulation) Bill [HL]* (Private Members' Bill, House of Lords, 2024–26 Session) bills.parliament.uk/bills/3942 accessed 17 October 2025.

[102] Turner (n 88) 7.

(e.g. statistical correlations)' to emulate tasks ordinarily requiring human cognition.[103] From a rationality perspective, intelligence refers to the ability to select the optimal course of action to achieve a defined objective (goal), given specific criteria for optimisation and the constraints of available resources.[104] This latter understanding is particularly relevant for legal analysis, as it frames intelligence not as a mental or moral attribute but as a process of goal-oriented optimisation. Within this framework, the notions of a 'certain goal', 'certain criteria', and 'available resources' acquire central importance: they delineate the parameters within which an AI system operates and thereby identify the locus of human control and responsibility in its design and deployment.

The concept of a 'certain goal' refers to the intended outcome or specific result that a system, model, or algorithm is designed to achieve. It defines what the AI system seeks to produce after processing data, performing computations, or making decisions. Specifying this desired outcome is essential, as it guides the system's training, optimisation, and evaluation, ensuring that its outputs align with the objectives set by human designers. In this framework, the term 'criteria' denotes the performance measures used to assess how successfully the goal has been achieved, while 'available resources' refers to the data and computational capacity accessible to the system. Although the latter may vary with each operation, the goal and the evaluation criteria remain constant.

Even from the most expansive rationalist perspectives – those that attribute to Artificial General Intelligence (AGI) or Artificial Superintelligence (ASI) a capacity for self-generated objectives – it is generally accepted that such systems still operate, at a high level of abstraction, within externally defined parameters or overarching goals.[105]

A threefold taxonomy of artificial intelligence is generally recognised, distinguishing between *Narrow AI*, *Artificial General Intelligence* (AGI), and *Artificial Superintelligence* (ASI).[106] *Narrow AI* – also termed *Weak AI* – encompasses systems designed and trained for clearly defined tasks, lacking the capacity to generalise knowledge or perform functions beyond their specific domain. By contrast, *AGI* refers to hypothetical systems capable of understanding, learning, and applying knowledge across a wide range of contexts, displaying a cognitive

[103] H Surden, 'Machine Learning and Law' (2014) 89 *Washington Law Review* 87, 95.

[104] M Milossi, E Alexandropoulou and KE Psannis, 'AI Ethics: Algorithmic Determinism or Self-Determination? The GDPR Approach' (2021) 9 *IEEE Journals & Magazine* 58455, 58445 ieeexplore.ieee.org/stamp/stamp.jsp?tp=&arnumber=9400809 accessed 2 May 2024.

[105] Turner (n 88) 14.

[106] See N Bostrom, *Superintelligence: Paths, Dangers, Strategies* (Oxford University Press, 2014); S Legg and M Hutter, 'Universal Intelligence: A Definition of Machine Intelligence' (2007) 17 *Mind and Machines* 391; JR Searle, 'Minds, Brains and Programs' (1980) 3 *Behavioral and Brain Sciences* 417. There are other classifications such as between Symbolic AI and sub-symbolic AI. Symbolic AI involves 'express' instructions on how to perform a task, whereas sub-symbolic approaches, such as machine learning and deep learning, are associated with more implicit, data-driven methodologies. In line with this categorisation, this research concentrates on sub-symbolic AI systems. For this classification see E Mik, 'Much Ado About Artificial Intelligence or: The Automation of Contract Formation' (2023) 30 *International Journal of Law and Information Technology* 484, 494–96.

versatility comparable to that of human intelligence. *ASI*, in turn, denotes a speculative stage in which machine intelligence would not only match but exceed human cognitive abilities across all dimensions, including reasoning, creativity, and autonomous decision-making.[107]

To mitigate the anxiety often associated with artificial intelligence, clarity of scope and functionality is essential. The analysis that follows in this book therefore focuses on 'Narrow AI' systems, and in particular on their operation in contract formation, where algorithmic decision-making most directly engages the legal concept of agreement.

### *ii. Navigating Controversial AI Concepts of Significance for Algorithmic Contracts*

The academic literature across multiple disciplines explores, often with diverging terminology, the conceptual and technical foundations of artificial intelligence.[108] Within this vast landscape, certain notions have acquired particular relevance for understanding algorithmic contracting. This section focuses on those that are both functionally significant and legally contentious, with the aim of clarifying how they shape the legal interpretation of algorithmic behaviour in contract formation.

The analysis is confined to *Narrow AI* systems operating within the contractual domain and begins with their two essential building blocks: *algorithms* and *data*. The interaction between these elements has been succinctly captured in the aphorism that '[a]lgorithms without data are empty; data without algorithms are blind.'[109] In this regard, algorithms are said to be eventful: they are processes that depend on data.[110]

'Algorithms are computational sets of rules that computer programmers input into technologies to "design in" particular patterns of decision-making, which generate outputs the technologies are designed to solve.'[111] In the contractual domain, understanding algorithms requires attention to three foundational components: 'rules', 'patterns', and 'designations'. These elements function as conceptual anchors for analysing how algorithmic processes operate and, more importantly, how human agency is embedded within them. Algorithms do not act independently of human intention; they embody the objectives, constraints, and

[107] Kaplan and Haenlein (n 95) 18.

[108] See, eg, Kutyniok (n 39); MM Mariani et al, 'Artificial Intelligence in Innovation Research: A Systematic Review, Conceptual Framework, and Future Research Directions' (2023) 122 *Technovation* 102623, 102623 www.sciencedirect.com/science/article/pii/S0166497222001705; VC Muller, 'Philosophy of AI: A Structured Overview' in NA Smuha (ed), *Cambridge handbook on the law, ethics and policy of Artificial Intelligence* (Cambridge University Press, 2024) 1, 1–25; P Malik, M Pathania and V Kumar Rathaur, 'Overview of Artificial Intelligence in Medicine' (2019) 8 *Journal of Family Medicine and Primary Care* 2328, 2328–31; MM Cheng and RD Hackett, 'A Critical Review of Algorithms in HRM: Definition, Theory, and Practice' (2021) 31 *Human Resource Management Review* 100698, 100698.

[109] JM Balkin, '2016 Sidley Austin Distinguished Lecture on Big Data Law and Robotics: The Three Laws of Robotics in the Age of Big Data' (2017) 78 *Ohio State Law Journal* 1217, 1220.

[110] T Bucher, *If... Then: Algorithmic Power and Politics* (Oxford University Press, 2018) 49.

[111] Wellstead, Heikkila and Wood (n 33) 194.

value choices defined by their designers. The human behind the system defines the rules and the patterns and determines the task to solve.[112] Recognising this human imprint is crucial, as it enables a more coherent integration of algorithmic systems into the doctrinal framework of contract law. The determinative structure of rules and patterns – each established by human design – underscores that decision-making by algorithms remains traceable to human judgement, even when executed autonomously.

Machine learning constitutes one of the principal approaches through which artificial intelligence is achieved. It is 'the field of study that gives computers the ability to learn without explicitly being programmed'.[113] Technically, '[a] computer program is said to learn from experience E with respect to some class of tasks T and performance measure P, if its performance at tasks in T, as measured by P, improves with experience E'.[114]

This triadic framework can be illustrated by an algorithm designed to refine pricing strategies for a retail enterprise. Such an algorithm learns from experience (*E*) by analysing historical sales, customer behaviour, competitor pricing, and market trends to optimise its strategy. The task (*T*) is to set prices that maximise profit margins while maintaining competitiveness, and its performance (*P*) is evaluated through measurable outcomes such as increased revenue or improved adaptability to market fluctuations. Through iterative adjustments, the system identifies patterns in past data and applies them to new situations, dynamically updating prices in response to real-time inputs.

This process exemplifies how machine learning systems operationalise optimisation: they continuously improve performance relative to human-defined objectives by refining internal parameters. The mechanism not only illustrates the adaptive potential of AI but also highlights its dependence on human-defined goals and evaluative criteria – an essential consideration when analysing decision-making and intention in algorithmic contracts.

The notions of 'class of task' and 'performance measure' are crucial to understanding how artificial intelligence functions within legally relevant contexts. These terms correspond, respectively, to the 'certain goal' and 'criteria' discussed earlier. The 'certain goal' is what the *Narrow AI* system must achieve, having been tailored and trained for this specific task. The 'criteria' concern the human-defined parameters or measures by which the performance of the algorithm is assessed. In practice, these parameters are established through processes of *parameterisation*, which determine the algorithm's decision rules, the weighting of variables, and the categories of data used to reach a result. As such, '[h]uman intervention is present in the use of algorithms, through the parameterization of the algorithm, the choice

[112] I Rahwan et al, 'Machine Behaviour' (2019) 568 *Nature* 477, 480.

[113] S Brown, 'Machine Learning, Explained' (MIT Sloan School of Management, 21 April 2021) mitsloan.mit.edu/ideas-made-to-matter/machine-learning-explained accessed 14 November 2023, citing Arthur Samuel.

[114] D Dellermann et al, 'The Future of Human-AI Collaboration: A Taxonomy of Design Knowledge for Hybrid Intelligence Systems' (2021) *arXiv* doi.org/10.48550/arXiv.2105.03354.

and weighting criteria as well as the categories of data that are taken into account in order to arrive at the desired result.'[115]

This human imprint is decisive for the alignment of algorithmic systems with the principles of contract law. It ensures that, despite the apparent autonomy of the algorithm, its outputs remain bound by objectives defined ex ante by its designers or operators. Returning to the earlier example of price optimisation, the desired outcome – the 'certain goal' or 'task' assigned to the system – remains fixed and immutable, even as the algorithm adapts its internal parameters to improve performance within that human-determined framework.

Machine learning stands in marked contrast to earlier forms of *symbolic artificial intelligence* – now often referred to as old-fashioned AI.[116] Symbolic AI systems relied on explicitly programmed rules and representations of knowledge, typically organised in logical structures such as decision trees: *if X, then Y*. These systems operated through a predefined sequence of instructions that mapped specific inputs to corresponding outputs. Their behaviour was fully deterministic, in the sense that each computational step could, in principle, be traced back to a decision made by the programmer.[117] Symbolic AI thus reflected a closed design logic: the system could execute decisions, but it could not generate or modify the rules by which those decisions were made.

Artificial neural networks represent an advanced form of machine learning architecture, consisting of numerous interconnected units – often called *neurons* – each responsible for performing specific computations. The connections between these units are governed by numerical parameters known as *weights*, which determine the strength of influence that one unit exerts on another. By iteratively adjusting these weights, neural networks modify their internal structure, thereby improving the accuracy of their outputs.[118] This process of adjustment, or *learning*, typically occurs through *back-propagation*, a supervised learning technique that minimises the error between predicted and target outputs,[119] although alternative methods such as unsupervised and reinforcement learning also exist.[120]

The essence of this process lies not in altering the system's ultimate function, but in optimising its performance within pre-established parameters. Learning, in this sense, entails refinement rather than transformation: the system continually enhances its ability to achieve a fixed goal without redefining that goal itself.

[115] Milossi, Alexandropoulou and Psannis (n 104) 58458.

[116] See Kaplan and Haenlein (n 95) 17; Turner (n 88) 18. Another term used to refer to old-fashioned AI is *Good Old-Fashioned Artificial Intelligence* (*GOFAI*), a label coined by John Haugeland. See J Haugeland, *Artificial Intelligence: The Very Idea* (MIT Press, 1985).

[117] Turner (n 88) 18.

[118] ibid 19.

[119] T Mukanata, *Fundamentals of the New Artificial Intelligence: Neural, Evolutionary, Fuzzy and More* (Springer, 2008) 255, 12.

[120] For a more in-depth analysis of the different recalibration or adjustment mechanisms, see Turner (n 88) 72–73. See also, from a technical perspective, TD Raheni and P Thirumoorthi, 'Stochastic Artificial Intelligence: Review Article' in T Sands (ed), *Stochastic Artificial Intelligence* (IntechOpen Ltd, 2020) 3, 7–9.

The functionality of neural networks bears particular relevance for understanding decision-making in contract formation. In technical terms, a neural network is trained through exposure to pairs of input and target data – for example, (input pattern 1, target pattern 1), (input pattern 2, target pattern 2), and so on. Each target pattern is represented as a vector $t = (t_1, t_2, \ldots, t_{no})$. The objective of the training process is to adjust the network's internal weights so that, for each input, it produces an output approximating the corresponding target pattern.[121]

In simplified terms, a neural network learns through repeated exposure to pairs of information – for example, an image of a cat (input) and the label 'cat' (target pattern). By processing many such pairs, the network gradually adjusts its internal parameters (weights) to strengthen the associations between input features and the correct output. Once trained, it can classify new images without external labels, identifying them as 'cat' based on similarities to the data it has previously encountered. The purpose of this process is not to memorise examples, but to generalise patterns from experience so as to produce accurate outputs when confronted with new inputs.

When neural networks are trained for contract-related functions, such as estimating target prices within contractual frameworks, the process follows the same logic. The system is provided with contract data as input and the corresponding target prices as output. By analysing these paired examples, the network discerns statistical relationships between contractual features and their associated prices. Through iterative adjustment of its internal parameters (weights), it gradually acquires the capacity to predict or approximate target prices when presented with new contract information. The goal of this training is for the network to infer and forecast pricing outcomes by abstracting patterns from the examples encountered during the learning phase. 'Once a network has been designed for a precise application, then the network is equipped to be trained.'[122]

For the purposes of contract formation, it is essential to emphasise that throughout this process of learning, the network's weights and parameters are refined, but its 'ultimate objective' – its 'certain goal' – remains fixed. The system optimises its internal performance in pursuit of a pre-defined task; it does not redefine the task itself.

Returning to the earlier example of price optimisation, the same process can be illustrated using a neural network. The system is trained with pairs of input patterns – representing data such as sales history, market trends, and product characteristics – and their corresponding target outputs, which represent the desired or optimal prices. Each target pattern can be expressed as a vector $t = (t_1, t_2, \ldots, t_{no})$, guiding the network towards the intended price points. Through iterative adjustments of its internal weights, the network refines its capacity to generate outputs that approximate these targets. By progressively recalibrating its parameters, the neural network improves its predictive accuracy, learning to infer the

[121] Mukanata (n 119) 12.
[122] Raheni and Thirumoorthi (n 120) 7.

optimal price for each new input configuration. In essence, the process seeks to enhance the model's ability to approximate the pre-defined ideal outcome, thereby achieving the ultimate goal of price optimisation.

It follows from the foregoing that algorithmic systems, including those employing machine learning techniques that depart from the traditional *if–then* logic of symbolic AI, remain ultimately bound to their pre-defined objectives. Their function is directed towards optimisation rather than deviation: they refine their performance but do not alter their fundamental goals. In this sense, algorithms may be described as 'inflexible', pursuing a constant end through adaptive means. This characteristic has significant implications for contract formation, particularly in understanding how consent is structured and manifested within algorithmic contracts.

Decision-making in contract formation is a critical issue. The fact that an algorithm's 'decision' coincides with the ultimate goal it has been designed to achieve has generated substantial conceptual confusion, particularly concerning the distinction between deterministic and non-deterministic processes. Deterministic algorithms, by definition, 'produce the same output given the same inputs.'[123] There is unanimous agreement that systems using deterministic algorithms do not pose a threat to the meeting of the minds, since their behaviour is fixed and predictable.[124] 'In contrast, the term non-deterministic is used to denote an event whose outcome depends on the choices made by its participants.'[125] In computer science, 'stochasticity and non-determinism, (…) can cause two similar training procedures to produce vastly different results in practice'.[126]

A significant source of terminological confusion arises at this point. In practice, strictly deterministic machine learning algorithms are rare. Their determinism extends only to the specific dataset used for training and to the defined interactions that occur within the training process itself. Once the trained model is deployed in a real-world environment – where it encounters novel data and external variability – the predictability inherent in determinism dissipates. Accordingly, any system employing machine learning can, in functional terms, be regarded as 'non-deterministic'.

Moving beyond the basic notion of determinism, it is essential to differentiate between the concepts of non-determinism and stochasticity. 'Non-determinism is a property of processes for which supplying the same inputs can produce different outputs (…) Stochasticity is a property for non-deterministic processes whose outcomes can be reasoned about using probability theory.'[127] In summary,

[123] Tan Ming En (n 85) 93.
[124] See, eg, Ebers (n 65) 30; N Liu, 'The "Contracting Problem" Revisited: Explaining the Formation of Algorithmic Contracts under the Common Law' in Z Slakoper and I Tot (eds), *Digital Technologies and the Law of Obligations* (Routledge, 2022) 133, 135.
[125] J Cohen, 'Non-Deterministic Algorithms' (1979) 11 *Computing Surveys* 79, 79.
[126] FA Cooper, J Frankle and C De Sa, 'Non-Determinism and the Lawlessness of Machine Learning Code' (Proceedings of the 2022 Symposium on Computer Science and Law ACM, Washington DC, Nov 1, 2022) dl.acm.org/doi/proceedings/10.1145/3511265 accessed 14 November 2023.
[127] ibid.

deterministic algorithms consistently link specific inputs to respective outputs, ensuring a predictable A-to-B relationship. Non-deterministic algorithms, by contrast, may yield divergent outcomes from identical inputs. Within this broader category, stochastic algorithms introduce probabilistic reasoning: their outputs are uncertain but statistically explicable.

Machine learning belongs to this latter class. It is 'grounded in probability and statistics, and thus is fundamentally stochastic in nature'.[128] The purpose of these systems is to identify probable associations between inputs and outputs, exploiting randomness where complete knowledge of real-world phenomena is unattainable. Stochasticity 'is the property that makes it possible for ML to model phenomena that are too complex to specify exhaustively using if/then deterministic rules'.[129] Decision-making in such systems therefore relies on probabilitics rather than certainties.[130] Yet, stochastic non-determinism must not be conflated with arbitrariness.[131] Together with the 'inflexibility' discussed above, this probabilistic quality is central to understanding how algorithms contribute to, and shape, the process of contractual agreement.

Having clarified the distinction between 'non-determinism' and 'stochasticity', it is necessary to introduce one further concept that generates particular unease in relation to the requirement of a meeting of the minds in algorithmic contract formation: the 'black-box algorithm'. Certain machine learning systems are described as *black boxes* when their functioning can be understood only in terms of observable inputs and outputs, with little or no insight into the internal processes linking the two.[132] In such cases, while we may have full visibility of both the data fed into the system and the results it produces, the mechanism by which inputs are transformed into outputs remains opaque.[133]

Scholz has highlighted the particular difficulties that this opacity poses for contract law.[134] Whereas a deterministic decision process permits the tracing of each computational step,[135] such reconstruction is often said to be impossible in the case of non-deterministic systems. Yet it is important to note that not every non-deterministic algorithm qualifies as a black box. The classification depends on the degree of 'explainability' of the model: as the complexity of an algorithm increases, so too does the likelihood that it will operate as a black box.[136]

[128] In computer science, randomness serves as a mechanism that diminishes standardisation, consequently reducing systemic exclusion from opportunities. See ibid 15.

[129] See the section entitled 'Non-deterministic Code Is Lawless' in Cooper, Frankle and De Sa (n 126).

[130] Cheng and Hackett (n 108) 100698.

[131] Cooper, Frankle and De Sa (n 126).

[132] B Mols, 'In Black Box Algorithms We Trust (or Do We?)' cacm.acm.org/news/in-black-box-algorithms-we-trust-or-do-we accessed 2 May 2024. See also, Bucher (n 110) 42–43.

[133] See section 'Introduction' in Cooper, Frankle and De Sa (n 126).

[134] LH Scholz, 'Algorithmic Contracts' *Stanford Technology Law Review* 128, 149–64.

[135] Turner (n 88) 18.

[136] On the relevance of explainability for contract law, and the extent to which opacity in algorithmic decision-making affects the legal assessment of agreement, see further ch 4, section III.A, where the contrasting positions of Yavar Bathaee and Eliza Mik are discussed.

Explainability, in computer science, refers to the capacity to understand how a trained neural network reaches its decisions – specifically, which features of the input data are decisive in producing a given output.[137] While concepts such as non-determinism or black-box algorithms are frequently employed in discussions concerning algorithmic decision-making, their relevance leans more towards the domain of explainability rather than in determining whether a system can deviate from its intended purpose. The mere fact that a decision process cannot be fully explained does not imply that the system operates arbitrarily or independently of its design. In fact, '[w]hile it might indeed be difficult to explain what patterns in the data are being caught by the model of a machine learning algorithm (…) the general principle and operational logics of these systems are very well-known. That's why they are used in the first place.'[138] The system's *inflexibility* continues to constrain its operation, ensuring that optimisation remains aligned with the goal originally defined by its designers.

## V. Autonomy, Artificial Intelligence, and Algorithmic Contracts: Concluding Remarks

The central conclusion of this chapter is what may be termed the 'inflexibility of algorithms' – the idea that, despite their apparent adaptiveness and capacity for learning, algorithmic systems remain bound by the objectives and constraints defined by their human designers. The adjustments that occur within machine learning – alterations of weights and parameters – do not amount to independent change but to optimisation within a fixed goal structure. These refinements enhance performance rather than transform purpose. In functional terms, optimisation precedes and constrains decision-making: it governs how the system selects the most efficient configuration to achieve a result without ever redefining the goal itself. This holds true across both deterministic and non-deterministic models, underscoring that apparent autonomy does not imply freedom of purpose.

The long historical arc traced in this chapter – from the earliest automata to neural networks – reveals a persistent human aspiration to delegate cognitive labour to machines. Automation and autonomy differ only in degree: the former replicates human action, while the latter simulates decision-making. Yet both are guided by the same logic of efficiency and optimisation. The Fourth Industrial Revolution has magnified this aspiration by endowing machines with adaptive capacities, but the direction of their operation remains humanly defined. In contract formation, this means that the locus of intention continues to reside outside the system, even when execution is technically autonomous.

[137] Kutyniok (n 39) 6. See also C Gallese, 'The AI Act Proposal: a New Right to Technical Interpretability?' (1st ISLC Online International Conference, Milan, 20-22 February 2023) arxiv.org/pdf/2303.17558 accessed 2 May 2024.
[138] Bucher (n 110) 57.

The discussion has also exposed how conceptual ambiguities in the literature – particularly concerning determinism, stochasticity, and explainability – complicate the articulation of a coherent legal framework for algorithmic contracting. These ambiguities often arise from conflating functional unpredictability with legal indeterminacy. The difficulty is not that algorithmic systems act beyond human control, but that the parameters of their control are insufficiently articulated in legal doctrine.

The concept of artificial intelligence has evolved alongside the technology itself, with definitions increasingly emphasising the system's capacity for autonomous learning. In practical terms, determinism is largely confined to the learning phase of these systems. The boundary between what is deterministic and what is autonomous is therefore blurred,[139] and perhaps unnecessary. Any system that incorporates the ability to respond to new situations through machine learning operates, to some extent, non-deterministically. Consequently, the doctrinal implications of determinism will require reconsideration in light of algorithmic contracts, as examined in the following chapter. This observation highlights the conceptual tension that persists in attempts to reconcile technological adaptability with the doctrinal framework of contract law.

Focusing on narrow, purpose-built AI systems clarifies the dynamics underlying algorithmic behaviour. These systems, which define the technological context of contract formation, operate within goals determined ex ante by their designers, even when the processes through which those goals are pursued involve probabilistic or adaptive computation. What might appear as independence is better understood as optimisation within pre-established parameters. Describing such systems as *black boxes* may therefore exaggerate their distinctiveness: their internal operations are undoubtedly complex and often opaque, but so too is human reasoning. In both cases, opacity does not imply the absence of direction or intent. The functional orientation of AI systems used in contract formation remains externally determined, reflecting human-defined objectives. The conceptual distinctions developed in this chapter thus provide the analytical basis for the following discussion, which examines how such algorithmic processes can be situated within the evolving framework of contract formation in the digital age.

[139] C Wendehorst, 'Discussion Draft: Principles for AI in Contracting (Version 2.1)' (2024) 13 *Journal of European Consumer and Market Law* 43, 49.

# 4

# Mapping the Evolution: A Critical Review of Algorithmic Contract Formation

## I. Introduction

The adaptability of contract law raises the fundamental question: what is new that makes things different now? The previous chapters have undertaken a meticulous examination of algorithmic contracts and their defining characteristics and an extensive categorisation of related models, distinguishing them from other forms of digital-era contracting that diverge from the essence of algorithmic contracts. Given the longstanding de facto existence of algorithmic contracts frameworks,[1] a detailed exploration of academic perspectives on this topic has become increasingly critical. The likely escalation in AI usage over the coming years poses significant, unresolved legal challenges, heightening the chances of court involvement to address these issues.

This chapter undertakes a systematic analysis of the existing literature, distinguishing between two primary categories: publications proposing speculative theories on the basis of anticipated future trends, and more contemporary research specifically focusing on the theoretical analysis of algorithmic contract formation and corresponding conceptual frameworks. By critically assessing the strengths, weaknesses, and gaps in the existing literature, this evaluative process deepens our understanding of the field and provides a foundation for developing more comprehensive, innovative, and integrative approaches to algorithmic contract analysis.

There is a quasi-consensus among reputable sources regarding the need to establish a legal framework suited to algorithmic contracts based on machine learning. 'Whether traditional contract theories can be applied to cases where the software can learn from experience, adapting its own responses to varying conditions, is an open question.'[2] Some argue that the validity of these contracts is implicitly accepted, yet they fail to provide substantial justification of this view.[3]

[1] The most remote antecedents of algorithmic contracts can be traced back to high-frequency trading (HFT). For an in-depth discussion, see ch 1, section III.A.

[2] M Ebers, 'Artificial Intelligence, Contracting and Contract Law: An Introduction' in M Ebers, C Poncibò and M Zou (eds), *Contracting and Contract Law in the Age of Artificial Intelligence* (Hart Publishing, 2022)19, 30.

[3] A Beckers and G Teubner, *Three Liability Regimes for Artificial Intelligence. Algorithmic Actants, Hybrids, Crowds* (Hart Publishing, 2021) 54.

Even strong proponents of the conventional view of the absence of novelty in the impact of certain technologies on contract law cautiously acknowledge a shift from the fundamental inquiry of 'do traditional principles apply?' to a more nuanced exploration of 'how do these principles apply?'[4]

Given the nascent nature of this research domain, a more profound understanding of its genesis is needed. By synthesising prior studies, this assessment will consolidate existing knowledge and encourage further investigation. This analysis aims to develop a cohesive framework of the theoretical foundations established in earlier work.[5] By doing so, it will illuminate the historical development of research in this particular field, ascertain its present status, and delineate the gaps that require addressing to enable the development of a holistic approach to the issue of the formation of algorithmic contracts.

The remainder of this chapter is structured as follows: first, the contributions made prior to defining the concept of algorithmic contracts are discussed, differentiating between speculative and visionary ideas and those rooted in tangible advancements in AI through machine learning. After introducing the perspective of the individual who coined the term 'algorithmic contracts', the discussion transitions to contemporary viewpoints, where two factions can be distinguished: those who deny the impact of algorithmic contracts and those actively engaged in addressing the challenges that arise from this innovative form of contracting. Finally, conclusions are presented, highlighting unresolved issues whose solutions will remain integral to further progress in this area of research.

## II. From Concept to Reality: The Emergence of Algorithmic Contracts

This analysis categorises the existing scholarship into two major groups: pre- and post-identification of algorithmic contracts, a division marked by the definition of the concept by Lauren Scholz. Formally, the concept of algorithmic contracts dates to 2017, when Scholz coined the term to refer to contracts in which the parties used an algorithm to determine the terms of the offer or acceptance.[6] However,

[4] In particular, in her recent works, Eliza Mik argues that an exhaustive analysis is unnecessary because the legal position remains unchanged. See E Mik, 'The Resilience of Contract Law in Light of Technological Change' in M Furmston (ed), *The Future of the Law of Contract* (Routledge, 2020) 112, 112–40; E Mik, 'AI in Negotiating and Entering into Contracts' in LA Di Matteo, C Poncibò and M Cannarsa (eds), *The Cambridge Handbook of Artificial Intelligence* (Cambridge University Press, 2022) 45 45–58; E Mik, 'The Unimportance of Being "Electronic" or Popular Misconceptions about "Internet Contracting"' (2011) 19 *International Journal of Law and Information Technology* 324, 324–47; E Mik, 'Much Ado About Artificial Intelligence or: The Automation of Contract Formation' (2023) 30 *International Journal of Law and Information Technology* 484, 484–506.

[5] This analysis will serve as an initial step for future work involving the amalgamation and categorisation of various theoretical approaches used in prior research. This process will, in turn, serve as a basis for analysing certain contentious issues in the subsequent phases of the study. See ch 4, section II.

[6] LH Scholz, 'Algorithmic Contracts' (2017) *Stanford Technology Law Review* 128, 128–69.

algorithmic contracts were operational before they were defined, and there had been speculation about them before they even existed. Scholz herself alludes to their presence in various contexts, such as HFT or algorithms designed for price fixing.[7] The first pre-definition epoch is marked by speculative theory, envisioning potential future developments, while the second post-definition epoch is firmly rooted in the contemporary reality of algorithmic contracts.

## A. Pre-algorithmic Contract Landscape: Glimpsing into the Future

### *i. 'Can Computers Make Contracts?'*[8]

In 1996, when AI was going through the so-called second AI winter,[9] Curtis Karanow predicted that intelligent technology 'will soon allow some commercial transactions to take place without any need for human traders to review, or even be aware of, particular transactions'.[10] Tom Allen and Robin Widdison also foresaw the shift from automation to the autonomy of computational systems. Following on from Michie and Johnston's idea of 'the Creative Computer',[11] they envisioned systems with the ability to modify and create their own instructions, foreseeing a future where these systems could execute predefined commands and also adapt, modify, and generate their own directives. Their evolved capabilities would resemble human cognitive abilities, including decision-making, forming intentions, selecting choices, and even giving consent. These researchers carried out an in-depth exploration of the implications of the anticipated autonomy of computer systems in contracting, emphasising the overlap between technological autonomy and legal frameworks.[12]

In their scrutiny of this then-hypothetical paradigm in contracting facilitated by autonomous computational systems, which they conduct primarily from the perspective that they are mere tools, Allen and Widdison discerned a confluence of four fundamental challenges. Firstly, they highlighted the issue of capacity, emphasising that parties to a contract must possess the legal capacity to engage in it, but computational systems lack this capacity. Secondly, the concept of achieving consensus ad idem, or a meeting of the minds, was confounded by the difficulty in distinguishing between an offer and a mere invitation to contract within the realm

[7] ibid 137–45.

[8] T Allen and R Widdison, 'Can Computers Make Contracts?' (1996) 9 *Harvard Journal of Law & Technology* 25, 25.

[9] For a more exhaustive analysis of the AI timeline, see ch 3, section II.B.

[10] Karnow in IR Kerr, 'Ensuring the Success of Contract Formation in Agent-Mediated Electronic Commerce' (2001) 1 *Electronic Commerce Research* 183, 184.

[11] D Michie and R Johnston, *The Creative Computer: Machine Intelligence and Human Knowledge* (Viking, 1984).

[12] Allen and Widdison (n 8) 27–28.

of automated interactions. Thirdly, they observed the nuanced incorporation of intentionality within computer programming, acknowledging its presence albeit in a different form compared to human intentionality. Finally, their analysis delved into the aspect of consideration, highlighting the complexity of its identification in the instances of promises to be performed by the parties.[13] It is remarkable that, nearly 30 years later, these profound questions persist largely unanswered, particularly concerning systems entwined with machine learning technologies.

The evolution of artificial intelligence, especially with the integration of machine learning, adds levels of complexity to these challenges, given the ability of these systems to 'self-modif[y] or self-create (...) instructions'.[14] This is a significant point. The core issue revolves around the recognition that while advanced machine learning techniques can alter sequences, selections, and iterations, the fundamental purpose of the system persists, and this is set by the system operator. This fundamental purpose or intention that shapes the design of these computer systems is what endures unchanged amidst the dynamic flow of the algorithms and data processing.[15]

From the perspective that treats computers as mere machines, the analysis delves into three potential approaches to the problem: modifying the existing contractual doctrine; regarding them as mere tools for communication; or outright invalidating agreements formulated by autonomous systems.[16] In exploring the first approach, they entertain the notion of bypassing the traditional examination of agreements through the lens of offer and acceptance. Instead, the focus shifts to acknowledging the mere existence of an agreement. On this point, they base their argument on the reasonableness that the computer user should be vicariously bound by the agreements generated and the commercial presumption. However, they consider that the weakness of this position is that it eliminates the 'meeting of human minds', as the system operator might remain unaware that such agreements were even generated,[17] casting doubt on the validity of this approach. This point warrants a more in-depth exploration, and will be revisited later, providing a substantiated rationale that elucidates how, despite the manifestation of agreements through AI systems, the fundamental concept of the 'meeting of the minds' perseveres.[18]

Viewing algorithmic contract systems as solely communication tools is inadequate since it overlooks their primary function as decision-makers. However, acknowledging their role as communication tools remains pertinent. Critical aspects such as the moment of contract formation or attributing knowledge of the agreement's content to the operator hinge on this. This function has to be

[13] ibid 30–34.
[14] ibid 27.
[15] For a more comprehensive examination of the functioning of Machine Learning AI systems, see ch 3, section IV.
[16] Allen and Widdison (n 8) 43–49.
[17] ibid 43–45.
[18] See to ch 7, section IV for further details and in-depth discussion on this topic.

specifically considered, recognising its significance within the context of algorithmic contract systems.[19]

Ultimately, while acknowledging that invalidating contracts facilitated by autonomous systems would be a dismissal of reality, the authors envision substantial challenges when justifying agreements made by contemporary machine learning systems.[20] Their analysis culminates in the recognition that the core of this challenge is rooted in the structural framework of contract doctrine tailored for agreements between parties operating at arm's length.[21] Their ultimate proposal involves relaxing the stringent requirement that the parties' intent must exclusively pertain to the offer and acceptance specific to the agreement under consideration.[22]

Although they did not yet envision the benefits and risks of employing artificial intelligence in contract formation, the vision of Jeff A Dodd and James A Hernandez of contracting in cyberspace pointed to some issues that could be exacerbated by the integration of AI, namely: 'Authority (...) What electronic actions will be attributed to me? [and] [m]ethods of [f]ormation: How are offers and acceptances electronically formed? Is a contract formed? When is it formed?'[23] In relation to the first of these questions, the authors could be considered to be pioneers in referring, albeit tangentially, to agency law.[24] Concerning the second question, they advocated for applying face-to-face communication principles. However, there is a drawback: the system operator needs to intervene if the electronic agent fails to detect terms that may harm them and agrees to them.[25] This proposed solution is a kind of oxymoron. As the existing scholarship makes clear, both the issue of attribution and the timing of contract formation persist as unresolved matters. The former has not been adequately addressed, while the latter remains unaddressed entirely.

From the contributions of these pioneers, several critical questions arise for further exploration. These revolve around fundamental aspects of autonomous systems, concerning their role as decision-makers and communication tools. Specifically, the key areas of investigation include understanding how to recognise the agreement or meeting of minds in contracts generated by autonomous software. Additionally, there is a need to determine the moment of contract formation while attributing the knowledge present at that time to the operator involved. These questions can be traced back directly to the foundational work and insights offered by these trailblazing figures in the field. Despite their initial explorations,

[19] For further exploration on the time of contract formation, see ch 5, section IV. Additionally, for the attribution of knowledge of the agreement's content to the system operator, see ch 6, section IV.C.

[20] Allen and Widdison (n 8) 47–49.

[21] ibid 50.

[22] ibid 52.

[23] JC Dodd and JA Hernandez, 'Contracting in Cyberspace' (1998) 1 *Computer Law Review and Technology Journal* 2.

[24] ibid 5–8.

[25] ibid 7–11.

these questions remain unresolved, indicating their complexity and yet also ongoing relevance.

### *ii. Navigating the Contracting Problem in the Pre-Algorithmic Contract Era*[26]

In the realm of e-commerce, Jean-Francois Lerouge highlighted the potential use of systems capable of automatically finalising contracts without human intervention. These systems, referred to as 'electronic agents', possess the capability to conclude agreements on behalf of the involved parties.[27] For him, '[e]lectronic agents are intelligent software that search the Internet for some alternatives across a range of prices and valued-added options, proposing an adequate transaction, while taking our demand into account. The agent will even conduct the entire negotiation based on designated criteria'.[28] He even describes them as semi-autonomous entities capable of forming contracts without the parties utilising them being cognisant of their existence and the terms they establish.[29]

Lerouge expressed his concern about the requirement of consent.[30] In his study, he conducted a thorough analysis of three key perspectives: agency, the legal personality of autonomous computers, and the aspect of appearance. From the agency viewpoint, he emphasised the fact that computers lack the capacity to consent to an agent-principal relationship or to assume liability. Regarding the legal personality of autonomous computers, he scrutinised the necessity for the existence of a patrimony and the registration of these entities, ultimately concluding that the drawbacks outweigh the benefits of granting legal personality to computers. From the appearance perspective, theory dictates that its application necessitates the party wishing to employ it to have acted unknowingly while contracting with a software agent. Therefore, this theory proves inapplicable in situations where the parties are aware of the involvement of software agents in the contract.[31]

His most notable contribution lies in highlighting the shortcomings of the objective theory of contracts. He emphasises that this approach falls short in addressing crucial unresolved issues, particularly in situations where there exists a lack of awareness regarding the existence and contents of the agreement at the time when it is formalised by the system operator.[32] This indicates the limitations

[26] The term 'contracting problem' is borrowed from Samir Chopra and Laurence White, denoting the challenge related to the agreement requirement in contract formation involving autonomous software agents. See S Chopra and LF White, 'Artificial Agents and the Contracting Problem: A Solution Via an Agency Analysis' (2009) 2009 *University of Illinois Journal of Law, Technology & Policy* 363, 363.

[27] J-F Lerouge, 'The Use of Electronic Agents Questioned Under Contractual Law: Suggested Solutions on a European and American Level' (1999) 18 *John Marshall Journal of Computer & Information Law* 403, 403–33.

[28] ibid 405.

[29] ibid 405–06.

[30] ibid 406–07.

[31] ibid 407–14.

[32] ibid 417.

of conventional contract theories in effectively grappling with the complexities arising from contracts facilitated by autonomous systems. Hence, the conclusion drawn by Lerouge is equally applicable to algorithmic contracts which not only act autonomously but can also act non-deterministically,[33] adding to the complexity of the issue. Indeed, this insight serves as a foundational standpoint for this study.[34] It is precisely the fulfilment of the requirement of agreement, meeting of the minds, consensus ad idem or consent with respect to algorithmic contracts that is the subject of this research,[35] so that Lerouge's contribution remains pertinent and significant even though it precedes the current state of AI development.

Ian Kerr, a contemporary of Lerouge, took a different approach. He argued that technicians should consider integrating the established legal boundaries of traditional contract law into the design of what he calls 'agent-mediated' e-commerce.[36] He highlighted several points of contention: these systems lack legal personality, making it impossible for them to enter into contracts or possess the capacity to do so. Additionally, he noted the absence of a meeting of the minds in transactions generated through them.[37]

Rather than pursuing proposals through modifications in the law or re-evaluation of current legal principles, Kerr recommended a few key measures to guide technicians in the design. Firstly, he suggested that the electronic agent clearly demonstrate the assent of the operator. Secondly, he proposed implementing mechanisms to mitigate liability arising from electronic errors. Finally, he advised devising a process to explicitly attribute actions to specific individuals or entities involved. In the first scenario, it implies an acknowledgement that the system possesses a broad authorisation to enter contracts. The second scenario entails a process akin to validation, which could potentially postpone the actual establishment of the contract. Lastly, attribution denotes the precise correlation between the system and its operator, ensuring clear identification and association between the two entities.[38]

The fact that Ian Kerr acknowledges that his work focuses primarily on technical aspects does not detract from its relevance. While he may not have fully foreseen the evolution of technology, his analysis remains pertinent considering the current state of the art, and one must either dismiss or delve deeper into his recommendations. Consequently, in relation to his proposed mechanisms to mitigate liability arising from electronic errors, these subsequent ratification processes may undermine the immediacy and efficiency pursued by algorithmic contracts. Indeed, this proposed solution, akin to the one suggested by Dodd and Hernandez,[39] would

[33] For a discussion elucidating the differentiation between deterministic and non-deterministic algorithms and exploring its implications, see ch 3, section IV.B.ii.

[34] For an analysis of the characteristics of algorithmic contracts, see ch 1, section II. For an examination of the proposed solution in this research regarding the attribution of knowledge of contract formation and content to the system operator, see ch 6, section IV.C.

[35] For the framing of the inquiry, see ch 1, section IV.

[36] Kerr (n 10) 200.

[37] ibid 187–90.

[38] ibid 197–200.

[39] Dodd and Hernandez (n 23) 7–11.

hinder the formation of the contract at the moment of convergence between the two systems. Instead, it would defer the contract formation, consequently impeding one of the primary advantages of these systems – namely, their efficiency, speed, and immediacy. Moreover, in relation to his correlation proposal, while express attribution assists in pinpointing the accountable entity, addressing concerns such as potential anonymity, it does not resolve matters concerning the concurrence of the meeting of the minds, as it solely impacts on liability determination.

However, the statement of the first of his proposals is worth exploring in greater detail: '[e]nsure that the electronic agent manifests the originator's assent'.[40] While he emphasises embedding a form of general authority in the design, the focus should be on examining the intrinsic technical aspects of these systems themselves. This examination leads to the conclusion that in narrow artificial intelligence systems specifically tailored for tasks such as negotiation and contract formation, the system, even with automatic learning or an inability to explain its actions, will always align with the primary interest of its operator. This remains a highly pertinent question that, as of now, lacks a definitive resolution. From a technical standpoint, however, it is feasible to assert Kerr's phrase that 'the electronic agent manifests the originator's assent'.[41]

During the 'slope of enlightenment' of e-commerce,[42] Anthony Bellia also considered '[t]he use of computer technology to "make contracts"'.[43] Bellia's work is relevant to this study because it concerns a feature of algorithmic contracts as proposed in this research: when both parties are served by an algorithm that interacts on their behalf.[44] Beginning with the assumption that common law contract principles do not conclusively address enforceability issues, and acknowledging the restricted relevance of agency principles,[45] he critiques the approach rooted in the objective theory already discussed by Lerouge, Allen, Widdison, or Kerr. His criticism asserts that the objective theory fails due to a scenario where an individual employs someone as their agent to purchase an item from a seller. In this context, the individual's liability is not solely determined by contractual rules but also influenced by regulations governing agency relationships. The objective theory alone proves to be insufficient.[46]

[40] Kerr (n 10) 197–98.

[41] In this regard, see ch 3, section IV.B.ii which discusses the characteristics of AI systems and related terminology, and in ch 7, section IV.A which addresses the consequences stemming from the inflexibility of algorithms.

[42] In the context of technology hype cycle and specifically in relation to e-commerce, the phrase 'slope of enlightenment' denotes a specific phase in its evolution where organisations or industries attain a deeper comprehension of the potential and practical applications of e-commerce technologies. It signifies a stage characterised by heightened awareness, enhanced understanding, and a more pragmatic outlook regarding the advantages and challenges associated with employing e-commerce strategies and tools. See 'Gartner Hype Cycle Research Methodology' www.gartner.com/en/research/methodologies/gartner-hype-cycle accessed 2 May 2024.

[43] AJ Bellia, 'Contracting with Electronic Agents' (2001) 50 *Emory Law Journal* 1047, 1047.

[44] ibid.

[45] ibid 1051.

[46] ibid 1047–48.

In the work of Bellia, he makes a statement which is clearly applicable to algorithmic contracts:[47] '[i]t seems that there is no basis upon which to know the assent of the other until after the existence of a legal obligation'.[48] While his analysis stems from the viewpoint of the Restatement (Second) of Contracts,[49] it bears a strong resemblance to the offer and acceptance framework utilised in English contract law, bringing to the discussion concepts such as cross offers. It is important to note that, unlike in English contract law, cross offers appear to be accepted under American regulations, but this alone does not serve to justify the admissibility of agreements reached by electronic agents.[50]

He then analyses the suggestions advocating for the use of agency principles to resolve enforceability issues concerning electronic agents. Scholars have proposed that applying agency principles to electronic agent bots in electronic contracts could resolve legal complexities. However, invoking actual or apparent authority in this context faces numerous legal hurdles. Agency law necessitates consent between principal and agent, a requirement impossible for software acting as an agent. Consent justifies legal obligations in agency relationships, including fiduciary duties, which electronic agents lack due to their absence of judgement or discretion. While they can faithfully perform programmed tasks, they do not assume legal obligations for program malfunctions. Consequently, applying representation principles to electronic agents leads to an unrecognisable principal-agent relationship. Even considering apparent authority encounters challenges, as it requires a representation of real authority absent in software. This dilemma prompts the question of whether electronic agents should be classified under a different form of authority, excluding duties to principals but binding them to third parties. However, justifying this as an agency solution seems inaccurate, as the fundamental aspects of agency law, centred as they are on trust relationships between autonomous beings, do not align with the functionality of electronic agents.[51]

It is precisely this setback that leads him to consider the proposal to grant legal personality to these entities because the core problem with regarding artificial agents as agents stems from the presumption in agency law that agents are natural persons. However, Bellia argues that debating whether the law should treat computer programs as human is unnecessary in the current context and specifically in their relation to contract law, and this perspective holds true today.[52] The crucial point pertains to whether acknowledging artificial agents as legal persons would resolve the legal quandaries associated with their use, something he rejects.

[47] For a comprehensive examination regarding the timing of algorithmic contract formation, see ch 5, section IV.

[48] Bellia (n 43) 1055.

[49] Restatement (Second) of Contracts § 21 (American Law Institute, 1981).

[50] Bellia (n 43) 1053–59.

[51] ibid 1059–65.

[52] To avoid distorting the object of analysis and refrain from creating complexities where solutions are sought, it is crucial to focus on the specific purpose for which AI is being analysed. In the case of contract formation, it is essential to remember that we are dealing with AI systems known as narrow AI. In this regard, see ch 3, section IV.B.ii for further consideration.

Advocates suggest granting embedded software the right to enter contracts to protect users relying on its actions. However, for Bellia, this proposal would not serve its purpose. Software lacks personal assets, making it impractical to hold it accountable for contractual obligations. Even if insured, the user bears ultimate liability, which makes the designation of the software as a 'person' redundant. Bellia emphasises that focusing on 'personhood' in legal debates diverts attention from the main objective of the law: serving human individuals. The argument that electronic agents should be considered 'persons' ignores that they are simply instruments for the affairs of natural persons.[53]

Although Bellia conducts an extensive analysis of various theories justifying the enforceability of contracts, including will theories, reliance theories, and finally the trust theory,[54] he concludes that '[t]he theories that appear consistent with enforcing such exchanges are those that seek to protect the ability of individuals to pursue reasonable objectives through reliable arrangements'.[55] This proposition implies the need to reconsider these theories to address the question of whether transactions executed by electronic agents should be legally binding, which shows that this is an unresolved issue.

Contemporary to Bellia's research is that of Emily M Weitzenboeck's 'Electronic Agents and the Formation of Contracts'.[56] In this paper, she stresses the fact that the role of this type of technology went beyond being a mere communication tool to become an active element in the formation of the contract.[57] Weitzenboeck discusses the challenges posed by the involvement of intelligent agents in contract formation, evaluating three doctrinal solutions: legal personality, mere tools, and agents. From the first perspective, she assumes that the legal capacity to enter into binding contracts is usually limited to natural or legal persons. She also emphasises the fact that a lack of personality does not equate to incapacity. This lack of personality poses a significant challenge when considering the involvement of intelligent agents in contract formation. The idea of conferring legal personality on these agents has been proposed, citing moral right, social capacity and legal expediency as possible justifications. However, attributing legal personality to intelligent agents raises complex issues regarding liability, identity and the difficulty of identifying the agent itself, ultimately raising practical problems.[58] From the second perspective, intelligent agents are considered as mere communication tools, similar to machines such as telephones or faxes. From this point of view, everything that proceeds from an electronic agent is considered to originate directly from its human controller. However, this approach holds human users responsible for the actions of the electronic agents they operate. Although it encourages users to ensure that agents operate correctly, she believes

[53] Bellia (n 43) 1065–67.
[54] ibid 1074–92.
[55] ibid 1092.
[56] EM Weitzenboeck, 'Electronic Agents and the Formation of Contracts' (2001) 9 *International Journal of Law and Information Technology* 204, 204–34.
[57] ibid 209–10.
[58] ibid 211–14.

that it can be unduly harsh, especially in cases where unexpected liabilities arise due to technical failures or errors in the agent's operation.[59]

Lastly, as an alternative perspective, she explores the classification of intelligent agents as agents within the framework of agency law. Despite its apparent appeal, she finds that this approach faces substantial hurdles posed by various legal doctrines, including consent, excess of authority, and undisclosed principal. She points out the inherent challenge in applying the requirement of consent between principal and agent in accordance with agency law to autonomous electronic devices, a concern also highlighted by Lerouge.[60] Furthermore, other unresolved issues surrounding delegation, and ratification persist within the context of intelligent agents.[61]

Weitzenboeck, building upon Kerr's insights, highlights a critical feature of the objective theory: the consent of the person using the system is what is crucially important, rather than the consent of the electronic agent itself.[62] This also should remind us of something that is often overlooked – the emphasis on the human operator's volition within the framework of the objective theory. Following an examination of multiple regulations, including the UNCITRAL Model Law on Electronic Commerce, the EU's Electronic Commerce Directive, UETA, UCITA, and Canada's Uniform Electronic Commerce Act, she emphasises the insufficiency of a regulation which merely acknowledges its validity without providing substantial doctrinal backing.[63] Her study identifies issues that remain unresolved via a straightforward application of the objective theory of contract. Instead of advocating for doctrinal constructions that validate contracts formed via electronic agents, her work leans towards solutions aligned with risk management, such as implementing standards or labelling systems.[64] This points toward pragmatic solutions to address the challenges posed by electronic agents in contract formation.

Weitzenboeck's view is persuasive: relying solely on the objective theory of contracts is inadequate. However, rather than approaching this solely as a risk management issue that could potentially be addressed through contractual liability,[65] there still exists a fundamental doctrinal gap concerning the contract's

[59] ibid 214.
[60] See section II.A.ii above.
[61] Weitzenboeck (n 56) 215–18.
[62] ibid 221–23.
[63] ibid 223–31.
[64] ibid 232–24.
[65] In this regard, it should be noted that in the EU, efforts are underway to address this concern through the proposed new Product Liability Directive and the emerging AI Liability Directive. The revised Product Liability regime updates strict liability to reflect digital and AI-enabled products. Alongside it, the Commission proposed an AI Liability Directive to complement national fault-based rules through targeted measures on disclosure and proof – although that proposal has since been formally withdrawn. See Directive (EU) 2024/2853 of the European Parliament and of the Council of 23 October 2024 on liability for defective products and repealing Council Directive 85/374/EEC [2024] OJ L2024/2853; European Commission, Proposal for a Directive of the European Parliament and of the Council on adapting non-contractual civil liability rules to artificial intelligence (AI Liability Directive) COM(2022) 496 final; European Commission, *Commission Work Programme 2025: Moving forward together: A bolder, simpler, faster Union* COM(2025) 45 final annex IV; and 'Withdrawal of Commission proposals' [2025] OJ C2025/5423.

formation phase. The absence of endorsement from the objective theory of contracts, without further support, indicates that a gap is present in the comprehensive framework intended to uphold the validity of contracts formed through electronic agents.

The state of the art in 2007 led Andrade and others to ask how to express consent in the era of the autonomous action of computers.[66] Once more, this study meticulously examines the three prevailing approaches: regarding them as mere tools, as legal persons, or contemplating the application of agency rules. For them, the lack of predictability of some of the actions of autonomous systems makes them question the viability of the possibility of considering them as mere tools.[67] This paves the way to contemplate the possibility of granting legal personality to the contracting agents. In this regard, their work explores the potential attribution of legal personality to intelligent software agents by comparing them with established legal entities such as natural and legal persons. It highlights the historical recognition of non-human entities in law, emphasising legal personality as more about rights and obligations than a physical concept. Examining the requisites for legal personality, the analysis considers various elements, including the personal or patrimonial perspective, purpose, intent, and legal acknowledgement. These authors consider the option of providing legal personality to such systems. The justification for this would be the fact that the agents have the ability to carry out independent action, and any such actions can have a legal impact. In this sense, these agents can be compared to corporate legal entities, enabling the legal theories that apply to the latter to be applied to the former. While recognising that conferring legal personality upon software agents could potentially resolve consent and contractual issues and diminish human responsibility, significant challenges remain. These challenges encompass aspects such as identification, liability, domicile, obligations, and the enforcement of contracts involving such agents. The article concludes by stressing the complexity of attributing legal personality to software agents and suggests potential strategies to tackle the associated challenges.[68] Their contribution also examines the possibility of applying the 'agency paradigm' from the broader concept of 'representation'. The analysis introduces various forms of representation, including direct and indirect, assessing their relevance to relationships between human and electronic agents. Cases in which a representative makes statements with legal effect on behalf of another person are examined, distinguishing between direct representation and the role of a 'messenger' or 'nuntius' who transmits statements without making personal decisions. The discussion delves into voluntary representation, highlighting the need to understand and desire capacity, which is essential for effective representation. In addition, it explores the complexities associated with representation without power of attorney and

[66] F Andrade et al, 'Contracting Agents: Legal Personality and Representation' (2007) 15 *Artificial Intelligence and Law* 357, 357–73.

[67] ibid 360–61.

[68] ibid 361–67.

the prospect of ratification by a principal. It discusses the challenges of granting powers of attorney to intelligent electronic agents, focusing on their lack of legal personality. Their work concludes by questioning the ability of the legal system to recognise the acts or statements of electronic agents and their possible ratification, ultimately exploring the intricacies of representation theory and its applicability to non-human entities in contractual contexts.[69]

The assertion by these authors that conferring legal personality on contracting agents is not necessary due to the present state of technology warrants careful consideration.[70] Granting legal personality to these agents is problematic for two main reasons: first, as this concerns narrow AI, it is crucial to contextualise the specific use case at hand, namely contract formation; and second, these agents lack autonomous goals and function primarily as tools with predefined objectives, regardless of their capacities for learning and self-improvement. As they are empowered solely to achieve predetermined aims, the argument for providing them with legal personality becomes redundant.[71] In their conclusion, the authors acknowledge an inability to provide a resolution to this issue, thereby emphasising the existing gap within the literature concerning the legal framework surrounding 'the acts of machines or devices predisposed by human or corporates bodies'.[72]

Giovanni Sartor presents an alternative viewpoint by suggesting that software agents possess 'cognitive states'. This perspective aims to move away from purely behaviouristic solutions, emphasising the importance of considering the subjective aspect of the agreement process.[73] 'When looking at an entity from the intentional stance, we are explaining the behaviour of that entity assuming that it has certain cognitive states (information on how things are) and conative states (information on what to do).'[74] Put another way, cognitive states refer to the information an entity possesses about how things are in its environment or within itself. These states encompass the knowledge, beliefs, perceptions, and understanding that the entity may have about its environment or its internal workings. For example, a computer program may have cognitive states about the structure of its database, the rules it follows, or the information it has been programmed to learn. Conative states, on the other hand, refer to the information or guidelines an entity possesses about what to do or how to act based on its internal cognitive states and external stimuli. These states include desires, goals, intentions or directives that guide the entity's actions or decision-making processes. For example, the same computer program may have conative states that instruct it to retrieve specific data from the database or perform certain operations based on certain conditions. Thus, when approaching an entity from the intentional point of view, its behaviour is explained

[69] ibid 367–70.
[70] ibid 371.
[71] For a more in-depth development of this argument, see ch 6, section II.D.
[72] Andrade et al (n 66) 371–72.
[73] G Sartor, 'Cognitive Automata and the Law: Electronic Contracting and the Intentionality of Software Agents' (2009) 17 *Artificial Intelligence and Law* 253, 253–90.
[74] ibid 260.

by assuming that it possesses these cognitive and conative states.[75] This perspective helps to attribute reasoning or intentionality to its behaviours based on the assumed cognitive and conative states it might have.

When analysing the behaviour of an intelligent system from the intentional stance, the assumption is that the system operates 'rationally', 'by adopting determinations appropriate to the purposes assigned to it, on the basis of the information available to it, in the context in which it is going to operate'.[76] The contribution of Sartor in this respect is of great importance and remains pertinent in the current context.[77] However, his theory faces a roadblock when he applies it to the contracts. This hurdle arises when he treats the act of delegating cognitive tasks to an intelligent system on par with delegating them to a human. Nonetheless, he suggests a potential solution by proposing that the contract be deemed formalised upon the system's receipt of acceptance (not its operator). This approach, while addressing some issues, still maintains the sequence of offer and acceptance, failing to address situations where both parties utilise such intelligent agents.[78]

Moreover, this setback resembles the observation made by Bellia, who, when applying the objective theory of contracts to individuals instead of software, revealed that not only is the objective theory of contracts affected but also the agency concept itself.[79] Indeed, the amalgamation of Bellia and Sartor's approaches, along with their method of identifying setbacks, is intriguing. They introduce a test by applying their findings to the realm of human delegation, allowing for the detection of shortcomings in proposals, which is an interesting method to uncover potential problems in this context.

Samir Chopra and Laurence White introduced the term 'the contracting problem' to refer to the issue surrounding contracts facilitated by artificial agents which lack legal personhood and, consequently, which cannot act as formal parties within the contract.[80] In contrast with Sartor's view, they argue that software agents lack mental states, meaning that knowledge cannot be attributed to them.[81] In their approach, they distinguish between open and closed systems. For closed systems, where rules and protocols can be predefined, they suggest acceptance through terms in a master agreement or via click-wrap or browse-wrap methods (which were contentious at that time).[82] In dealing with open systems, they present six possible approaches: relaxing the intention requirement as proposed by Allen and Widdison; treating these agents as tools, despite the drawback of them transcending mere communication systems; regarding them

[75] ibid 260–63.
[76] ibid 265.
[77] In contrast, Mik argues that 'role of mental states in the process of contract formation' is absent. See Mik 'Much Ado About Artificial Intelligence or: The Automation of Contract Formation' (n 4) 487.
[78] Sartor (n 73) 277–82.
[79] See above n 46.
[80] Chopra and White (n 26) 365.
[81] S Chopra and LF White, *A Legal Theory for Autonomous Artificial Agents* (University of Michigan Press, 2011) 72.
[82] Chopra and White (n 26) 366–68.

as conveyors of a unilateral offer, yet without clarifying how the offer is attributed to the system operator; returning to the objective theory of contractual intention, which fails to address not just expressing the party's intention but also the formal aspect; considering them as agents devoid of legal personality; or ultimately viewing them as legal persons.[83]

To avoid redundancy, the focus will now centre solely on propositions related to the doctrine of unilateral offer and artificial agents functioning as legal agents without legal personality, as these represent the most innovative and groundbreaking contributions. The approach focused on the doctrine of unilateral offer deals first with the transmission of pre-established conditions. Under this perspective, if the artificial agent is considered solely as a medium for communication, its role remains confined to facilitating the transmission of predefined terms and conditions. Therefore, its function is restricted to that of a conduit for relaying information rather than that of an active participant in the contractual process.[84] This approach fails in attributing the content of an offer autonomously generated by the system to its operator.[85]

Regarding their proposal of agents without legal personality, this focuses on the 'apparent authority' to circumvent the lack of consent due to the absence of capacity. They draw parallels with historical contexts like Roman slaves and actions conducted by minors. However, their crucial reference to 'the agent's programmed instructions' that 'specify the scope of the agent's activities and the breadth of its discretion',[86] hints at a significant avenue for argumentation within this realm, because they ultimately refer to the establishment of objectives and constraints by the system operator.[87]

Ultimately, however, the application of agency law is the option presented as preferable by Chopra and White, who also confine it to agents without legal personality, reinforcing the idea of the lack of necessity to grant legal personality to artificial agents.[88] They base their argument on intuitive rationales, economic grounds, and the possibility of overcoming the difficulties the issue presents. Regarding the 'common sense' arguments and despite the fact that ratification by the principal has already been shown to be ineffective since it undermines the objective of this contracting method and revives the risk of ratification delays, their differentiation between authority and instructions is insightful: authority defines the contractual objective or goal, while instructions are programming, which may evolve due to machine learning.[89] Authority is what delimits the scope of the

[83] ibid 368–79.

[84] ibid 372–74.

[85] For a detailed explanation regarding the attribution of the knowledge of the agreement to the system operator, see ch 6, section IV.C.

[86] Chopra and White (n 26) 376–78.

[87] In relation to the characteristics of systems justifying the attribution of the meeting of the algorithms to the system operator, see ch 7, section IV.A.

[88] This approach is further reinforced in their work Chopra and White (n 81) ch 2, 29–70.

[89] Chopra and White (n 26) 393.

ultimate goal intended with the use of the system. From an economic perspective, their theory follows Rasmusen's argument, which aims to clarify the process of assigning accountability for errors or mistakes committed by an agent to the party capable of resolving these issues with the least expenditure or cost.[90] Technical arrangements related to programming should ideally be excluded from this equation, instead being addressed through the attribution of contractual responsibility in the agreement binding the operator and the programmer. This point indicates that Chopra and White primarily adopt an approach centred on resolving liability concerns rather than fulfilling the requirement of consent. As a result, their focus deviates somewhat from addressing the core contracting issue and leans towards tackling a liability problem.

A temporal span of almost two decades, from the initial envisioning by early scholars of scenarios involving human interaction through algorithms to optimise outcomes in contracting processes until the definitive identification of the 'contracting problem' by Chopra and White, gave rise to a rich body of literature. Although scholars have made diligent efforts to navigate the challenges presented by artificial agents in contracting, none of the proposed approaches offers a comprehensive solution to the contracting problem. Instead, these approaches themselves lay bare their own limitations and drawbacks. Yet this extensive scholarship still serves a dual role: it acts as a wellspring of inspiration due to its exploration of hypotheses and provides a foundational framework for further development. Despite the various perspectives and theoretical frameworks provided in this area, a noticeable gap persists in that no conclusive solution has been proposed that comprehensively and definitively addresses the intricacies inherent in the involvement of artificial agents in contractual affairs. These complexities include attributing decision-making outcomes from the system to the operator, addressing subjectivity, and determining the time of contract formation.

## B. Unveiling Algorithmic Contracts: Lauren Scholz's Conceptual Innovation

It was in 2017 that a term was introduced to encapsulate an established practice that had long been in operation: the use of algorithms to define the contractual obligations between parties. These were termed 'algorithmic contracts' by Scholz.[91] She noted that 'when algorithms are introduced in institutional decision-making, individuals outsource their valuation processes to the algorithm'.[92] Her argument is based on the inadequacy of considering algorithms as mere tools, pointing out that algorithms can produce results that were not foreseen by their creators, and

[90] ibid 394–402.
[91] Scholz (n 6) 128–69.
[92] ibid 132.

that they can lead to fraud or illegal practices.[93] In particular, she refers to black-box algorithms as a key example of the challenges arising from this innovative contracting mechanism within contract law.[94]

Moving away from the idea of algorithms as mere tools and acknowledging the need to address the legal validity of algorithmic contract formation, Scholz reintroduces the specific principles of agency law into the debate. Her proposal aims to substantiate the fulfilment of the objective intent requirement within these contracts. From her perspective, algorithmic contracts function as what she calls 'constructive agents',[95] that are able to 'move far beyond the intents and capacities of their authorizing entities'.[96] In this context, these contracts are seen as entities that carry out transactions on behalf of their principals (the parties involved), with their actions being implicitly authorised or ratified by those principals. This implies that the actions performed by the algorithmic contracts are deemed legitimate and binding as if expressly authorised by the parties involved. In the absence of a framework agreement such as in EDI,[97] the proposed solution is based on ratification models, and is focused on intention and algorithmic accountability rather than mutual assent and enforceability.[98]

While acknowledging the pivotal role of Scholz's foundational work in clarifying the prerequisites for forming algorithmic contracts, adopting agency contract rules for this context may not be necessary. Critically, the advocated ratification mechanism contradicts the core principles of speed and efficiency that algorithmic contracts aim to provide. Introducing a two-stage contract formation process – algorithm performance followed by ratification – brings forth new risks, such as delayed or absent ratification, potentially compromising the swift and seamless nature these contracts strive to achieve. Without this immediacy and bidirectionality of communication, there would be no justification for arguing that algorithmic contracts are formed at the moment when the two algorithms converge.[99]

'[A] tool is a poor metaphor for an algorithm with the ability to program itself that has been delegated substantial responsibility for developing contractual terms.'[100] This is Scholz's argument when, revisiting her own algorithmic contracts from the perspective of their relationship to contract law, she dismisses the idea of their being mere tools. However, she does not elaborate further on this point other than to indicate that they make 'independent decisions' or that they manifest

[93] ibid.
[94] ibid 149–64.
[95] ibid 165. See also LH Scholz, 'Algorithms and Contract Law' in W Barfield (ed), *The Cambridge Handbook of The Law of Algorithms* (Cambridge University Press, 2020) 141, 142.
[96] Scholz (n 6) 150.
[97] For a detailed analysis on the functioning of EDI and its distinctions from algorithmic contracts, see ch 2, section II.
[98] Scholz (n 6) 164–69.
[99] For a more detailed examination regarding the formation of algorithmic contracts, see ch 5, section IV.
[100] Scholz (n 95) 146.

assent.[101] Her 'constructive agents' are nothing more than a sophisticated tool, or complex tool if we use her own terms.[102] But she never builds on the term 'constructive agents' other than to say that this concept 'provides a specific, technology neutral reason why it is appropriate to hold companies to the terms an algorithm has chosen for them'.[103] It should be noted that she does not make any reference to the possible granting of legal personality to systems employing autonomous algorithms as a solution for issues related to consent, intention, or liability, a perspective at least considered by other scholars.[104]

Additionally, the solution proposed by Scholz emphasises the requirement of intent but fails to adequately address the issue of mutual agreement, a notable gap in the proposed approach. Furthermore, concerning intent, it is uncertain whether these systems go beyond the intent of their operators.[105] Despite their capacity for self-learning, their design and definition are structured in a way that, while enabling self-improvement, they consistently align with the primary purpose for which they were created. Consequently, despite what Scholz says, they do not significantly stray from the intent of their authorising entities. This discrepancy highlights a significant lacuna within the proposed solution concerning the essential element of mutual agreement for algorithmic contracts. The present study aims to address this problem.

## III. Algorithms and Contract Law: A Contemporary Perspective

Although this remains a controversial and unresolved issue within the field, contributions dedicated to this specific subject matter are scarce. Intelligent inter-systemic contracting was perhaps still in its infancy when Andrade and others noted that 'the existing legal norms are not fit for an endeavouring challenge as the appearance of intelligent electronic agents in electronic relations',[106] but it was an established reality when Scholz spoke of 'contracting agents'.[107] Yet how to accommodate algorithmic contracts within the contract law framework remains an unanswered and open question,[108] even if there are dissenting voices who believe that no further analysis is needed.[109]

[101] ibid.
[102] ibid 150.
[103] ibid 151.
[104] See section II.A.ii above, particularly comments on Lerouge, Weitzenboeck, and Andrade et al.
[105] Scholz (n 6) 150.
[106] Andrade et al (n 66) 372.
[107] Scholz (n 6) 136–49.
[108] Ebers (n 2) 30. See also ch 1, section V.
[109] Mik, *The Resilience of Contract Law in Light of Technological Change* (n 4) 112–40; Mik, *AI in Negotiating and Entering into Contracts* (n 4) 45–58; Mik, 'Much Ado About Artificial Intelligence or: The Automation of Contract Formation' (n 4) 484–506.

## A. Algorithmic Contracts: Business As Usual

In stark contrast to the prevailing opinion of those who have scrutinised the ramifications of contract formation through algorithms within contract law, there exists an important voice who steadfastly maintains a stance of 'business as usual'. Having also played an active role in fuelling the academic hype surrounding smart contracts,[110] Eliza Mik insists on 'The Resilience of Contract Law in the Light of Technological Change',[111] while pointing to an excess of hype surrounding the use of AI in contract formation.[112] However, while the resilience of contract law is evident, time-tested and proven, a re-evaluation of theories and doctrines is essential to accommodate something which is genuinely new: technology which is not only used as a communication tool but to which decision-making is also delegated. This is not a counter-example to the resilience of contract law, but, contrary to Mik's position, it is not business as usual either.

On the opposite end of the spectrum from Scholz, Mik considers artificial intelligence systems to be mere tools, on the basis that there is a great deal of terminological and legal confusion and that '[i]n the context of contract law, technical details are rarely (if ever!) relevant'.[113] While echoing the concern about the absence of a meeting of the minds, she downplays the significance of system autonomy by linking it to machine automation. In her work, she criticises the recourse to the separation theories that enshrine the need to recognise legal personality for this kind of software and at the same time rejects any recourse to agency precisely because the systems lack legal personality.[114] Mik emphasises the intention requirement over the agreement itself, dismissing the significance of the decision-making process,[115] and ultimately asserting the importance of the objective theory of contract.[116] Her straightforward approach is appealing, and yet it fails because the subjective element remains intrinsic to contract formation; its elimination would render remedies obsolete.[117] It would

[110] For the contribution of Mik in this respect see E Mik, 'Contracts in Code?' (2021) 13 *Law, Innovation and Tech* 478, 478–509; E Mik, 'Smart Contracts: Terminology, Technical Limitations and Real World Complexity' (2017) 9 *Law, Innovation and Technology* 269, 269–300; E Mik, 'Deconstructing Smart Contracts' in N Kim and E Stacy-Ann eds, *The Cambridge Handbook of Emerging Issues at the Intersection of Commercial Law and Technology* (Cambridge University Press, 2025) 375, 381. She also continues to refer to smart contracts in Mik, *The Resilience of Contract Law in Light of Technological Change* (n 4) 112–40.

[111] ibid.

[112] Mik, 'Much Ado About Artificial Intelligence or: The Automation of Contract Formation' (n 4) 484–506.

[113] Mik, *The Resilience of Contract Law in Light of Technological Change* (n 4) 113–14.

[114] ibid 118–20.

[115] Mik, 'Much Ado About Artificial Intelligence or: The Automation of Contract Formation' (n 4) 487–90.

[116] Mik, *The Resilience of Contract Law in Light of Technological Change* (n 4) 120–23.

[117] Note, however, that despite Mik's radical objectification, she herself recognises that the decision-making process is important in the case of vitiating factors, and therefore not completely negligible. See Mik, *AI in Negotiating and Entering into Contracts* (n 4) 56.

be 'a *reductio ad absurdum* of the fundamental principle of *consensus ad idem* under contract law'.[118]

As her view has evolved, she has made a distinction between AI's role in entering contracts and AI's involvement in negotiating contracts. She dismisses the latter, concentrating on the former as a means to 'assist human negotiators'. For Mik, there appears to be no distinction between whether the trader uses a program to determine the optimal stock price and communicates the resulting offer personally, or if the program both determines the price and communicates the offer.[119] However, there exists a significant distinction because there is a form of oversight or supervision in the first case which is not present in the latter. Precisely because there is novelty in the absence of human involvement before the AI system communicates its decision to the other party and the contract is formed, this impacts upon contract formation. This particular aspect remains completely unresolved in Mik's. She herself acknowledges that the debate over whether the decision is made by a human or the AI system is left for future discussions.[120] This represents a substantial gap within her scholarly contribution.

However, it is interesting that what for others represents a challenge for contract law, such as the lack of explainability,[121] especially in black-box algorithms,[122] she views as irrelevant. From her perspective, contract law does not require the statements made by the contracting parties to be understandable or explainable.[123] Moreover, although she also appears to contradict what others are asserting regarding the meeting of the minds during the contract formation process, Mik's approach assumes that the stated intention is the same as the true intention, and so that the contract reflects what both parties intended. Thus, in essence, she does not rule out mental states but assumes that the objective intent coincides with the subjective intent. An understanding of true subjective intent often undermines the protection afforded by the objective approach.[124] She extends her argument by suggesting that an automatically generated statement might not accurately reflect the true intention of the individual who operated it, but still it is attributed to the operator.[125] However, a notable weakness in her position is the lack of clarity in the rules concerning the attribution of the

[118] Ebers (n 2) 31.
[119] Mik, *AI in Negotiating and Entering into Contracts* (n 4) 52.
[120] ibid.
[121] Explainabilitiy as a technique to fulfil the requirement of right to explanation is defined by Chiara Gallese as 'the attempt to explain the output of a black box', by creating a second model that mimics the first and opaque one with the aim to explain the latter. See C Gallese, 'The AI Act Proposal: a New Right to Technical Interpretability?' (Speech at the 2023 1st ISLC Online International Conference, Milan 20-22 February 2023) arxiv.org/pdf/2303.17558 accessed 2 May 2024.
[122] See, eg, Y Bathaee, 'The Artificial Intelligence Black Box and the Failure of Intent and Causation' (2018) 31 *Harvard Journal of Law & Technology* 889, 889; Scholz (n 6) 128–69.
[123] Mik, *AI in Negotiating and Entering into Contracts* (n 4) 56. See also Mik, 'Much Ado About Artificial Intelligence or: The Automation of Contract Formation' (n 4) 504–05.
[124] ibid 489.
[125] ibid 504.

system's decision-making output to the operator. The argument rests primarily on the operator's choice to utilise the system, without providing additional doctrinal support.

She starts from the premise that technological advances have not altered the fundamentals of contract law. One can concur with this view by understanding that adaptation does not always mean change. For instance, the postal rule is an adaptation rather than a fundamental alteration in contract law. However, the evolution of Mik's over time reveals that, while she tries to suggest that nothing has changed, she does tentatively acknowledge that there is something new that demands special attention: the existence of a 'complex multi-attribute decision-making process' within AI negotiating contracts.[126]

While her later approach seems to adopt the devil's advocate position, providing thoughtful analysis of her work from that standpoint, it also sheds light on certain gaps in her view that warrant further consideration. Her primary focus is on the perspective of intent, neglecting the requirement of agreement and, therefore, the attribution of the outcome of system decision-making to the operator. However, despite acknowledging that in *Quoine* 'the judges [...] struggled to identify both a person to whom knowledge could be attributed and a time at which it was appropriate to do so',[127] she distances herself from that debate by stating that '[t]he question whether the decision is made "by" a human or "by" the AI must be relegated to future debates',[128] completely omitting any reference to time in the formation of these types of contracts.

## B. The Persistent Dilemma: The Lack of Innovation in Addressing the Contracting Problem

Vincent Ooi was the next in line to tackle the 'contracting problem'.[129] In his paper, he scrutinises both the mere tools theory and the agency approach. Regarding the former, he differentiates between a passive and an active role for autonomous software. In the passive role, the software is a communication tool, while the active stance takes advantage of its decision-making capabilities. He appraises the agency approach, evaluating its advantages and disadvantages, finally finding that the latter have greater weight. This is due to the lack of legal personality of the system, meaning that it cannot be adduced as a solution to the problems arising from a system malfunction.

[126] Mik, *AI in Negotiating and Entering into Contracts* (n 4) 45–58.
[127] KFK Low and E Mik, 'Lost in Transmission: Unilateral Mistakes in Automated Contracts' (2020) 136 *Law Quarterly Review* 563, 563–69.
[128] Mik, *AI in Negotiating and Entering into Contracts* (n 4) 52.
[129] V Ooi, 'Contracts Formed by Software: An Approach Form the Law of Mistake' (2022) 2 *Journal of Business Law* 97, 97–117.

To overcome these limitations, he draws on earlier contributions by Allen and Widdison,[130] to propose what he calls 'extended objective theory of contract'.[131] Through this concept, he attempts to introduce the subjective element of the agreement. In his approach, the parties involved would explicitly convey their intention to legally bind themselves to the contracts generated by the system, as a sort of 'prior intention', specifically using the phrase 'in choosing to trade'.[132] Ooi criticises the rules of the United Nations Convention on the Use of Electronic Communications in International Contracts or the EU Electronic Commerce Directive for their lack of explanation regarding 'the theoretical legal basis or rule of attribution through which these contracts are given validity or enforceability'.[133] However, this criticism can be similarly applied to Ooi's own proposal, who could have examined this issue in greater depth. The actions of the parties extend beyond merely choosing to trade through the system; they also encompass the selection of general terms of trade and the ultimate objectives the parties intend to pursue.

Ooi's contribution is significant in that it provides an elaborate critique of the inadequacy of the mere tools or agency theories, while focusing on the exercise of choice by operators. However, it lacks a robust theoretical legal basis for attribution beyond a forced extension of the objective theory of contract.

Nicholas Liu also proposes revisiting the 'contracting problem', and in his contribution he specifically refers to the formation of algorithmic contracts.[134] One of the three categories delineated by Liu,[135] called 'pure algorithmic contracts' overlaps with the approach taken in this study.[136] Building upon Ooi's classification of the active or passive role of systems, Liu concentrates solely on the active role, specifically on decision-making capacities, identifying these as vulnerable to potential challenges within the scope of contract law. From the outset, two discernible gaps are evident in Liu's work. Firstly, he passes over any consideration of the passive role of systems as mere communication tools. Secondly, Liu explicitly excludes non-deterministic algorithms, contending that such algorithms demand a broader consideration encompassing a wider array of factors.[137] This book, in contrast, will examine both the passive role of algorithms and the full spectrum of algorithmic types, including non-deterministic algorithms, to provide a more comprehensive understanding of their place within contract law.

Liu's observation regarding the potential confusion between the requirements of intention and agreement in contract formation is a valuable one. Certain facets

[130] See section II.A.i above for further details.

[131] Ooi (n 129) 109–12.

[132] ibid 109.

[133] ibid 111.

[134] N Liu, *The 'Contracting Problem' Revisited: Explaining the Formation of Algorithmic Contracts under the Common Law* (Z Slakoper and I Tot eds, Routledge, 2022) 133, 133–54.

[135] Nicholas Liu classifies the three categories as offeror-side and offeree-side, contingent upon whether the software is utilised by either party, while 'pure' designates the utilisation of algorithmic contracts jointly by both involved parties. ibid 134.

[136] See ch 1, section II.B for further insight into the concreteness of the object pertinent to this work.

[137] Liu (n 134) 135.

of these elements do indeed exhibit an overlap, contributing to the ambiguity surrounding their distinctiveness in certain contexts.[138] On this basis, he focuses his contribution on scrutinising the agreement requirement, with a specific emphasis on dissecting the components of offer and acceptance. For him, from the point of view of the offer, the potential lack of precise knowledge of the offeror about the terms of the offer does not present any inherent disadvantage. This scenario, including situations involving black-box algorithms, resembles cases recognised by contract law where a party is bound even in the absence of a full understanding of the terms, which resembles cases similar to gap-filling under contract law.[139] However, from his perspective, the absence of knowledge regarding the terms of the offer does indeed pose a drawback concerning the acceptance phase.[140] Regrettably, his best alternative seems to involve making an exception to the necessity of having knowledge of the offer for its acceptance, with this being inadequately justified. This book seeks to go beyond the rules for forming the agreement and explore the convergence of the offer and acceptance to overcome this obstacle. Additionally, it seeks to clarify the rules of attribution, both regarding the awareness of the parties of the agreement and its content.[141]

In a 2019 paper, John Linarelli acknowledges that there is no such thing as general artificial intelligence yet,[142] but he concentrates on the premise of AI autonomously engaging in contracting on its own behalf, rather than on just using AI within the contracting environment.[143] This scenario is not the focal point of this thesis. However, his methodological contribution regarding the consideration of AI involvement in contractual processes is highly pertinent. His concept of 'AI agency' concerns the capacity of an entity or individual to exert control or perceive that it has control over its actions. It pertains to human agency rather than legal agency.[144] While insightful for constructing an argument against applying agency law to algorithmic contracts, it is not necessary for our purposes. This form of agency does not pertain to narrow artificial intelligence, nor does it apply to systems operated for a specific contracting purpose. This allows us to disregard such an agency-centred proposal in this context.

He has also made an interesting contribution regarding the concept of intent. When discussing the concept of 'shared intentionality' as a premise for contract

[138] See ch 7, section IV.B for a detailed examination of the necessary distinction between intention and agreement, crucial for establishing the requisite legal foundation supporting the formation of algorithmic contracts. See also Liu (n 134) 139.

[139] ibid 143–47.

[140] ibid 147–52.

[141] See ch 6, section IV.C for further details.

[142] General Artificial Intelligence (GAI or AGI) represents AI systems with the ability to understand, learn, and apply knowledge across a broad range of tasks, demonstrating a level of cognitive versatility comparable to human intelligence. For a comprehensive explanation of the distinction between artificial intelligence, general artificial intelligence, and superintelligence, see to ch 3, section IV.B.i.

[143] J Linarelli, 'Artificial Intelligence and Contracts Formation: Back to Contract as Bargain?' (2023) *Emerging Issues at the Intersection of Commercial Law and Technologies* ssrn.com/abstract=4363410 accessed 2 May 2024.

[144] ibid 2.

formation, he states that '[w]hat gives artificial intelligence intent is not some internal workings of its programming but *us* – the ascription of intentionality to artificial intelligence by humans'.[145] This reinforces Mik's position on the irrelevance of explicability or black boxes and supports the approach to attribution adopted in this monograph.

Building on the earlier work of Scholz, Yavar Bathaee has explored the implications for intention and causality arising from the inherent challenge of understanding the decision-making processes of systems using artificial intelligence.[146] He argues that the unpredictability of algorithmic decisions can create a disconnect between the intentions of the system operator and the actual outcomes produced by the system.[147] In order to address this challenge, Bathaee suggests revising the intent and causality test by implementing a sliding scale that correlates with varying degrees of human supervision and transparency. According to this proposal, the less transparent and controlled the system is by its operators, the higher their level of responsibility should be.[148]

In her latest article on the subject, Cristina Poncibò refers to artificial intelligence as a communication tool, but this seems to be misleading, as it goes beyond considering AI systems from a passive standpoint.[149] She focuses on consent,[150] but on its expression rather than the decision process itself, and discusses the impact of AI on the connection between consent and human will. It highlights how AI has the potential to separate consent from individual human intentions, with technology facilitating this distancing. To overcome the problem that this poses for contract law, she presents two key options: the possible acceptance of contracts without explicit consent and the redefinition of consent to be less dependent on human will. Her article emphasises the importance of differentiating between authentic consent and simulated or technology-enabled consent and the fact that, while consent may incorporate elements of technology, it must stay connected to individual will ('the link must never be completely broken'),[151] as it signifies personal freedom within legal relationships. Within the realm of remedies, her emphasis lies in pinpointing the fundamental issue: a deficiency in understanding between the system itself and the party employing its mechanisms. In this context, she takes the view that this internal issue between the operator and the system does not impact the

[145] J Linarelli, 'A Philosophy of Contract Law for Artificial Intelligence: Shared Intentionality' in M Ebers, C Poncibò and M Zou (eds), *Contracting and Contract Law in the Age of Artificial Intelligence* (Hart Publishing, 2022) 59, 61.

[146] Bathaee (n 122) 889.

[147] ibid 893.

[148] ibid 894.

[149] The passive and active roles were differentiated by Vincent Ooi. This distinction delineates the two roles that AI may play, as a communication tool and as a delegated decision-maker, as mentioned earlier in this text. See n 129 above for further details.

[150] C Poncibò, 'Artificial Intelligence as a Communication Tool in Contract Law' (2023) 31 *European Review of Private Law* 239, 239–60.

[151] ibid 245.

contract's validity, as it is preserved by its outward appearance, yet the internal matter remains.[152]

Poncibò's contribution is significant in several ways, even if it is not entirely exhaustive in its exploration because it does not focus solely on contract formation, as it also considers execution through AI and remedies.[153] However, it is subject to criticism in that the system is labelled merely as a communication tool to 'express contractual consent or decisions'.[154] However, these systems go beyond being a mere tool to express consent; what is most significant and innovative is that not only is communication outsourced to such systems, but also that they may even define the precise content of the contract.

Some of the ideas which she offers while attempting to answer the question of whether AI can 'express' consent are worth highlighting: understanding 'consent, in terms of voluntary choice',[155] and 'there must always be an initial and explicit decision by the human party/parties to resort to algorithms in order to express contractual consent or decisions, which cannot be attributed to the will of the machine under any circumstances'.[156] However, Poncibò does not determine how to maintain the connection between will and consent, a 'link' that she recognises it is imperative not to break.[157] A potential solution to maintaining this connection may lie in upholding principles of contractual freedom. It exists in the initial and explicit decision of the party involved, which goes beyond the mere expression of will to be bound by the outcome of the system. This decision also delimits the scope of the terms of the agreement, thus ensuring the continuity of this link between will and consent.[158]

## IV. Practical Implications

In the context of algorithmic contracts, an AI system serves a twofold purpose in the contracting process: firstly, it converts into a single reality the precise parameters of one party's undetermined open offer; and secondly, it functions as an intermediary that facilitates the communication of this open offer while conveying the other party's acceptance of it. The first function refers to the decision-making process and the second to the communication of the outcome and the localisation of its matching demand, or cross-offer. Both together constitute the meeting of the algorithms.

These two functions exhibit internal and external components, which pertain to the algorithm's association with the operator and the counterparty, respectively. On one hand, the internal aspect of the decision-making process involves the

[152] ibid 247.
[153] ibid 251–58.
[154] ibid 245.
[155] ibid 244.
[156] ibid 245.
[157] ibid.
[158] For a more comprehensive analysis of this proposal, see ch 7, section IV.B.

stipulation of the rules and objectives set by the human operator that are to guide the AI system in the contracting process. The external aspect of the decision-making process involves the use of external data to achieve the objective defined by its operator: there is a relationship between the AI system and the environment in which it has to operate. The external aspect of its function as an element of communication between the system can also be articulated in two phases. In the first instance, the communication of the offer to the environment that is considered the potential audience, and, in the second instance, the communication with the system that presents the matching cross-offer. Finally, the internal aspect of communication refers to the communication between the system and the system operator, which is key to the attribution of knowledge to the latter.

The evolution of artificial intelligence, especially with the integration of machine learning, seems to add further levels of complexity to the challenges announced by Allen and Widdison in 1996,[159] arising from the ability of systems to 'self-modif[y] or self-create (...) instructions'.[160] Yet, while it may seem that this capacity significantly impacts contract formation, the actual influence may be less substantial than often assumed. Although advanced machine learning techniques can alter the sequences, selections, and iterations of instructions, the system's underlying purpose remains consistent. This continuity applies to both the internal and external dimensions of the decision-making process described above. In essence, the foundational intent – the purpose guiding the design of these computer systems – remains an immutable core, enduring even amidst the dynamic processes of algorithms and data handling.[161]

This examination of the diverse contributions made before and after the actual implementation of AI for decision-making indicates that the issue remains unresolved. Over the years, a range of solutions have been proposed, supported and criticised, involving mere tool theory, agency law or the consideration of these systems as legal, but all have proven insufficient.

Despite having garnered numerous supporters in the past,[162] approaches rooted in agency law appear to have been largely abandoned in contemporary discussions,[163] as appealing and groundbreaking as it may seem to consider autonomous software to be a legal entity.[164] This concept now often remains confined

[159] See above for more on the challenges identified by the authors, namely: capacity, consensus ad idem, intentionality and consideration. See n 12.

[160] Allen and Widdison (n 8) 27.

[161] For a more comprehensive examination of the functioning of machine-learning AI systems, see ch 3, section IV.B.ii.

[162] For reference, see, for instance, the contributions by Andrade et al, and Chopra and White.

[163] See also SJ Bayern, 'Algorithms, Agreements, and Agency' in W Barfield (ed), *The Cambridge Handbook of the Law of Algorithms* (Cambridge University Press, 2020) 153, 153–61; M Oliver, 'Contracting by Artificial Intelligence: Open Offers, Unilateral Mistakes, and Why Algorithms Are Not Agents' (2021) 2 *Australian National University Journal of Law and Technology* 45, 45–87.

[164] See J Linarelli, 'Artificial General Intelligence and Contract' (2019) 24 *Revue de droit uniforme* 330, 330–47; C Novelli, G Bongiovanni and G Sartor, 'A Conceptual Framework for Legal Personality and Its Application to AI' (2022) 13 *Jurisprudence* 194, 194–219; Sartor (n 73) 253–90.

to generalisations or dystopian visions without substantial integration into more practical discussions. 'Autonomous software are (…) not real agents nor persons even if they can communicate and interact with people, because they are incapable of juridical cooperation and partnership with others.'[165]

This survey of existing literature reveals critical gaps in our understanding of algorithmic contracts. The quest for legal fit through agency law or recognition of legal personality for autonomous algorithmic systems primarily addresses issues of responsibility rather than comprehensively answering how consent fits into the formation of such contracts. Additionally, the prevalent emphasis on intent often overshadows the equally crucial aspect of consent. The most recent contributions focus on the expression of consent and demonstrate that there is an unmet challenge in the construction of consent.

While the objective theory may adequately clarify the intent requirement, it falls short in providing a legal resolution to other intricacies inherent in algorithmic contracts, such as the attribution of knowledge or the establishment of mutual understanding. 'The *objective* manifestations of contract may be present, but the direct operation of human choice is not.'[166] These systems are tools. 'The tools of the digital age are still tools',[167] yet they transcend the status of being mere tools; they are intricate and demand a sophisticated integration into contract law. The proposed solution involves dissecting and addressing all conceivable facets of these intricate tools. Taking a mathematical or engineering-oriented approach, the aim is to offer a tailored, individual, narrow solution to address each specific problem they present. We have seen that one-size-fits-all solutions such as mere tools or agency are unable to address these complexities.

This exploration has highlighted several critical inquiries within the domain of algorithmic contracts that have surfaced but remain largely unaddressed, revealing substantial gaps in current research. Firstly, the fundamental issue of the exact moment of contract formation in algorithmic contracts lacks a robust theoretical grounding. Despite initial considerations likening these contracts to face-to-face communications, there exists a conspicuous absence of well-founded frameworks supporting this comparison. Indeed, the solution proposed by Dodd and Hernández in 1998 relies on an ex-post intervention by the principal, which would fundamentally disrupt the core attributes of algorithmic contracts, namely their velocity and immediacy. Since then, this issue has received little attention. Consequently, there exists a substantial gap in the literature concerning the timing of contract formation in algorithmic contracts. An examination of this topic requires a consideration of the passive role of algorithmic systems, essentially as external communication tools. By better understanding how these systems

[165] C Alvisi, 'Drive and Agency in the Age of Algorithmic-Based Decision Making' (2022) 8 *The Italian Law Journal* 895, 905.

[166] Dodd and Hernandez (n 23) 5.

[167] JM Lipshaw, 'Lawyering Somewhere between Computation and Will to Act' in LA Di Matteo and others (eds), *The Cambridge Handbook of Lawyering in the Digital Age* (Cambridge University Press, 2021) 327, 338.

function as external communicative tools, we can shed light on their role in and impact on the timing of contract formation. This approach is essential to bridge the gap and gain deeper insights into the temporal dynamics of algorithmic contracts.

Secondly, the challenge of achieving consensus ad idem, or the meeting of the minds, within algorithmic contracting remains a pressing concern. This issue was first raised by Allen and Widdison in 1996 and continues to be a thorny issue due to the complex nature of machine learning. Moreover, scholars such as Lerouge have shown the inadequacy of the agency approach due to the legal limitations of autonomous systems, emphasising the significance of consent in contract formation. Lerouge also highlighted a crucial gap in our understanding regarding the lack of awareness by system operators of the existence and contents of agreements at the moment they are formalised. This gap has not been addressed in recent contributions, which have deliberately excluded non-deterministic algorithmic systems, underlining the continued absence of a comprehensive answer.

The riddle of attributing knowledge to system operators when they cannot possess actual, real-time knowledge poses yet another significant challenge, particularly concerning the requirement of consent. While some contributions, such as Kerr's, have presented technical solutions, the puzzle has not been entirely resolved. One of the major drawbacks of the technical solutions proposed so far is that they alter the very purpose of algorithmic contracts, making them slower and more inefficient. As we will see, an examination of the technical characteristics of these systems may offer insights into the problem of attributing unknown outcomes to the operator.

These gaps in understanding algorithmic contracts raise a pivotal question: 'Can an AI-based algorithmic system effectively determine the fundamental content of a contract and the legally binding clauses for the parties involved, thus qualifying it as an enforceable algorithmic contract?' This core inquiry requires a comprehensive exploration of various facets within the realm of algorithmic contracting. The breakdown of this phenomenon into its distinct functions and internal-external relations illuminates specific areas which demand our attention. From the perspective of algorithmic systems as communication tools, there arises a critical need to discern the precise moment of contract formation, a problem which the current literature fails to adequately address. Furthermore, intertwined with the system's decision-making role is the pivotal question of attributing knowledge regarding the formalisation and content of the contract to the system operator. The absence of a robust theoretical foundation in this respect highlights a lack of understanding of how knowledge can be vested in the operator in the absence of direct human comprehension. Lastly, the endeavour to elevate the interaction of algorithms to a level where it mirrors the traditional 'meeting of the minds' in contract law poses yet another challenge. Any sense of an evolution from algorithmic interaction to a comprehensive understanding and agreement akin to human negotiations remains largely uncharted territory in current research.

Given these gaps in understanding and the broader challenges in this field, it is clear that a deeper investigation is essential. This book will approach the complex issues surrounding algorithmic contracts by breaking them down into key components, each explored in detail.

The following chapters will begin with an analysis of algorithmic contracts as communication tools. From there, the discussion will progress to the issue of attribution, or the 'proxy issue', followed by an examination of subjectivity – what might be termed the 'meeting of the algorithms'. Each of these sections will be addressed with a focus on the operator-system relationship, both internal and external. Through this structured approach, the aim is to construct a comprehensive legal framework for algorithmic contracts, ultimately offering a robust and inclusive structure to address the unique challenges they pose.

# 5

# An Analysis of Algorithmic Systems as Communication Tools

## I. Introduction

An algorithmic contract is a contractual agreement where both involved parties engage in decision-making processes operating an algorithmic system rooted in artificial intelligence.[1] '[W]hat is new and different about algorithmic contracts is [that] in the process of forming an algorithmic contract, computer programs step into decision-making roles previously performed by humans.'[2] Yet algorithmic contracts also serve as sophisticated communication tools.

In the contractual context, AI systems typically perform a dual role. Firstly, they facilitate communication between the parties. Secondly, they assume decision-making functions within the process of contract formation. When both roles operate together, there is what this book later describes as a 'meeting of the algorithms'. To analyse this phenomenon, it is useful to distinguish the internal and external components of each role, and to examine in turn the interaction between the algorithm and its operator and the interaction between the algorithm and the counterparty (or that counterparty's system).

On the decision-making side, the human operator internally establishes rules and objectives that guide the system's behaviour throughout the contracting process. Externally, the system draws on data from its environment to pursue those objectives, thereby creating a relationship between the AI system and its operating context. 'Human intervention is present in the use of algorithms, through the parameterization of the algorithm, the choice and weighting criteria as well as the categories of data that are taken into account in order to arrive at the desired result.'[3] Algorithms are said to be eventful: they are processes that depend on data.[4]

[1] See ch 1, section II.B for the reasons for adopting the definition of 'algorithmic contract' used in this book.

[2] LH Scholz, 'Algorithms and Contract Law' in W Barfield (ed), *The Cambridge Handbook of The Law of Algorithms* (Cambridge University Press, 2020) 141, 141.

[3] M Milossi, E Alexandropoulou and KE Psannis, 'AI Ethics: Algorithmic Determinism or Self-Determination? The GDPR Approach' (2021) 9 IEEE Journals & Magazine 58455, 58458 ieeexplore.ieee.org/stamp/stamp.jsp?tp=&arnumber=9400809 accessed 2 May 2024.

[4] T Bucher, *If...Then: Algorithmic Power and Politics* (Oxford University Press, 2018) 49.

On the communication side, there is again an internal and an external dimension. Internally, the system interacts with its operator – for example, through logs, dashboards or alerts – an interaction that will be crucial when addressing the attribution of knowledge. Externally, two phases can be distinguished. Firstly, the system communicates an offer to a potential audience. Secondly, there is an interaction with the system that generates the corresponding matching offer. Both offer and acceptance, however, remain conceptually distinct from the communications that convey them.[5]

Although algorithmic systems perform both internal and external functions in their role as means of communication, the focus of this chapter is on the external function: the communication of the offer and the 'encounter' with the corresponding acceptance. The purpose is not to revisit the entire law of contract formation, but to identify how the communicative acts that bring algorithmic contracts into existence can be located within existing doctrine.

As Mik points out, '[c]ontractual relationships have never been regulated on the basis of the technology used to facilitate the process of contract formation and/or performance'.[6] The analysis throughout this book adopts a coherentist approach.[7] Rather than proposing a technology-specific regime, it asks how the external communicative role of algorithmic systems can be understood within the existing framework of contract formation, and in particular how to determine the time of formation of the contract when communications occur between systems rather than directly between human parties.

This aspect remains comparatively underexplored in both case law and academic writing. The present study is deliberately prospective and conceptual in character, with the aim of providing a framework capable of informing emerging case law. It should nevertheless be acknowledged that some courts have already been confronted with closely related questions. In *Quoine*, for example, 'the judges (…) struggled to identify both a person to whom knowledge could be attributed and a time at which it was appropriate to do so'.[8]

Although there have been initial comparisons between these contracts and face-to-face communications,[9] there is a notable lack of established frameworks to substantiate this analogy. The proposal made by Dodd and Hernández did

[5] See *Air Transworld Ltd v Bombardier Inc* [2012] EWHC 243 (Comm), [2012] 1 Lloyd's Rep 349 at [75], [79].

[6] E Mik, 'The Resilience of Contract Law in Light of Technological Change' in M Furmston (ed), *The Future of the Law of Contract* (Routledge, 2020) 112, 113.

[7] This term is borrowed from Roger Brownsword to describe the approach undertaken here which seeks to preserve the integrity of legal doctrine integrity. R Brownsword, 'Smart Transactional Technologies, Legal Disruption, and the Case of Network Contracts' in LA DiMatteo, M Cannarsa and C Poncibò (eds), *The Cambridge Handbook of Smart Contracts, Blockchain Technology and Digital Platforms* (Cambridge University Press, 2020) 320.

[8] KFK Low and E Mik, 'Lost in Transmission: Unilateral Mistakes in Automated Contracts' (2020) 136 *Law Quarterly Review* 563, 563–69.

[9] JC Dodd and JA Hernandez, 'Contracting in Cyberspace' (1998) 1 *Computer Law Review and Technology Journal* 12.

not explicitly concern algorithmic contracts but rather what they envisioned as the future application of artificial intelligence in contracting.[10] Their solution, however, introduces an ex post intervention by the principal (in the case of algorithmic contracts, the operator). Therefore, this proposal cannot be regarded as an adequate solution in this area. It is insufficient because it offers little doctrinal justification beyond a reference to a US rule that has no direct equivalent in English contract law,[11] and it is unsuitable because its adoption would significantly compromise key characteristics of algorithmic contracts, notably their speed and immediacy.

The importance of the time of contract formation is undeniable. A particular problem for the case of intelligent software that can conclude agreements on behalf of the parties was identified a quarter of a century ago: the system operator is not aware of the existence and content of the agreement at the time it is concluded.[12] This chapter therefore concentrates, in the first instance, on establishing the moment of contract formation in such settings. The following chapter then addresses the challenge posed by the operator's lack of contemporaneous knowledge of both the conclusion of the agreement and its terms.

A renewed theoretical account is required because the way in which consent is given through algorithms differs significantly from traditional scenarios, both in terms of timing and in the mode of expression. 'One prominent justification for the dispatch rule is that dispatch marks the moment of a "meeting of the minds" between offeror and offeree, as expressed through the objective manifestation of their intent.'[13] The timing of that meeting matters because it determines the content of the parties' obligations. At the same time, as Amelia Rawls has argued, identifying the exact moment of the meeting of the minds can, in many contemporary contexts, have little practical importance and risk becoming a largely theoretical exercise.[14] Both perspectives are relevant to algorithmic contracting, where factual patterns diverge sharply from those in which the classical rules were developed.

Against this background, the remainder of the chapter proceeds in three steps. It first revisits the evolution of the theory of contract formation, examining the underlying rationales for contract enforceability and reconsidering the concept of agreement, with particular attention to the objective test and the role of consent. It then charts the historical evolution of the external expression of human consent in contract formation, from the dispatch rule to the receipt rule and into the digital

[10] ibid 5–8.

[11] For the US position, see Restatement (Second) of Contracts § 64 (American Law Institute, 1981) treating acceptance by telephone or other 'substantially instantaneous' two-way communications as effective on receipt.

[12] J-F Lerouge, 'The Use of Electronic Agents Questioned Under Contractual Law: Suggested Solutions on a European and American Level' (1999) 18 *John Marshall Journal of Computer & Information Law* 403, 417.

[13] A Rawls, 'Contract Formation in an Internet Age' [2009] *The Columbia Science and Technology Law Review* 200, 217.

[14] ibid 218.

age. Finally, it examines algorithmic contracts as dynamic communication tools, arguing that communications between algorithmic systems can, for the purposes of formation, be treated as substantially instantaneous and bidirectional, even though the parties are not face-to-face and act through systems that search for an optimal contractual match.

This analysis also prepares the ground for the following chapters. The next chapter considers the attribution of knowledge to the operator, thereby bridging the roles of an algorithmic system as a communication tool and as a decision-maker. The subsequent chapter then explores how the 'meeting of the algorithms' identified here can be related back to the traditional notion of a 'meeting of the minds'.

## II. Evolution in the Theory of Contract Formation

### A. Back to Basics: What is a Contract?

There is no unanimously accepted definition of 'contract' in English law.[15] Beatson and others define a contract as 'a promise or a set of promises for the breach of which the law gives a remedy, or the performance of which the law in some ways recognizes as a duty'.[16] Burrows, in his *Restatement of the English Law of Contract*, defines a contract as an agreement that is legally binding because:

(a) it is supported by consideration or made by deed (see section 8);
(b) it is certain and complete (see section 9);
(c) it is made with the intention to create legal relations (see section 10); and
(d) it complies with any formal requirement needed for the agreement to be legally binding (see section 11(2)(a)).[17]

Nicholas, contrasting English and French law, suggests that in English law a contract can 'more nearly' be described as a promise in return for good consideration.[18] Other authors focus on the basic formation requirements. McKendrick, for example, states that '[t]o conclude a contract the parties must reach agreement, the agreement must be supported by consideration, and there must be an intention to create legal relations'.[19]

Taken together, these accounts indicate that three basic elements are generally required in English contract law: agreement, consideration, and intention to create

[15] RE Barnett, 'A Consent Theory of Contract' (1986) 86 *Columbia Law Review* 269, 269; E McKendrick, 'English Contract Law: A Rich Past, an Uncertain Future?' (1997) 50 *Current Legal Problems* 25, 27.
[16] A Burrows, J Cartwright and J Beatson, *Anson's Law of Contract* (Oxford University Press, 2020) 2.
[17] A Burrows, *A Restatement of the English Law of Contract* (Oxford University Press, 2020) 5.
[18] B Nicholas in A De Moor, 'Contract and Agreement in English and French Law Review Article' (1986) 6 *Oxford Journal of Legal Studies* 275, 275.
[19] McKendrick (n 15) 27.

legal relations. In addition, contracts must satisfy requirements of certainty and completeness and, in some cases, particular formalities.[20] Formation of a contract requires an offer by one party and an acceptance by the other, and from the perspective of the objective theory of contracts, this is sufficient to say that an agreement exists. An offer has been defined as 'an expression of willingness to contract, made with the intention that it shall become binding upon the person making it, as soon as it is accepted by the person to whom it is addressed'.[21] Acceptance is 'a final and unqualified expression of assent to the terms of an offer'.[22] Seen from another angle, 'a consensus ad idem [or] "a meeting of the minds" is required for the contract to be formed'.[23]

Consideration may be 'some right, interest, profit, or benefit accruing to the one party, or some forbearance, detriment, loss or responsibility given, suffered, or undertaken by the other (…)',[24] and 'need not be adequate but it must be of some value in the eye of the law'.[25] Intention to create legal relations is generally presumed from 'the fact of the agreement and the existence of consideration';[26] it must, however, be manifested or communicated,[27] and is tested objectively.[28] Finally, some argue that an agreement must be certain and complete.[29] This is also the approach of the Law Commission that has stated that '[a]n agreement is not legally binding unless it is certain and complete'.[30] In a strict sense, these are not legal requirements for an agreement to be enforceable under the law of England and Wales, and a contract will only be voidable if it is 'impossible to give reasonable content to the parties' agreement'.[31]

Against this background, the role of algorithms at the formation stage of contracts is often recognised but rarely examined in depth.[32] Some contend that although the existence of these contracts is acknowledged, there is an unwillingness to modify

[20] See Law Commission No. 401 'Smart Legal Contracts. Advice to Government' (Law Com No. 401, 2021) 39.

[21] *Air Transworld Ltd v Bombardier Inc* [2012] EWHC 243 (Comm), [2012] 1 Lloyd's Rep 349 at [75] by Cooke J.

[22] ibid at [79].

[23] M Durovic and A Janssen, 'Formation of Smart Contracts under Contract Law' in LA DiMatteo, M Cannarsa and C Poncibò (eds), *The Cambridge Handbook of Smart Contracts, Blockchain Technology and Digital Platforms* (Cambridge Law Handbooks, Cambridge University Press, 2019) 61, 68.

[24] *Currie v Misa* [1875] LR 10 Ex 153, [162]

[25] Burrows Beatson and Cartwright (n 15) 104.

[26] J Cartwright, *Contract Law* (Hart Publishing, 2016) 156.

[27] E Mik, 'The Resilience of Contract Law in Light of Technological Change' in M Furmston (ed), *The Future of the Law of Contract* (Routledge, 2020) 112.

[28] Burrows, Beatson and Cartwright (n 15) 34.

[29] Cartwright (n 26) 122.

[30] This statement, although from the report of the Law Commission on Smart Contracts, is significant for its contemporary view of contract formation and the influence of technology in this context. See Law Commission No. 401 (n 20) 50.

[31] ibid.

[32] M Rizzi and N Skead, 'Algorithmic Contracts and the Equitable Doctrine of Undue Influence: Adapting Old Rules to a New Legal Landscape' (2020) 14 *Journal of Equity* 301, 312. See also SJ Bayern, 'Algorithms, Agreements, and Agency' in W Barfield (ed), *The Cambridge Handbook of the Law of Algorithms* (Cambridge University Press, 2020) 153, 160.

contractual rules because of them.[33] The reference by the Law Commission to 'computer programs that reach an agreement' implies the possibility of automating the offer and acceptance process without human intervention.[34] However, this assertion lacks solid legal support beyond references to specific cases, and those cases concern deterministic algorithms such as those in *Software Solutions* and *Quoine*.[35] Non-deterministic algorithms are not considered, and this represents a significant gap that must be addressed. The question of how these technologies fit within the traditional elements of contract thus requires closer conceptual analysis.

## B. The Underlying Rationales for Contract Enforceability

To understand why contract formation plays such a central role in contract theory, it is useful to recall the main rationales for enforcing contracts. Barnett's 'theory of consent' offers a classification of the different theories for the enforceability of contracts,[36] which is useful to understand the importance of the agreement requirement in the formation of contracts.[37] His five theories can be grouped into three broad categories: party-based theories (will and reliance), standards-based theories (efficiency and fairness), and process-based theories (bargain theory). Party-based theories focus on the position of one of the parties, either the promisor or the promisee.

Will theories are grounded in the idea that contractual obligations are enforceable when they are willed or freely assumed by the promisor. The central inquiry concerns the promisor's actual state of mind at the time of agreement, that is, a 'subjective' perspective.[38] In principle, it is assumed that the promisor's actual intention corresponds to what can be objectively perceived. Where this correspondence is absent and the subjective intention can be proved, will theories suggest that the latter should prevail.

Reliance theories start from the premise that a person should be held liable for conduct that induces foreseeable expectations in others.[39] Reliance is itself a subjective notion, and such theories face well-known difficulties, including the

[33] A Beckers and G Teubner, *Three Liability Regimes for Artificial Intelligence. Algorithmic Actants, Hybrids, Crowds* (Hart Publishing, 2021) 54.

[34] Law Commission No. 401 (n 20) 46. Again, it is necessary to reiterate that this viewpoint is articulated by the Law Commission within the realm of smart legal contracts. However, it is important to note that some smart legal contracts can also fall under the category of algorithmic contracts, thereby emphasising the significance of this statement within this domain. For further discussion of this matter, see ch 2, section IV.

[35] *R (Software Solutions Partners Ltd)* v *HM Customs & Excise* [2007] EWHC 971 (Admin) ('Software Solutions'); *Quoine Pte Ltd v B2C2 Ltd* [2020] SGCA (I) 02.

[36] Barnett (n 15) 269–321.

[37] There are other points of view from which to examine contract enforceability, such as expectation damages, but this perspective is much more complete as it includes the subjective factor in a broader way. See, eg, SJ Bayern, 'Offer and Acceptance in Modern Contract Law: A Needless Concept' (2015) 103 *California Law Review* 67, 93–98.

[38] Barnett (n 15) 272–74.

[39] ibid 274–76.

problem of distinguishing legally binding acts from non-binding ones. Nevertheless, like will theories, they underline that the mental states of the parties cannot be entirely disregarded. A common criticism of both approaches is that they overlook the relational nature of contract, in that they tend to prioritise the position of one party.[40] For present purposes, it is significant that both emphasise the subjective dimension of agreement in this analysis.

Standards-based theories justify enforcement by reference to the content of the agreement. Contracts are enforced because they are efficient in economic terms or because they are substantively fair, irrespective of the actual will of the parties.[41] It is not a question of whether the parties agree, but whether the outcome is desirable from an economic or justice perspective, but this is not useful because such a perspective is far removed from the reality of transactional relationships.

Process-based theories, in particular the bargain theory, regard contract as a reciprocal exchange. Each party undertakes performance in expectation of the other's manifested commitment, thereby highlighting the reciprocity of the bargaining process.[42] Here again, subjective elements are present in the background, even if the analysis proceeds largely in objective terms.

Barnett's theory of consent seeks to synthesise these strands. Contract interpretation should respect the actual intent of the parties, but where subjective intentions have not been communicated, the content of the agreement is determined by a reasonable, objective interpretation.[43] Formation analysis is therefore inherently interpretative. Bayern likewise emphasises that the reasonable person standard, which is interpretative in nature, operates as a default rule where there is no demonstrable subjective disagreement between the parties.[44]

Against this backdrop, Tommaso Dalla Massara's reading of Siegmund Schlossmann offers an important reminder of the fragility of contractual autonomy.[45] Schlossmann's radical critique of the concept of contract, and his reconstruction of liability around the culpable frustration of legitimate expectations, challenge the idea that consensus or will alone can provide a secure foundation for obligation.[46] Dalla Massara captures this with the notion of 'annihilated consent': situations in which consent is formally present, because the acts that the law treats as assent have been performed, but substantively hollow, because the party bound lacks meaningful understanding or control over the commitments undertaken.[47]

[40] ibid 277.
[41] ibid 277–86.
[42] ibid 287–89.
[43] ibid 306–07.
[44] SJ Bayern, 'The Nature and Timing of Contract Formation' in LA Di Matteo and M Hogg (eds), *Comparative Contract Law* (Oxford University Press, 2016) 77, 79.
[45] T Dalla Massara, *Il consenso annichilito. La critica radicale del contratto in Siegmund Schlossmann* (Il Mulino, 2022).
[46] S Schlossmann, *Der Vertrag* (Breitkopf und Härtel, 1876).
[47] G Albers, 'Tommaso Dalla Massara: *Il consenso annichilito, La critica radicale del contratto in Siegmund Schlossmann*' (2023) 19 *European Review of Contract Law* 90–101.

Although Schlossmann and Dalla Massara do not address algorithmic systems, the structural concern they identify is directly relevant to contracts concluded in highly automated, opaque environments. In algorithmic contracts, agreements may be formed by systems operating at speed and on the basis of complex processes that are not transparent to the parties. There is, therefore, a risk that consent becomes merely procedural – recorded in logs and system outputs – while the conditions for genuinely voluntary and informed consent are weakened. This reinforces the need, in analysing algorithmic contracts, to look beyond the formal presence of offer and acceptance and to revisit the foundations of consent and agreement on which the enforceability of contracts ultimately rests.

## C. Revisiting the Concept of Agreement

In 1979 Lord Denning observed that 'our traditional analysis of offer, counter-offer, rejection, acceptance and so forth is out of date'.[48] That remark has renewed significance in the context of algorithmic contracts. In such contracts the decision-making process is delegated to an algorithmic system, and the operator may have little or no insight into how the system's output is generated, particularly in the case of opaque or 'black-box' algorithms.

Traditionally, English contract law has identified agreement through the mechanism of offer and acceptance.[49] Despite Lord Denning's doubts and occasional academic criticism – some authors have gone so far as to describe offer-and-acceptance theory as a 'doctrinal distraction' – the paradigm has rarely been questioned in practice.[50] The topic has been comparatively neglected, with the last major general treatments dating back to the first half of the twentieth century.[51] Recent debate on algorithmic contracting has brought the issue back into focus and underscores the need for renewed analysis.[52]

'[A]n agreement is more than a coincidence of intentions.'[53] Two parties may have a converging interest without realising it. For an agreement to exist, communication is essential. Courts have therefore focused on how offers and acceptances are communicated. Hence, '[c]hanges in methods of communication may require changes in the rules relating to contract formation'.[54] Communication is, in this

[48] *Butler Machine Tool Co Ltd v Ex-Cell-O Corp* [1979] 1 WLR 401 at 404.

[49] See, eg, R Stone, 'Forming Contracts without Offer and Acceptance, Lord Denning and the Harmonisation of English Contract Law' (2012) *Web Journal of Current Legal Issues* 2 www.bailii.org/uk/other/journals/WebJCLI/2012/issue4/stone4.html accessed 2 May 2024; Bayern(n 37) 68.

[50] Bayern (n 44) 77.

[51] See, eg, S Williston, 'Mutual Assent in the Formation of Contracts' (1920) 14 *The Illinois Law Review* 85, 85–95; PH Winfield, 'Some Aspects of Offer and Acceptance' (1939) 55 *Law Quarterly Review* 499, 499–520.

[52] Bayern (n 37) 67–101.

[53] Cartwright (n 26) 95.

[54] S Waddams, *Contract Law and the Challenges of Computer Technology* (Oxford University Press, 2017) 318.

sense, one of the fundamental functions of algorithmic contracts and a natural starting point for analysis.

At the same time, the concept of 'agreement' itself requires re-examination in order to avoid an excessive objectification that would distort the principle of *consensus ad idem*. In the digital environment there is a risk of what has been described as a *reductio ad absurdum* of that principle:[55] the law may continue to speak of a 'meeting of the minds' even where only formal manifestations of assent exist and underlying consent is fragile. Duress, fraud, and mistake can still vitiate the will and contaminate 'the appearance of consent'.[56] Agreement is the result of communicated intention of the parties, but the inquiry into that intention always sits at the intersection of subjective and objective elements, between subjectivity and objectivity theories. In the realm of algorithmic contracts, additional questions arise: is 'subjectivity' intrinsically human? Can there be such a thing as a computer-generated subjectivity?

There is no single, dominant subjective or objective theory of agreement as a necessary element in contract formation. Rather, there exists a spectrum of approaches. At a high level, agreement can be conceived from a subjective perspective, as a 'meeting of the minds', or from an objective perspective, as a manifestation of intention. Furmston's *Law of Contract* describes the purely subjective approach as 'an alien approach to the problem of agreement',[57] yet an unqualified commitment to pure objectivity risks treating as binding arrangements that the parties themselves would not recognise as contracts.[58] The classic tension between subjectivity and objectivity thus remains unresolved.

In principle, identifying what constitutes an agreement between parties is a subjective exercise: the question is what they actually intended. In practice, however, intention can only be assessed through its external manifestations, and the concept of agreement ultimately concerns communicated intentions. The choice of an objective or subjective view will depend on the reason for which the test is used. This matter has long been the subject of debate, which is ongoing.[59] Will-based theories favour a subjective approach, but even where the law seeks to uncover actual intentions, it must rely on outward evidence. Cartwright therefore suggests that the subjective test becomes objective from the perspective of proof.[60] Yet the objective test is not simply the use of objective proof. Under that test, the question is what a reasonable observer would conclude from the parties' words

[55] M Ebers, 'Artificial Intelligence, Contracting and Contract Law: An Introduction' n M Ebers, C Poncibò and M Zou (eds), *Contracting and Contract Law in the Age of Artificial Intelligence* (Hart Publishing, 2022) 19, 31.

[56] JM Perillo, 'The Origins of the Objective Theory of Contract Formation and Interpretation' (2001) 69 *Fordham Law Review* 427, 469.

[57] MP Furmston, *Cheshire, Fifoot and Furmston's Law of Contract* (Oxford University Press, 2017) 42.

[58] Cartwright (n 26) 98.

[59] For a deeper analysis see Perillo (n 56) 427–78.

[60] Cartwright (n 26) 97.

and conduct. For this reason, communication has long been the primary focus of analysis when considering the agreement requirement.

'The objective theory of contracts examines the output of the decision-making process, not the decision-making process itself.'[61] That approach presupposes that 'communications, whether oral or in writing, made face-to-face or at a distance, are made between the parties themselves as they are trying to come to an agreement'.[62] This assumption no longer holds in its original form when one or both parties rely on algorithmic systems during contract formation. In such cases, both the matching and the communication of intentions may be performed by systems rather than by individuals.

'To understand the contemporary role of contract we need to integrate the communications systems of hardware and software into our understanding of what it is that gives commitments their binding character.'[63] In algorithmic contracts, humans can still decide to enter into a contractual relationship and configure the parameters under which systems will operate, but the concrete acts of offer and acceptance may be generated, transmitted and matched entirely by machines. Just as humans can decide on and communicate agreement simultaneously, algorithmic systems may do the same within their domain, where interactions occur between systems rather than between individuals.

The challenge is to conceptualise agreement in a way that preserves the centrality of human relationships and intentions, while acknowledging that the communicative acts evidencing those intentions are increasingly mediated, or even performed, by machines. Concerns that consent may become merely formal or procedural – what some have described as 'annihilated' consent – are sharpened in this context, especially where systems operate in ways that are opaque to those who are legally bound by their outputs.[64] The subsequent sections therefore turn to the objective test and to the role of consent in order to examine how far existing doctrines can accommodate these developments.

## D. The Objective Test

The objective test has a functional character. It is designed to protect trust and legitimate expectations while avoiding the difficulties and potential abuses associated with a purely subjectivist approach. As discussed in the preceding section, an agreement is the result of the communicated intention of the parties. Intention has a clear subjective component which is not entirely disregarded,[65] but the commu-

[61] E Mik, 'AI in Negotiating and Entering into Contracts' in LA Di Matteo, C Poncibò and M Cannarsa (eds), *The Cambridge Handbook of Artificial Intelligence* (Cambridge University Press, 2022) 45, 50.

[62] Cartwright (n 26) 99.

[63] J Savirimuthu, 'Online Contract Formation: Taking Technological Infrastructure Seriously' (2005) 2 *University of Ottawa Law and Technology Journal* 105, 108.

[64] Dalla Massara (n 45); Albers (n 47) 92–95.

[65] Cartwright (n 26) 99.

nications between the parties are assessed from the perspective of the objective test. For this reason, communication has become the central focus of both contract formation and contract construction. The same objective standpoint is used, firstly, to decide whether a contract has been concluded at all and, secondly, to determine what the contract, once formed, should be taken to mean.

Blackburn J's classic statement in *Smith v Hughes* is generally taken as the basis of the objective test:[66]

> [I]f one of the parties intends to make a contract on one set of terms, and the other intends to make a contract on another set of term, or, as it is sometimes expressed, if the parties are not ad idem, there is no contract, unless the circumstances are such as to preclude one of the parties from denying that he has agreed to the terms of the other… If, whatever a man's real intention may be, he so conducts himself that a reasonable man would believe that he was assenting to the terms proposed by the other party, and that other party upon that belief enters into the contract with him, the man thus conducting himself would be equally bound as if he had intended to agree to the other party's terms.

This formulation has two dimensions. It provides a criterion for deciding whether a contract exists, but it also anticipates the later development of objective rules of construction, which ask what a reasonable person, with the background knowledge reasonably available to the parties, would understand the words and conduct in question to mean. The objective test thus links formation and interpretation: the same vantage point is used to identify both the existence and the content of contractual obligations.[67]

Historically, this was not always the dominant view. Perillo argues that until the nineteenth century, recourse to objective rules for the interpretation of the will of the parties had predominated, drawing attention to cases such as Pigot's case.[68] He also notes an apparent late eighteenth-century shift towards subjectivity, illustrated by *Cooke v Oxley*,[69] although that decision concerned the requirement of consideration and, more specifically, the need for simultaneity of acceptance rather than agreement as such. The modern law can therefore be seen as reasserting and systematising an objective tendency that had long been present and extending it from formation into the domain of construction.[70]

In contracts concluded by technological means, including algorithmic contracts, reliance on the objective test alone may suggest that nothing of doctrinal significance has changed. If attention is confined to outward appearance, there may be a sequence of communications that fit neatly within the traditional pattern of offer and acceptance: messages are sent and received, logs record matching

[66] *Smith v Hughes* (1871) LR 6 QB 597, 607.

[67] See *Investors Compensation Scheme Ltd v West Bromwich Building Society* [1998] 1 WLR 896 (HL) 912–13 (Lord Hoffmann); E McKendrick, *Contract Law: Text, Cases, and Materials*, 11th edn (Oxford University Press, 2024) 382.

[68] *Pigot's (Henry) Case* (1614) 1 Co Rep 26b, 77 ER 1177.

[69] *Cooke* v *Oxley* (1790) 3 T. R. 653.

[70] For a more in-depth analysis of the evolution of the objective theory, see Perillo (n 56) 427–78.

declarations, and a reasonable observer might conclude that a contract has been formed on particular terms. Yet algorithmic systems can make mistakes, operate on unexpected data, or generate outputs in ways that are not transparent to their operators or counterparties.

In such environments, the role of contract construction becomes particularly important. Objective interpretation provides a mechanism for controlling the legal effect of communications generated or processed by algorithms, by asking what meaning can reasonably be attributed to those communications in light of their technical and commercial context. At the same time, construction cannot by itself resolve all the problems raised by automated contracting. Where the appearance of agreement masks defects in consent or fundamental misunderstandings about the way algorithmic systems operate, recourse to doctrines concerned with the validity of consent, rather than its interpretation, may still be necessary. The interaction between the objective test at the stages of formation and construction is therefore central to any assessment of how algorithmic contracts should be treated within the existing framework of contract law.

## E. Why Consent Matters

Formation, interpretation, and the law of mistake constitute three different perspectives from which to consider the use of the objective theory in contract law. As seen in the preceding sections, the formation and interpretation are generally approached from an objective standpoint. Once the objective requirements for formation have been satisfied, the enforceability of an agreement can be challenged only on subjective grounds, such as mistake, misrepresentation, duress or undue influence. In this sense, the parties' actual intentions re-enter the analysis through doctrines that treat a contract as defective where subjective states diverge from what a reasonable observer would otherwise infer.[71]

Perillo has observed that theorists who endorse the objective approach nevertheless accept that '[d]uress, fraud and mistake vitiated the will and contaminated the appearance of consent'.[72] Defences of this kind describe factual circumstances which, if established, deprive the manifestation of assent of its usual legal meaning.[73] The law, therefore, does not treat outward indications of consent as conclusive. It recognises that the appearance of agreement may, in some cases, be an unreliable proxy for genuine consent.

The availability of these defences cannot simply be set aside because no human being is directly involved at the moment of communication because, as Sartor points out, some cognitive states such as goals, beliefs, or intentions can be inferred

[71] Bayern (n 37) 74.
[72] Perillo (n 56) 469.
[73] Barnett (n 15) 318.

with respect to the software.[74] At the same time, the decision to delegate contract formation to an algorithmic system can itself be understood as an exercise of private autonomy. The central question, developed in the following sections, is how far this initial act of delegation can ground consent to transactions generated by such systems. From this perspective, it becomes important to distinguish between genuinely consensual consent and merely procedural consent: there is a risk, highlighted in Dalla Massara's account of 'annihilated' consent, that consent may survive in form while its substantive, voluntary character is weakened.[75] In later chapters, this question will be revisited through doctrines concerned with defects in consent, particularly mistake, and their application to contracts formed by algorithmic systems. This requires looking back at the evolution of the ways in which human consent has been expressed in contract formation and assessing whether algorithmic communications can be understood as a new, legally acceptable manifestation of that consent.

# III. Looking Backward: The Evolution of the Expression of Human Consent in Contract Formation

## A. From the Dispatch Rule to the Receipt Rule

As seen in the preceding sections, the external manifestation of the parties' will is one of the basic pillars for identifying an agreement under the objective theory. Although consent is, in principle, a matter of subjective assent, in practice we only have access to manifested intentions.[76] It is therefore necessary to examine how the forms of manifestation of human consent have evolved, and how they have been affected by the use of technologies. On this basis, we can consider whether new forms of manifestation of human consent, via algorithms, can be accommodated within contract law.

It can hardly be denied that the introduction of postal mail was revolutionary as a method of communication. New, now old, technologies such as the telefax, and later the telephone and email, emerged as further deferred methods of communication, in which offer and acceptance were not simultaneous. Over time they have largely replaced 'snail mail'. All these means of communication, from ordinary post to internet-based contracting, have gradually come under judicial scrutiny.

[74] To justify the position that software agents are capable of reaching agreements in the legal sense of the term, Giovanni Sartor identifies beliefs with the ability to follow reality, goals with objectives, and intentions with internal states that trigger actions. For a more in-depth analysis, see G Sartor, *Contracts Without Agreement, or Agreement by Artefacts?* (Academy of Sciences in Göttingen ed, Universitätsverlag Göttingen, 2020) 41, 41–46; G Sartor, 'Cognitive Automata and the Law: Electronic Contracting and the Intentionality of Software Agents' (2009) 17 *Artificial Intelligence and Law* 253, 253–90.

[75] Dalla Massara (n 45).

[76] Barnett (n 15) 309.

A milestone in the evolution of contracting, *Adams v Lindsell* established what has become one of the most invoked, flexible and adaptable rules in contract law: the postal rule. Also known as the mailbox rule, it governs the timing of when a contract is considered to be formed.[77] In *Adams v Lindsell* the court held that a contract was formed when the acceptance letter was dispatched, rather than when it was received. The ruling set a precedent for the formation of contracts through correspondence, instead of requiring the parties to be physically present in the same space.

To reach this result, the law creates the fiction that acceptance occurs when the manifestation of assent leaves the control of the offeree, that is, when the letter is placed in the postbox. The objective test can be seen as lying behind this reasoning.[78] The objective theory places emphasis on communication between the parties; it is the communicated intention that determines the 'meeting of the minds'. What matters is the issuing and transmission of the intention, even if the message has not yet come to the knowledge of the other party. In this fiction, then, dispatch is decisive; actual knowledge is not.[79] Mik argues that the definition of when acceptance is considered communicated is conditioned by where we stand between the classical 'meeting of minds' theory and the objective theory.[80] The fact that the acceptance has not, strictly speaking, reached the offeror has long been a matter of controversy.[81] The dispatch rule even means that the contract is formed if the letter is delayed or not properly delivered.[82] It places a greater burden on the offeror, with little justification beyond a fiction: that the contract is formed during 'a period when both parties intended to form a contract', which is treated as sufficient to amount to a meeting of minds.[83]

In *Henthorn v Fraser*, an argument in favour of the dispatch rule was that the offeror's choice of method of communication implies acceptance of the risks inherent in that method, such as delay or loss in transit.[84] Ultimately, however, the more practical but less doctrinal justification is that the dispatch rule was established in *Adams v Lindsell*. For Law J, the rule prevents a successive and endless chain of communications that has to be stopped at some point.[85] As Macdonald suggests, it is a solution for a 'co-ordination problem'.[86] Other justifications range from

[77] *Adams v Lindsell* (1818) 1 B & Ald 681; 106 ER 250.

[78] Perillo (n 56) 439–40.

[79] Rawls (n 13) 205.

[80] E Mik, 'The Effectiveness of Acceptances Communicated by Electronic Means, or - Does the Postal Acceptance Rule Apply to Email?' (2009) 26 *Journal of Contract Law* 68, 73.

[81] For an analysis of controversy about the dispatch rule see, eg, A Nussbaum, 'Comparative Aspects of the Anglo-American Offer-and-Acceptance Doctrine' (1936) 36 *Columbia Law Review* 920, 920–29.

[82] *Dunlop v Higgins* (1848) 1 H.L.C. 381; *Household Fire & Carriage Accident Insurance Co Ltd v Grant* (1879) 4 Ex D 216, 223.

[83] K Rai and A Alla, 'From Phones to Emails: The Curious Case of Instantaneous Communication and Law on Contract Formation' (2021) 25 *Journal of Northeastern University* 1841, 1841–52.

[84] *Henthorn v Fraser* [1892] 2 Ch 27, 33.

[85] *Adams v Lindsell* (1818) 1 B & Ald 683

[86] E Macdonald, 'Dispatching the Dispatch Rule? The Postal Rule, e-Mail, Revocation and Implied Terms' (2013) 19(2) *European Journal of Current Legal Issues*.

arbitrariness, simple convenience, consideration of couriers as agents of the parties, or risk allocation and control over the message, among others.[87]

The postal rule laid down in *Adams v Lindsell* has been adapted over time, first being extended to the use of the telegraph,[88] and it has continued to evolve alongside new means of communication. *Entores Ltd v Miles Far East Corporation* constitutes the next milestone in the doctrinal evolution of the determination of when the contract is formed based on the orthodox method of offer-and-acceptance analysis. In that case, the ordinary postal rule was held not to apply to instantaneous means of communication such as telex or radio.[89] Instead, the formation of the contract took place at the time and place of receipt of the acceptance.

The earlier decision in *Entores v Miles Far East Co.* was later transposed to telephone communications. In *Brinkibon Ltd v Stahag Stahl GmbH*, Lord Wilberforce expressly extended the receipt rule to communications made by telephone or radio on the basis of their instantaneous nature, even if the parties were not physically present together.[90] An explicit recognition of the simultaneous character of the telephone appears in *Commission for New Towns v Cooper*, in which Stuart-Smith LJ states that '[e]xchange can also take place by telephone, in which case it will be simultaneous'.[91] The recognition of fax as a means of instant communication can be found in *JSC Zestafoni Nikoladze Ferroalloy Plant v Ronly Holdings Ltd.*[92] In that case, the mere sending of the fax did not determine the moment of contract formation; this was instead marked by correct receipt, which could be known immediately.

The reasoning behind this decision lies in the instantaneous nature of fax, telephone and radio communication. The justification for not applying the postal rule to instant communications is that in such cases it is possible to know immediately whether the delivery of the message has been effective and, therefore, to adopt the appropriate measures to guarantee the transmission and reception. It is even considered sufficient that the reply has reached the addressee's location even if it has not been attended to.[93] Hence, whether the dispatch or receipt rule applies is determined by the possibility of verifying the success of the communication process.

There is, however, a difference between these means of communication. While the telephone is instantaneous and simultaneous, meaning that information flows both ways concurrently, the fax is instantaneous only in the sense that there is

[87] For a review of the postal acceptance rule justifications see Mik (n 80) 79–81.

[88] *Cowan v O'Connor* (1888) 20 QBD 640.

[89] *Entores v Miles Far East Corporation* [1955] 2 QB 327.

[90] *Brinkibon Ltd v Stahag Stahl und Stahlwarenhandelsgesellschaft mbH* [1983] 2 AC 34, 41.

[91] *Commission for New Towns v Cooper* (GB) Limited [1995] Ch. 259 at 285.

[92] *JSC Zestafoni Nikoladze Ferroalloy Plant v Ronly Holdings Ltd.* [2004] EWHC 245 (Comm), [2004] 2 Lloyd's Rep 335.

[93] *Brinkibon Ltd v Stahag Stahl und Stahlwarenhandelsgesellschaft mbH* [1983] 2 AC 34, 42; *Entores v Miles Far East Corporation* [1955] 2 QB 327, 331.

no delay in delivery; it is not simultaneous. Even so, the general regime of *inter praesentes* communications has been applied to both types. However, there is no general rule applicable to all such communications, and although the *Entores* and *Brinkibon* cases are routinely cited in discussions of the matter, both decisions ultimately turned on their particular facts.[94]

The partial overturning of the dispatch rule on the basis of the alleged instantaneousness of communications via fax or telephone shows an implicit recognition that the dispatch rule already represented a departure from the essence of the meeting of the minds, in favour of an over-application of the objective theory, allowing the law to treat a contract as formed before the offeror had any actual knowledge of the acceptance.[95]

## B. Contract Formation in the Era of the Internet

Until the advent of the internet, two basic rules governed the formation of contracts. As Lord Wilberforce observed in *Brinkibon*, there was 'a general rule covering instantaneous communication *inter praesentes*, or at a distance, with an exception that applied to non-instantaneous communication at a distance'.[96] While some argue that in the internet age these rules are no longer justifiable,[97] others raise the question of whether the exception should also apply to acceptance carried out by electronic means.[98] There is now an extensive literature on the suitability of these rules for internet-based communications.[99] This point is significant, since interactions between algorithmic systems and their operational environment typically occur over the internet and are mediated electronically.

Although email, website interactions and instant messaging can all be regarded as contemporary modes of communication in the internet age, we must start from the fact that 'the Internet is not a technology'.[100] The internet is '[a] system of linked computer networks, worldwide in scope, that facilitates data

[94] Mik (n 80) 71.

[95] SWB Hill, 'Flogging a Dead Horse: The Postal Acceptance Rule and Email' (2001) 17 *Journal of Contract Law* 151, 151–62.

[96] *Brinkibon Ltd v Stahag Stahl und Stahlwarenhandelsgesellschaft mbH* [1983] 2 AC 34, 41–42.

[97] Rawls (n 13) 202.

[98] Mik (n 80) 71.

[99] See, eg, P Fasciano, 'Internet Electronic Mail: A Last Bastion for the Mailbox Rule' (1997) 25 *Hofstra Law Review* 971, 971; Macdonald (n 86); M Robertson, 'Is Assent Still a Prerequisite for Contract Formation in Today's E-Conomy?' (2003) 78 *Washington Law Review* 265, 265–96; S Christensen, 'Formation of Contracts by Email - Is It Just the Same as the Post?' (2001) 1 *Queensland University of Technology Law Review*; Rawls (n 13) 200–31; P Goodrich, 'Habermas and the Postal Rule' (1996) 17 *Cardozo Law Review* 1457, 1457; E Mik, 'The Unimportance of Being "Electronic" or Popular Misconceptions about "Internet Contracting"' (2011) 19 *International Journal of Law and Information Technology* 324, 324–47.

[100] Mik (n 80) 80.

communication services such as remote login, file transfer, electronic mail, and newsgroups. The Internet is a way of connecting existing computer networks that greatly extends the reach of each particular system.'[101] In other words, the internet is an infrastructure that allows the exchange of information through applications installed on computers that are not part of a network, and whose communication is standardised through the TCP/IP protocol.[102] It is through this infrastructure that the parties' intentions can be communicated using methods such as email, instant messaging and web pages.[103] This, in turn, has given rise to what is known as e-commerce.

In *Thomas v BPE Solicitors*, the question was when an email message is legally considered to be received, specifically in the context of accepting an offer to form a contract.[104] The case regarded email communications as instantaneous, thereby subjecting them to the receipt rule. This approach rests on the premise that problems with the communication can be promptly identified, given the supposedly immediate nature of email transmissions. The instantaneous nature of the communication, on the one hand, and the presumption that the sender can control whether the message has reached the addressee, on the other, underpin the use of the receipt rule for email.

However, the characterisation of email as 'instantaneous' is open to question. The term is applied in a nuanced way that tolerates some degree of delay. In reality, 'email is an asynchronous, non-real-time, delayed-access, store-and-forward method of communication'.[105] Once an email is sent, it is transmitted to an intermediate mail server, and several stages may then follow, including attempts to deliver the message to the addressee or placing it in temporary storage. This process is typically overlooked.[106] Even instantaneous transmission is not equivalent to immediate notification.[107] Email is not truly instantaneous, and it is also fragmented, as messages travel in packets.[108] From a legal perspective, this technical fragmentation is largely irrelevant,[109] but it underscores the fictional character of the assumption of instantaneity.

[101] Internet definition from B Pfaffenberger, in 'Que's Computer User's Dictionary' in Fasciano (n 99) 989.

[102] The term computer is used in the broad, non-technical sense of the word, not as a device. This is because today the functionalities of a computer can be present in cell phones, or vice versa, you can make calls from computers or send or receive faxes.

[103] For a more in-depth analysis of the technical features of the internet and related applications, see Mik (n 80) 79–81.

[104] *David Baxter Edward Thomas and Peter Sandford Gander v BPE Solicitors* (a firm) [2010] EWHC 306 (Ch) [85]–[90].

[105] Mik (n 80) 84.

[106] For a more in-depth analysis of the process of delivering messages and notifying delivery or failure through SMTP protocol see ibid 86–88.

[107] ibid 91.

[108] AD Murray, 'Entering into Contracts Electronically: The Real W.W.W.' in L Edwards, and C Waelde (eds), *Law and the Internet: a Framework for Electronic Commerce* (Hart Publishing, 2000) 17, 17–36.

[109] Mik (n 99) 325.

The second argument, regarding the sender's control over the receipt of email communications, is also contestable. The parties are not necessarily sitting in front of their computers, as in the case of telex transmissions in *Entores*, to ensure receipt of the message.[110] Criticism may be directed towards the application of the same principle governing face-to-face interactions to the formalisation of contracts by email based on the presumed instantaneousness and control over communications, which in reality do not exist.[111] If anything, what can be established is a procedural framework encompassing acknowledgements of receipt and failure notifications, but full control remains elusive.[112] No generalisations can therefore be made about the instantaneous or delayed nature, or the uni- or bidirectionality, of email communications. The specific participation of the recipient matters.[113] Some email communications can replicate bidirectional communications by automatically generating confirmations of receipt or, conversely, failure notifications.[114]

Electronic Data Interchange (EDI) transactions, though sometimes compared to email, are in fact closer to telex.[115] Here, a direct link is established between the parties' systems, allowing information to be exchanged directly from one computer system to another. This characteristic renders EDI a quasi-instantaneous mode of communication, distinguishing it from email, where communication does not involve a direct transmission from one computer to another but passes through intermediaries. In the case of EDI, reference to the general rule that acceptance takes place upon receipt of the message is therefore more straightforwardly supported by its instantaneous character.[116]

Once the applicability of the postal rule to email has been analysed, the same reasoning can be extrapolated to other immediate means of communication such as WhatsApp or Telegram as well as to web-based communications.[117] The latest instant messaging applications mirror and have partly replaced face-to-face interactions. Mik argues that instant messaging applications are more reminiscent of bidirectional communication.[118]

There is another form of electronic contracting that must be considered. No analysis of the evolution of the provision of consent contract formation would be complete without examining e-commerce. Contracting through websites

[110] *Entores v Miles Far East Corporation* [1955] 2 QB 327, 333.

[111] Mik (n 80) 92–93.

[112] Similar critical positions are held by other scholars. See, eg, Fasciano (n 99) 1001; Rai and Alla (n 83) 1841–52; Murray (n 108) 17–36.

[113] In this regard note that in *Thomas v BPE Solicitors* (n 104) the generic answer would be that it depends on the expectations of the parties. In that case, the parties were in the final throes (or so they thought) of negotiating a substantial share purchase agreement, and the deal was expected to close that day, even after hours. Thus, the court held that the sender could reasonably have expected that the addressee would still be at his office at the time that the email was delivered.

[114] Mik (n 99) 330.

[115] For an overview of EDI transactions, see ch 2, section II.

[116] Christensen (n 99) 1.

[117] Mik (n 80) 71.

[118] ibid 94–95.

introduced new challenges for contract law.[119] One early controversy concerned whether the offer of products through a website should be characterised as an 'invitation to treat' or as an offer, with the associated consequences that the former is not binding while the latter is. Although the Electronic Commerce Directive (EC Directive)[120] could have shed light on the issue, its Article 11 does not clearly establish whether a website offering goods or services is actually making an 'offer' or an 'invitation to treat'.[121] There is, nonetheless, a certain degree of doctrinal unanimity in considering that, in contracts using the 'shop-window' of the World Wide Web, the display on the website has been regarded as a mere invitation to treat, while what appears to be the buyer's act of acceptance is, in legal terms, the offer.[122] Once the seller electronically receives an offer from a buyer, the seller can decide whether to accept or reject it and may email the customer once the buyer's offer has been considered and approved.[123] That communication may constitute acceptance. Some authors, however, consider that it is not the receipt of the order confirmation that constitutes acceptance, 'but the acceptance is executed by the dispatch of the goods themselves'.[124]

Interactions with a website can be viewed as a form of instant, two-way communication. They require active participation by clicking or filling in fields to which the system reacts in real time.[125] In the same vein, 'click-wrap' processes are considered instantaneous communications because the party clicking will know immediately whether there has been a failure in the communication.[126]

[119] Away from the subject of this research, contract formation, issues such as the incorporation of contractual terms, unfair terms in consumer contracts or choice of law are also the subject of discussion in relation to contracts concluded through websites. See, eg, the contribution by Elisabeth Macdonald on the question of contracts formed by the browse-wrap process: E Macdonald, 'When Is a Contract Formed by the Browse-Wrap Process?' (2011) 19 *International Journal of Law and Information Technology* 285, 285–305.

[120] Directive 2000/31/EC of the European Parliament and of the Council of 8 June 2000 on certain legal aspects of information society services, in particular electronic commerce, in the Internal Market (Directive on electronic commerce).

[121] Article 11 EC Directive: 'Placing of the order —(1) Unless parties who are not consumers have agreed otherwise, where the recipient of the service places his order through technological means, a service provider shall- (a) acknowledge receipt of the order to the recipient of the service without undue delay and by electronic means; and (b) make available to the recipient of the service appropriate, effective and accessible technical means allowing him to identify and correct input errors prior to the placing of the order. (2) For the purposes of paragraph (1)(a) above— (a) the order and the acknowledgement of receipt will be deemed to be received when the parties to whom they are addressed are able to access them; and (b) the acknowledgement of receipt may take the form of the provision of the service paid for where that service is an information society service. (3) The requirements of paragraph (1) above shall not apply to contracts concluded exclusively by exchange of electronic mail or by equivalent individual communications.'

[122] See, eg, Murray (n 108) 17–36.

[123] C Pacini, C Andrews and W Hillison, 'To Agree or Not to Agree: Legal Issues in Online Contracting' (2002) 45 *Business Horizons* 43, 46.

[124] D Defossez, 'Acceptance Sent through Email; Is the Postal Rule Applicable?' (2019) 11 *Law, State and Telecommunications Review* 23, 24.

[125] Mik (n 80) 95–96.

[126] Murray (n 108) 17–36.

However, it is notable that, in these attempts to justify instantaneity, little attention is paid to the fact that system responses are generated by software. The fact that a system responds to pre-programmed instructions is not a challenge to contract law, and this was recognised in *Digiliandmall.*[127] Something similar happens in algorithmic contracts when algorithmic systems either initiate an action or respond to electronic actions without human review or action.[128] The difference, however, is that not every answer in algorithmic contracts is deterministic. This non-deterministic dimension raises new questions as to how far traditional rules on dispatch and receipt, and the associated fictions about instantaneity and control, can be straightforwardly applied to contracts concluded through algorithmic systems.

## IV. Algorithmic Contracts: Their Role as Dynamic Communication Tools

'[A]lgorithmic contracts are contracts that contain terms that were determined by algorithms rather than a person.'[129] This assertion is significant at this stage of the analysis. Earlier sections suggested that, in algorithmic contracts, contract communications appear to bring the law 'full circle': algorithmic contract communications resemble face-to-face communications. However, this statement requires refinement. The crucial point is that algorithmic contracts involve machine-to-machine communication rather than interpersonal interaction.

In the same way that analysis has been traditionally carried out on how humans communicate in order to conclude whether an agreement has been reached, it is now necessary to examine how algorithmic systems communicate to determine how agreements in the form of algorithmic contracts come into being. In what follows, *algorithmic contracts* are taken to be contracts in which each party relies on an AI-based algorithmic system to make and communicate contracting decisions. Communication in such cases takes place, in functional terms, between systems rather than between individuals.[130] Therefore, our focus is on algorithm-to-algorithm communication.

The relevant paradigm of communication thus shifts from interpersonal exchanges to interactions between autonomous systems. In this context, the communication dynamics unfold between systems configured and deployed by

[127] *Chwee Kin Kegong v Digiliandmall.com Pte Ltd* [2004] SGHC 71, [2004] 2 SLR 594 at [134]. In the case involving Digilandmall.com Pte Ltd, the defendant erroneously listed an HP laser printer at $66 instead of the correct price of $3,854. Over 4,000 printers were ordered before the mistake was noticed. The defendants, claiming a unilateral mistake, refused to fulfil the orders, leading to a legal dispute. The court ruled in favour of the defendants, declaring the contract void due to the fundamental pricing mistake. The complainants were deemed aware of the error, and the absence of the meeting of the minds negated the formation of a binding contract. Consequently, the complainants were not entitled to enforce the contract at the mistakenly low price.

[128] Scholz, *Algorithms and Contract Law* (n 2).

[129] LH Scholz, 'Algorithmic Contracts' [2017] *Stanford Technology Law Review* 128, 134.

[130] See ch 1, section II.B.

the parties, rather than between the parties themselves. Before turning to the algorithmic determination of contractual content, it is necessary, as a preliminary step in concluding this chapter and its analysis of the communicative dimension, to reconsider some of the concepts discussed earlier – instantaneity or immediacy, synchrony or asynchrony, unidirectionality or bidirectionality, and reliability – in the specific setting of communications between algorithmic systems.

As discussed above, the concept of instantaneity is relative from a legal perspective. Rawls defines 'substantially instantaneous communications' as 'technologies that, when operating normally, can transmit a message somewhere in the time frame of a few seconds to a few minutes'.[131] The fact that one of the paradigmatic use cases of algorithmic contracts is high-frequency trading (HFT) supports the view that they are based on instantaneous communication methods.[132] On this basis, contracts concluded through the interaction of algorithms can be understood, by analogy with face-to-face contracts, as being formed at the point at which an acceptance is received by the offeror.

However, 'speed of transmission alone is not decisive'.[133] Mere instantaneity is insufficient to categorise a situation as akin to face-to-face communication. As the analysis of postal, fax, telephone and email communications showed, a second pivotal factor is the degree of control over communications. Only where communications are bidirectional and in real time can failures be detected and corrected immediately. In the case of algorithmic contracts in which both parties engage through algorithmic systems, this requirement is typically satisfied: where the interacting systems are unable to communicate effectively, the contract simply does not come into existence.[134] System-to-system communication therefore replicates face-to-face interactions to the extent that it is synchronous, substantially instantaneous and bidirectional.

Reliability and risk allocation constitute additional elements traditionally scrutinised in evaluating the appropriateness of applying the postal rule for the formation of contracts. In the context of algorithmic contracts, reliability concerns the efficacy of communication rather than the substantive reliability of the contract content, a controversial issue, particularly in the context of black-box algorithms.[135] Given that communications between systems emulate face-to-face

[131] Rawls (n 13) 210.

[132] For a more in-depth analysis of HFT as a use case for algorithmic contracts, see ch 1, section III.A.

[133] Mik (n 80) 72.

[134] It is pertinent to recall that the focus of this study is confined to algorithmic contracts wherein both contracting parties operate through algorithmic systems, and therefore potential challenges arising from communications issues between the system and a party not operating through algorithmic systems are not subject of this research. Further exploration of this latter issue is warranted.

[135] In academic discourse, certain algorithms are referred to as 'black boxes', denoting a lack of understanding about their internal mechanisms, with comprehension reliant solely on inputs and outputs. In the context of machine learning systems, despite having access to both inputs and outputs, the underlying process that connects the two may remain unclear – a concept highlighted by Scholz, who emphasised the challenges that black-box algorithms pose for contract law. Unlike deterministic decision processes, where retracing each step is feasible, some argue that such traceability is not possible for nondeterministic algorithms. See ch 3, section IV.B.ii.

negotiations, the high reliability of such communications stands as an unequivocally positive attribute.

Based on the above, algorithmic contracts can be understood, from the perspective of communication, as being formed upon the convergence of the algorithms, in a manner analogous to the formation of contracts through face-to-face communications. The analogy rests on the instantaneous, synchronous and bidirectional nature of communications between algorithmic systems and on the fact that the 'meeting of the algorithms' is contingent upon successful communication.

## V. Conclusion. The Evolution from Face-To-Face to Machine-To-Machine Operations. Moving Beyond Communication

The analysis in this chapter has treated algorithmic contracts primarily from the standpoint of communication. Building on the evolution from postal correspondence through fax, telephone, email and internet-based contracting, it has shown that algorithmic systems can now perform the external communicative functions of offer and acceptance. When both parties rely on interacting algorithms, their exchanges are, in functional terms, substantially instantaneous, synchronous and bidirectional. From this perspective, algorithmic contracts can be assimilated to face-to-face contracts: formation occurs at the point of convergence between the systems – a 'meeting of the algorithms' that plays a role analogous to the traditional meeting of the minds.

Treating algorithmic systems as communication tools in this sense, however, leaves important questions open. Firstly, the existence of a meeting of the algorithms does not itself explain when, and on what basis, that event can be considered the equivalent of a meeting of the minds. Secondly, if the contract is formed at the moment of system-to-system convergence, it remains to be clarified how knowledge of the fact of the agreement and of its content is attributed to the human parties who designed, configured and deployed the systems. Thirdly, once algorithms occupy decision-making roles in the formation process, it must be asked whether the traditional offer-and-acceptance framework, and the associated doctrines on defects in consent – particularly mistake – remain adequate to capture situations in which the system's behaviour departs from the assumptions under which delegation took place.

The analysis that follows moves beyond the treatment of algorithms as external communication tools and turns to these unresolved dimensions. It examines how knowledge and decision-making can be attributed in settings where agreements are formed through algorithmic systems, and how far the legal conception of consent must be re-worked to ensure that the meeting of the algorithms can, where appropriate, be treated as the functional equivalent of a meeting of the minds.

# 6

# Inside the Workings of Algorithmic Contract Formation

## I. Introduction

As discussed in the previous chapter, analysis of the agreement element of contract formation has traditionally centred on the communications through which offer and acceptance are exchanged. A contract is formed upon the concurrence of offer and acceptance, and acceptance marks the moment at which obligations arise that did not exist before. In this orthodox framework, 'the offer and acceptance rules tell us not only whether a contract was formed at all, but they also tell us when a contract was formed and where that took place'.[1] Determining the moment of acceptance has therefore been a central doctrinal concern, and the postal rule and its successive adaptations have served to allocate risk and ensure effectiveness in identifying when parties become bound.[2] In algorithmic contracting, however, the difficulty extends beyond *when* formation occurs. It concerns how knowledge of that formation, and of the content of the resulting agreement, can be attributed to the system operator when the relevant communicative acts are executed by an autonomous system.

To date, legal theorists have tended to rely on the efficiency of the objective theory of contracts, rather than confront the complexities of subjective intention. In algorithmic contracts, in which algorithms intervene as 'constructive agents',[3] it is not only the mode of communicating intentions that matters but also the fact that concrete contractual outcomes are generated in the absence of contemporaneous human awareness. The significance of the concreteness of the parties' obligations is magnified by their initial lack of specificity, since the system operator only defines the general parameters or objectives.[4] In the face of this new form of

[1] D Nolan, 'Offer and Acceptance in the Electronic Age' in A Burrows and E Peel (eds), *Contract Formation and Parties* (Oxford University Press 2010) 61, 61.

[2] E Mik, 'The Effectiveness of Acceptances Communicated by Electronic Means, or - Does the Postal Acceptance Rule Apply to Email?' (2009) 26 *Journal of Contract Law* 68, 71.

[3] The term 'constructive agent' is borrowed from Lauren H Scholz due to its expressive quality. See LH Scholz, 'Algorithmic Contracts' [2017] *Stanford Technology Law Review* 128, 165. The present study nevertheless avoids 'agent'-based characterisations of algorithmic systems, since the language of agency risks misleadingly importing agency-law intuitions; the reasons are developed in ch 2, section III.

[4] See ch 3, section IV.B. for the human influence on the system and on the output via the parameterisation and determination of the system objectives.

contracting, '[p]erhaps we might focus on the fact of agreement rather than the process of making the agreement'.[5] With algorithmic contracts, the issue at hand is not only how the parties' intentions are communicated, but also how those intentions are matched by the system and how the resulting agreement can be traced back, in legal terms, to the human party.

Understanding this challenge requires attention to the framework within which the system operates. The operator defines the objectives and performance criteria that determine how the algorithm will recognise offers, generate acceptances, and specify contractual terms. 'Human intervention is present in the use of algorithms, through the parameterization of the algorithm, the choice and weighting criteria as well as the categories of data that are taken into account in order to arrive at the desired result.'[6] This parameterisation provides the basis for attributing knowledge of the contract to the operator, despite the absence of contemporaneous human involvement.

We have not reached the technological singularity point,[7] current AI systems operate on behalf of humans rather than autonomously pursuing their own objectives, and they do not possess independent initiative.[8] The crucial question then, is to determine how the party is linked to a contract if the algorithm acts or behaves 'autonomously': in other words, how the offer or acceptance generated by the system can be attributed to the operator. For some, 'computers do not make their "own" decisions but execute earlier human decisions or manifest human decision in pursuance of human goals'[9] and for others, '[l]ike agents, algorithms must not be understood as mere extensions of the will of an individual or company'.[10] These positions converge on the idea that algorithmic systems both depend on human design and operate with a degree of functional independence. It is precisely this combination that makes the problem of attributing the system's communicative acts – and the knowledge they embody – to the human operator so acute in the context of algorithmic contracts.

As the preceding chapter showed, algorithmic contracts operate in a realm of instantaneity and simultaneity comparable to face-to-face contracting, albeit without direct human involvement at the decisive moment. It is this absence of human intervention that raises new questions for contract law. As Scholz has observed, '[t]he gap between the programming of the algorithm and the algorithm's act has

[5] T Allen and R Widdison, 'Can Computers Make Contracts?' (1996) 9 *Harvard Journal of Law & Technology* 25, 44.

[6] M Milossi, E Alexandropoulou and K E Psannis, 'AI Ethics: Algorithmic Determinism or Self-Determination? The GDPR Approach' (2021) 9 IEEE Journals & Magazine 58455, 58458 ieeexplore.ieee.org/stamp/stamp.jsp?tp=&arnumber=9400809 accessed 2 May 2024.

[7] For the term 'technological singularity', see M Shanahan, *The Technological Singularity* (The MIT Press, 2015).

[8] Even as Teubner elaborates on his theory of the legal status of autonomous software agents, he recognises that AI systems do not act in their own self-interest, but in the interest of their users. See G Teubner, 'Digitale Rechtssubjekte? Zum Privatrechtlichen Status Autonomer Softwareagenten / Digital Personhood? The Status of Autonomous Software Agents in Private Law' (2018) 2018 *Ancilla Iuris* 35, 43.

[9] E Mik, 'AI in Negotiating and Entering into Contracts' in LA Di Matteo, C Poncibò and M Cannarsa eds, *The Cambridge Handbook of Artificial Intelligence* (Cambridge University Press, 2022) 45, 55.

[10] Scholz (n 3) 153.

not been closed in substantive contract law'.[11] This chapter considers how, in an environment of instantaneous and system-level interactions, knowledge of the existence and content of the contract can be attributed to the operator.

The analysis so far has examined the moment of formation through the system's role as a communication tool. Extending the focus to the system's decision-making function raises a further question: how can knowledge regarding the formation of the contract and its content be attributed to the operator? This question structures the remainder of this chapter.

# II. Theoretical and Doctrinal Approaches to the Proxy Issue

## A. Approaching the Proxy Issue

'Algorithmic contracts are contracts in which one or more parties use an algorithm to determine whether to be bound and how to be bound.'[12] The concept implies the use of transmission systems and the delegation of decision-making functions to technology. What distinguishes these contracts is that computer programs intervene in decision-making roles previously carried out by humans, affecting the *how*, *when* and *what* of the formation process. 'The best way to understand what is new and different about algorithmic contracts is that in the process of forming an algorithmic contract, computer programs step into decision-making roles previously performed by humans.'[13]

Although the operator may define the system's objectives at a high level of abstraction, the operative terms of any transaction are ordinarily produced as determinate outputs at the point of execution, generated within parameters set by the operator and shaped by incoming data. The principal difficulty is therefore not uncertainty of content as such, but the attribution of that system-generated content – and of legally relevant knowledge of it – to the contracting party.

Chopra and White labelled the doctrinal difficulties arising from this shift as 'the contracting problem'.[14] Algorithmic contracts challenge traditional concepts of intention and consent by creating a distinct relationship between a contracting party and the system acting on their behalf.[15]

[11] LH Scholz, 'Algorithms and Contract Law' in W Barfield (ed), *The Cambridge Handbook of The Law of Algorithms* (Cambridge University Press, 2020) 141, 149.

[12] Scholz (n 3) 134.

[13] Scholz (n 11) 141.

[14] S Chopra and LF White, 'Artificial Agents and the Contracting Problem: A Solution Via an Agency Analysis' (2009) 2009 *University of Illinois Journal of Law, Technology & Policy* 363, 365. For a more in-depth discussion of the contribution of Chopra and White, see ch 4, section II.A.ii.

[15] M Rizzi and N Skead, 'Algorithmic Contracts and the Equitable Doctrine of Undue Influence: Adapting Old Rules to a New Legal Landscape' (2020) 14 *Journal of Equity* 301, 312. However, it is important to emphasise that this study is confined to those algorithmic contracts in which the two parties operate through algorithmic systems. See ch 1, section II.A. for a more detailed explanation.

In analysing this issue, three doctrinal starting points are commonly invoked – the mere tools perspective, the agency approach, and arguments based on legal personality. These approaches have already been discussed in earlier chapters; they are revisited here only to assess their capacity to address the specific problem examined in this chapter: how to attribute to the operator the knowledge embodied in the system's acts of offer and acceptance.

Addressing the proxy issue also requires consideration of the relevant judicial precedents. Establishing this doctrinal and case-law foundation provides the basis for the analysis that follows.

## B. The 'Mere Tools' Theory

Under the mere tools perspective, the actions or decisions made by algorithmic systems involved in contract formation are attributed directly to their human operators, who are treated as the true source of the relevant contractual conduct. Early descriptions of such systems as 'electronic agents' suggested an analogy with conventional communication devices.[16] However, as noted earlier in this book, algorithmic contracts involve not only transmission functions but also the delegation of decision-making processes. For this reason, characterising these systems as mere tools does not accurately capture the way in which contractual content is generated.

Some early analyses recognised that denying the validity of contracts facilitated by autonomous systems would be a dismissal of commercial reality.[17] The difficulty lies elsewhere: contract doctrine is structurally designed for agreements formed between human parties dealing with one another at arm's length,[18] whereas algorithmic contracts involve interactions between systems instructed by humans. This reveals a central weakness of the mere tools perspective: the system may generate agreements of which the operator has no contemporaneous awareness.[19] The theory therefore identifies whose act the system's output is but does not explain how knowledge of the existence and content of that output can be attributed to the human party. Ultimately, if one moves away from the conventional scrutiny of agreements through the lens of offer and acceptance, the attention pivots towards the recognition of the mere existence of an agreement – and this is significant, irrespective of the means by which it is attained. However, it is imperative to delineate a process which can establish the essential connection wherein consent, and therefore knowledge of the terms of the contract, can be traced back from the system to the human operator.

[16] Allen and Widdison (n 5) in EM Weitzenboeck, 'Electronic Agents and the Formation of Contracts' (2001) 9 *International Journal of Law and Information Technology* 204, 214.

[17] Allen and Widdison (n 5) 47–49.

[18] ibid 50.

[19] ibid 43–45.

Weitzenboeck has observed that, under the mere tools perspective, any output from an electronic agent can be considered to directly emanate from its human controller, a view that promotes user responsibility but may be 'unduly harsh' where the operator has no contemporaneous awareness of the system's actions or of errors arising from its operation.[20] Andrade and others have likewise questioned whether such systems can meaningfully be treated as mere tools, given the unpredictability of their actions and the corresponding difficulty of presuming operator knowledge.[21] More recent formulations of the mere tools position, such as Mik's, reinforce a focus on outcomes rather than on the underlying technical process. As she argues, 'in the context of contract law, technical details are rarely (if ever!) relevant',[22] and 'if a person looks like they want to enter into a contract on particular terms, the person will be regarded as intending to form such a contract'.[23] These positions support an outcome-based approach, but they do not resolve the central problem considered in this chapter: how knowledge of the existence and content of the contract generated by the system can be attributed to the operator when that knowledge is not contemporaneously possessed.

The 'meeting of the minds' doctrine emphasises the existence of a shared understanding and mutual agreement between contracting parties. While Mik's focus on expediting the execution of legal agreements through AI implementation is commendable, her position neglects to recognise the pivotal role of human consent in contractual relationships. By disregarding subjective elements inherent to the decision-making process that contribute to defining contractual terms, her perspective overlooks significant aspects of contract formation. Mik acknowledges the importance of human intention in contractual relations,[24] but seemingly disregards the subjective element: this reveals a contradiction, highlighting a lack of consistency in her justification of the attribution of consent to the human operator within her framework. Consequently, it is evident that a more nuanced approach is necessary, one that accounts for both the objective and subjective dimensions involved in the utilisation of autonomous artificial intelligence systems in the realm of contract law.[25]

[20] Weitzenboeck (n 16) 214.

[21] F Andrade et al, 'Contracting Agents: Legal Personality and Representation' (2007) 15 *Artificial Intelligence and Law* 357, 360–61.

[22] E Mik, 'The Resilience of Contract Law in Light of Technological Change' in M Furmston (ed), *The Future of the Law of Contract* (Routledge, 2020) 112 113–14. In the evolution of her scholarly contribution, Mik has come to affirm a clear distinction between the role of AI in entering into contracts and its involvement in negotiating contracts. She dismisses the latter, directing her focus on the former as a tool to 'assist human negotiators'. Mik does not seem to differentiate between scenarios where a trader uses a program solely to determine the optimal stock price and then personally communicates the resulting offer, or if the program both determines the price and communicates the offer. See Mik (n 9) 50–51.

[23] ibid 45, 50–51.

[24] Mik points this out indirectly in her work at several points, but it can also be clearly seen in the quote cited above: '[i]f a person *looks* like her or she wants to enter into a contract on particular terms, the person *will be regarded as* intended to form such contract'. See above n 23.

[25] A Beckers and G Teubner, *Three Liability Regimes for Artificial Intelligence. Algorithmic Actants, Hybrids, Crowds* (Hart Publishing, 2021) 55.

Vincent Ooi further exposes the limits of the mere tools perspective by distinguishing between passive and active contract formation mechanisms.[26] In the passive case, the system functions mainly as a means of communication, and the mere tools view can broadly be reconciled with the objective theory of contract. In the active case, however, the system 'autonomously decide[s] the terms and conditions of the electronic contracts', and the operator does not have precise knowledge of the terms at the moment of formation.[27] Ooi notes that this leads to a heavy and arguably inequitable allocation of risk to the operator, who bears the consequences of errors or unexpected outputs that could not have been anticipated. His analysis, however, remains focused on risk allocation and the law of mistake, and does not resolve the more fundamental problem addressed in this chapter: how knowledge of the existence and content of the contract, generated at system level, is to be attributed to the operator at the point of formation.

However, contrary to what Ooi says, the role of the technology is not so much to make conscious decisions, but rather to specify or delineate a course of action. In fact, it can be argued that the decision-making role, is not a role as such, but a process. In essence, algorithms, which are the driving force behind these technological processes, represent a set of instructions or steps to be followed in order to achieve a desired outcome. It is as simple as Justice Aedit Abdullah and Goh Yihan have put it: 'Algorithms execute these rules on the basis of data inputs.'[28]

The mere tools theory leaves the 'meeting of the minds' requirement unaddressed because of its view of these systems as communication tools within contract formation. For this very reason, this perspective has been criticised for its omission in scrutinising the active participation of the system in the process of contract formation.[29] But 'this theory (…) requires that a connection must thus be established between the action (non-human) and the intention (human)'.[30] Therefore, the mere tools theory, while heading to some extent in the right direction, cannot currently appropriately account for algorithm-based contracting. While the fact that it places greater emphasis on the outcomes rather than the decision-making process itself highlights the importance of these systems as communication tools, it does not adequately resolve the question of the attribution of knowledge to the system operator, neither in respect of the fact of the agreement itself nor of its content. From this perspective, the necessary 'connection'[31] or 'link'[32] is still broken.

[26] V Ooi, 'Contracts Formed by Software: An Approach From the Law of Mistake' (2022) 22 *Journal of Business Law* 97.

[27] ibid 100.

[28] A Abdullah and G Yihan, 'Making Smart Contracts a Reality' in JG Allen and P Hunn (eds), *Smart Legal Contracts* (Oxford University Press, 2022) 70 74.

[29] Rizzi and Skead (n 15) 314.

[30] Andrade et al (n 21) 360.

[31] To express the conclusion, the term 'connection' is adopted in the sense used by Andrade and others. See ibid.

[32] Similarly, in framing the conclusion, the term 'link' is adopted in the sense used by Poncibò. See C Poncibò, 'Artificial Intelligence as a Communication Tool in Contract Law' (2023) 31 *European Review of Private Law* 239, 245.

## C. The Agency Approach

Scholz has argued that algorithmic systems should be understood as 'servants rather than mere tools',[33] and she treats the agency framework as a possible means of reconciling the operation of autonomous systems with contract law. In her work, she proposed the agency approach as a potential solution to reconcile the disparity between artificial agents and contract law, seeing potential in classifying autonomous algorithms as 'constructive' agents rather than human agents.[34] However, in its current form the agency model faces structural limitations when applied to contract formation because it is presented solely from the standpoint of algorithmic accountability.[35]

'Agency is the relationship which exists where one person (the principal) authorizes another (the agent) to act on its behalf and the agent agrees to do so.'[36] The compatibility of algorithmic contracts with contract law has been examined using the agency law framework, specifically focusing on the process of contract formation. This is because '[a]lgorithms may seem to "act for" a company roughly as a human agent would'.[37]

Bellia's early analysis illustrates the central doctrinal difficulty: agency law presupposes that the agent can agree to act on behalf of the principal, and consent is what justifies the legal consequences of representation. Software systems, however advanced, cannot assent to an agency relationship, nor can they assume the fiduciary duties that accompany it.[38] This creates a one-way relationship in which the system may execute programmed instructions but cannot meaningfully accept or refuse authority – a point echoed in the observation that the human–algorithm relationship is inherently asymmetric.[39]

Attempts to overcome this problem by adapting existing doctrines do not resolve the difficulty.[40] Mechanisms based on post-hoc ratification,[41] require a two-stage formation process, that undermines the speed and immediacy characteristic of algorithmic contracting. Proposals to attribute partial legal capacity to software agents face the obstacle that the principal–agent relationship continues to

[33] Scholz (n 3) 133.

[34] ibid 164–68.

[35] ibid 169.

[36] A Burrows, J Beatson and J Cartwright, *Anson's Law of Contract* (Oxford University Press, 2016) 715.

[37] SJ Bayern, 'Algorithms, Agreements, and Agency' in W Barfield (ed), *The Cambridge Handbook of the Law of Algorithms* (Cambridge University Press, 2020) 153, 157.

[38] AJ Bellia, 'Contracting with Electronic Agents' (2001) 50 *Emory Law Journal* 1047, 1059–65.

[39] Teubner (n 8) 48.

[40] See, eg, G Sartor, 'Cognitive Automata and the Law: Electronic Contracting and the Intentionality of Software Agents' (2009) 17 *Artificial Intelligence and Law* 253, 253; G Sartor, *Contracts Without Agreement, or Agreement by Artefacts?* (Academy of Sciences in Göttingen ed, Universitätsverlag Göttingen, 2020) 41 42; Chopra and White (n 14) 377. See also A Katz and M MacDonald, 'Autonomous Intelligent Agents and the Roman Law of Slavery' in L Edwards, S Burkhard and E Harbinja (eds), *Future Law: Emerging Technology, Regulation and Ethics* (Edinburgh University Press, 2022) 295, 295–312.

[41] Scholz (n 3) 167.

rest on consent, which an artificial system cannot provide.[42] Even approaches that distinguish between 'authority' (defined by the principal's objectives) and 'instructions' (the algorithmic implementation of those objectives) ultimately reframe the problem rather than solve it, as they do not establish how the system's acts become the principal's knowledge at the moment of formation.[43]

Ooi notes further that while algorithms may share certain functional similarities with human agents – especially where they operate beyond the principal's direct control – their inability to consent creates gaps both in internal relations and in the protection of third parties.[44] These difficulties help to explain why agency law, in its current doctrinal form, has not yet provided a satisfactory account of how the outputs of an algorithmic system can be treated as generating knowledge attributable to the operator at the point of contracting.

The approach of equating algorithmic systems with agents has appeared to offer a straightforward solution. However, its proponents have acknowledged persistent drawbacks with this approach that remain unresolved. In fact, this discussion has revealed that the agency law approach takes the problem out of the scope of contract law and fails to offer a viable solution to the contentious issue of the consent requirement in the establishment of algorithmic contracts. Consequently, this perspective leaves unresolved critical issues, such as the timing of contract formation, the attribution of knowledge of the contract and its contents, and, notably, the lack of correlation between the meeting of the algorithms and the traditional concept of the meeting of the minds in contractual agreements.

Instead of dealing with the contracting problem from the agency law perspective and irrespective of the degree of autonomy exhibited by software agents, their operations are fundamentally rooted in the initial programmed instructions. These instructions serve as the origin of an authority that not only establishes a rationale linking the 'agent' and the principal but also apparently or explicitly renders the actions of the 'software agent' legally binding upon the principal. But the term 'authority' seems not to be useful when one of the entities involved does not include the human factor. Whether we are talking about personality or cognitive capacities, the agency law solution moves the contractual predicament from a purely contractual realm to a more intricate and philosophical domain. Agency law solutions suffer from some conceptual misunderstanding, often confusing the agency from a legal point of view with human agency.[45]

Accordingly, while the agency approach highlights important features of algorithmic contracting and may assume greater significance as technologies evolve, it does not presently resolve the core issue addressed in this chapter: how the existence and content of system-generated agreements can be attributed to the

[42] Teubner (n 8) 61.
[43] Chopra and White (n 14) 393
[44] Ooi (n 26) 102–06.
[45] It is rather illuminating on this point to go through the work of J Linarelli, 'Artificial Intelligence and Contracts Formation: Back to Contract as Bargain?' (23) *Emerging Issues at the Intersection of Commercial Law and Technologies* ssrn.com/abstract=4363410 accessed 2 May 2024.

human party. Nor does it clarify how the actions of interacting systems relate to the traditional requirement of a meeting of the minds – a question developed in the following chapter.

## D. Attribution of Legal Personality to Autonomous Agents

The proposal to attribute legal personality to autonomous software agents is not new.[46] Allen and Widdison anticipated that the increased use of computational systems in contracting might create 'pressure to treat computers and computer-person "partnerships" as legal persons, at least for determining when contracts are formed'.[47] Subsequent technological developments have renewed interest in this possibility. More recently, the European Parliament briefly considered, but ultimately rejected,[48] the idea of creating an electronic personality for highly autonomous systems, signalling that EU policy has moved away from this solution.[49]

Among scholars, Sartor has advanced one of the clearest arguments for recognising legal personality in artificial entities, at least for those capable of information processing, communicative activity, and autonomous operation.[50] In his view, a software agent treated as a legal person could 'enter into contracts in its own name and acquire its own rights and duties'.[51] Chopra and White outline the potential advantages of this approach: it could clarify questions of consent by locating it in the artificial agent, delineate liability when the agent acts outside its instructions, and provide third parties with a direct point of recourse. Yet they also acknowledge that such a shift would constitute a major legal transformation extending beyond contract formation.[52]

Other authors have adopted more cautious positions. Teubner and Becker argue that conferring full legal personality on software agents would be excessive, as these systems lack self-interest and operate within human–machine associations.[53] Andrade and others have explored analogies with corporate personality, noting

[46] See LB Solum, 'Legal Personhood for Artificial Intelligences' (1992) 70 *North Carolina Law Review* 1231, 1231–87; CEA Karnow, 'The Encrypted Self: Fleshing out the Rights of Electronic Personalities' (1994) 13 *The John Marshall Journal of Computer & Information Law* 1, 1–16.

[47] Allen and Widdison (n 5) 52.

[48] European Parliament resolution of 20 October 2020 with recommendations to the Commission on a civil liability regime for artificial intelligence (2020/2014(INL)) OJ C404/107.

[49] European Parliament resolution of 16 February 2017 with recommendations to the Commission on Civil Law Rules on Robotics (2015/2103 (INL)) OJ C252/239 [59f].

[50] See, eg, G Sartor, *Contracts Without Agreement, or Agreement by Artefacts?* (Academy of Sciences in Göttingen ed, Universitätsverlag Göttingen, 2020) 41, 41–46; G Sartor, 'Cognitive Automata and the Law: Electronic Contracting and the Intentionality of Software Agents' (n 40) 253–290; C Novelli, G Bongiovanni and G Sartor, 'A Conceptual Framework for Legal Personality and Its Application to AI' (2022) 13 *Jurisprudence* 194, 194–219.

[51] Sartor, 'Cognitive Automata and the Law: Electronic Contracting and the Intentionality of Software Agents' (n 40) 282.

[52] Chopra and White (n 14) 378–79.

[53] Beckers and Teubner (n 33) 8–12.

that the law already recognises non-human actors.[54] They suggest that unpredictability in autonomous systems makes the mere tools perspective less tenable,[55] but they also identify significant remaining obstacles, including problems of identification, accountability, and enforceability. Turner's analysis likewise highlights both the pragmatic attractions of legal personality – such as filling responsibility gaps and facilitating innovation – and its risks, including the so-called android fallacy, the potential for liability evasion, and the absence of assets to satisfy obligations.[56]

While the attribution of legal personality to autonomous systems remains a matter of normative choice, it would constitute a disproportionate response to the issue of attributing decision-making responsibility to contracting parties utilising such algorithms during the contract formation phase. For present purposes, the question is whether legal personality provides a workable basis for attributing knowledge of contract formation and content to the human party. None of the proposals surveyed explains how the system's knowledge becomes legally imputable to the operator at the moment of formation. A more pragmatic and context-specific framework, grounded in the contractual relationship between the operator and the system, offers a more coherent path for addressing the proxy issue.

## E. Mistake as a Stress-Test of Proxy Theories

The limits of existing proxy theories become particularly visible when they are tested against the doctrine of unilateral mistake. Courts in English and Commonwealth traditions have long recognised that outward appearance is not always conclusive: a contract may be set aside where one party labours under a fundamental error and the other has, or ought to have had, knowledge of that error. Yet algorithmic contracting compresses the temporal, cognitive and informational structures on which the doctrine depends, exposing weaknesses in the mere tools, agency and personality perspectives. The point is not that algorithmic contracting makes consent impossible, but that unilateral mistake is a poor doctrinal vehicle for reconstructing consent once formation and informational uptake occur at system level rather than through contemporaneous human cognition.

A first difficulty arises from the mere tools approach. If an algorithm is treated as nothing more than a machine executing prior instructions, the legally relevant knowledge is located exclusively in the mind of the programmer or operator. This reasoning is central to *Quoine Pte Ltd v B2C2 Ltd*, where the trading algorithms were characterised as 'mere machines' and the court held that any inquiry into

[54] Andrade et al (n 21). In addition to the contractual perspective, the relationship between autonomous algorithmic systems and corporations has been analysed from the perspective of these entities operating without human control, with a focus on attaining a liability framework akin to that applicable to corporations. See LM Lopucki, 'Algorithmic Entities' (2018) 95 *Washington University Law Review* 887, 887.

[55] Andrade et al (n 21) 360–61.

[56] J Turner, *Robot Rules: Regulating Artificial Intelligence* (Palgrave Macmillan, 2019).

knowledge must be anchored in the mental state of the programmers at the time of programming (both in the High Court and on appeal).[57] On this view, the doctrine becomes almost inapplicable in automated environments: if knowledge is fixed at the moment of programming, there is no doctrinal space for recognising a mistake that only becomes apparent at the moment of algorithmic execution, particularly where the system's behaviour reflects subsequent machine-learning evolution rather than the programmer's original instructions.

Paterson and Bant draw a similar conclusion in their discussion of 'automated mistakes'. They show that unilateral mistake is extremely narrow in the context of algorithmic contracts because the law situates the relevant knowledge at the human or corporate level, not in the functioning of the system itself. Software or coding errors – such as the mispricing event in *Quoine* – are treated as inherent risks of algorithmic contracting, analogous to mistakes as to quality or value, which ordinarily fall outside the scope of the doctrine of mistake and are to be managed through contractual allocation of risk rather than rescission.[58] Their analysis suggests that unilateral mistake becomes exceedingly narrow once the operative communicative act occurs at system level and the operator has no contemporaneous awareness of the transaction.

Oliver's examination of algorithmic contracting highlights an additional asymmetry. Because an AI system's internal 'awareness' is legally irrelevant, a party deploying such a system cannot be said to know of a counterparty's mistake, even where the system identifies and exploits that mistake.[59] This results in a structural imbalance between algorithmic and human traders. To address this, Oliver proposes an 'open-offer' model under which an operator who authorises an algorithm to contract on whatever terms it generates is taken to have assumed the risk of the system's pricing or execution behaviour.[60] While this approach simplifies risk allocation, it further illustrates the difficulty of accommodating the doctrine of mistake within proxy theories that deny legal significance to system-level knowledge. Such risk-allocation moves may be commercially expedient, but they are analytically downstream from – rather than answers to – the prior question of attribution: on what basis can the system's exploitation or detection of error count as the deploying party's legally relevant knowledge for consent-sensitive doctrine?

Agency-based approaches do not resolve the problem. If an algorithm were treated as an agent, the doctrine would require an inquiry into whether the *algorithm* knew or ought to have known of the counterparty's error. As Oliver notes, this would compel courts to attribute cognitive states to systems, a task that is

[57] *Quoine Pte Ltd v B2C2 Ltd* [2019] SGHC(I) 02; [2020] SGCA(I) 02, especially the discussion of algorithms as 'mere machines' and the reference to the programmers' state of mind.

[58] JM Paterson and E Bant, 'Automated Mistakes: Vitiated Consent and State of Mind Culpability in Algorithmic Contracting' in E Bant (ed), *The Culpable Corporate Mind* (Hart Publishing, 2023) 260–65.

[59] M Oliver, 'Contracting by Artificial Intelligence: Open Offers, Unilateral Mistakes, and Why Algorithms Are Not Agents' (2021) 2 *Australian National University Journal of Law and Technology* 45, 83.

[60] ibid 83–87.

conceptually incoherent and practically unworkable.[61] Rejecting the analogy, however, returns the analysis to the mere-tools position, where the doctrine becomes functionally redundant. The agency framework therefore oscillates between importing cognitive concepts that algorithms cannot satisfy and collapsing back into an approach that eliminates the doctrine's operative space.

Personality theories do not resolve the problem either. Even if a system were granted limited legal personality, the doctrine would still require identification of the entity whose knowledge renders the mistake operative. The analysis of legal personality for software agents shows how contested even basic questions of identification, attribution and liability would be, without offering a workable account of how system-level information becomes legally attributable to a contracting party.[62] As Loke's discussion of *Quoine* in the context of algorithmic trading of cryptocurrencies highlights, the central difficulty is that algorithmic trades are concluded without the traders' minds being 'engaged at the moment the contract was formed'; the doctrinal requirement of knowledge sits uneasily with such a setting.[63]

Recent work has sought to refine the doctrinal landscape. Frattone distinguishes between *automation mistakes* – errors arising within programmed parameters – and *autonomy mistakes*, which occur when an algorithm's behaviour evolves through machine learning beyond what the programmer could reasonably foresee.[64] Traditional doctrine can, in principle, address automation mistakes because the relevant behaviour remains traceable to prior human instruction. Autonomy mistakes, by contrast, expose the core problem identified above: if the law requires a human state of mind, and that state of mind cannot meaningfully be said to encompass the system's evolved behaviour, the doctrine lacks a point of doctrinal attachment, leaving autonomy mistakes conceptually unaddressed. The distinction thus reinforces the inadequacy of proxy theories that locate all knowledge either at the programming stage or within the human operator.

Taken together, these analyses confirm that the doctrine of mistake functions as a revealing stress-test of the proxy theories examined in this chapter. The mere-tools approach collapses the doctrine by attributing all knowledge to programmers; the agency model requires cognitive capacities that algorithms do not possess; and personality theories do not offer a workable mechanism for translating system-level information into legally relevant knowledge of a contracting party. The treatment of mistake in algorithmic contracting therefore underscores the need for a more coherent account of knowledge attribution – an account capable of explaining how legally relevant knowledge can arise in an environment where human minds are not present at the moment of formation.

[61] ibid 55–58.

[62] See, eg, S Chopra and LF White, *A Legal Theory for Autonomous Artificial Agents* (University of Michigan Press, 2011); and the critique discussed in Paterson and Bant (n 58) 267–68.

[63] A Loke, 'Mistakes in Algorithmic Trading of Cryptocurrencies' (2020) 83 *Modern Law Review* 1343.

[64] C Frattone, 'Algorithmic Mistakes in Machine-Made Contracts: The Legal Consequences of Errors in Automated Contract Formation' (2023) 28 *Uniform Law Review* 407.

## III. Case Law Illustrating the Knowledge Problem

Contract doctrine has long accommodated contracting in which one party does not possess contemporaneous knowledge of all terms or does not directly perform the operative act of formation. The cases considered in this section illustrate how courts locate the legally relevant knowledge in such settings, and how doctrines concerned with defective consent – particularly mistake and bindingness despite ignorance – operate where contractual formation is mediated by machines or pre-programmed processes. These precedents do not resolve the algorithmic contracting problem, but they clarify the doctrinal pressures created when contractual content is generated and executed at system level.

According to Lord Justice Denning MR's ruling, in *Thornton v Shoe Lane Parking Ltd*, in which the central dispute revolved around the formation of a contract and the validity of an exclusion clause, it was determined that the contract was finalised when Thornton made the payment at the ticket machine upon entering the car park.[65] The case is sometimes invoked as an early illustration of contracting mediated by machines.[66] Its factual setting is, however, materially different from algorithmic contracting: the terms embedded in the machine were fixed and limited, and the counterparty was determined simply by a user's decision to enter the facility.

The more instructive aspect of *Thornton* for present purposes lies in Willmer LJ's observations on the effect of machine-mediated formation on the user's ability to withhold consent. He contrasted a transaction conducted through a human ticket agent – where the customer can, at least in principle, refuse the terms once they are disclosed – with the process of contracting through a machine, which he characterised as effectively irrevocable once the mechanism is engaged.[67] That feature anticipates a central difficulty in algorithmic contracting: irrevocability arises promptly upon the execution by the algorithm of pre-programmed instructions and the realisation of the intended outcome.

*Carlill v Carbolic Smoke Ball Co* establishes that an offer may be addressed to an indeterminate class rather than to a specific offeree, with contractual formation occurring upon performance by any person who satisfies the stated conditions.[68] That principle provides a limited but instructive analogy for algorithmic contracting. While some algorithmic systems may be deployed to transact with identified counterparties, many are designed to locate and contract with any party meeting predefined criteria. In such cases, the system's deployment and parameterisation can be understood as a standing offer addressed to the public at large.[69]

[65] *Thornton v Shoe Lane Parking Ltd* [1971] 2 QB 163, 169.

[66] See, eg, N Liu, 'The "Contracting Problem" Revisited: Explaining the Formation of Algorithmic Contracts under the Common Law' in Z Slakoper and I Tot (eds), *Digital Technologies and the Law of Obligations* (Routledge, 2022) 133, 143. See also Oliver (n 59) 63.

[67] *Thornton* (n 65) at 174.

[68] *Carlill v Carbolic Smoke Ball Co Ltd* [1893] 1 QB 256.

[69] See, eg, Oliver (n 59) 83–86.

A significant distinction nonetheless remains. In *Thornton*, the user actively chose to enter into the contractual relationship by engaging the machine. In algorithmic contracting, by contrast, the identification of the counterparty may itself be delegated to the system where the operator chooses to rely on the system for that purpose. Although both settings involve offers addressed to an indefinite class akin to the precedent set by *Carlill*, the mechanism by which the contracting party is selected differs materially. That distinction does not undermine formation, but it underscores the extent to which consent and knowledge are mediated through pre-authorised system behaviour rather than contemporaneous human choice.

*L'Estrange v F Graucob Ltd* illustrates the extent to which English contract law may hold a party bound by terms of which they had no actual knowledge at the moment of contracting. Where a party signs a contractual document, they are ordinarily bound by its terms, even if they have not read them, and an exclusion clause may take effect notwithstanding ignorance of its content.[70] The case is relevant here not because it concerns automated contracting, but because it demonstrates that contemporaneous understanding of all terms is not a general condition of contractual validity.

The analogy has limits. *L'Estrange* rests on signature as a clear external manifestation of assent. In algorithmic contracting, by contrast, the operative terms may be generated and executed at system level without any comparable moment of human review. The case therefore does not resolve the knowledge problem, but it confirms that the difficulty in algorithmic contracting lies not simply in ignorance of detailed terms, but in attributing to the operator legally relevant knowledge of system-generated content at the point of formation.

*Software Solutions* concerned VAT, but the court's observations on contract formation are instructive for present purposes. The system enabled brokers to input risk data and generate quotes from participating insurers without the insurers being consulted at the point of quotation.[71] The court accepted that, in that setting, 'the "offer" is automatically generated by the program itself without further human intervention'.[72]

The case therefore provides a closer analogy than signature-based authorities because it involves an offer generated by software rather than drafted and communicated directly by a human. Its relevance is also bounded. The broker, acting for the insurer, is able to view the software-generated terms before presenting them to the counterparty. In algorithmic contracting, by contrast, contractual terms may be generated and executed at system level without any human intermediary acquiring contemporaneous knowledge of their content at the moment of formation. The case thus illustrates judicial willingness to treat system-generated offers as capable of forming contracts, while leaving open the harder question addressed

[70] *L'Estrange v E. Graucob Ltd* [1934] 2 KB 394.

[71] *Software Solutions Partners Ltd, R (on the application of) v HM Customs & Excise* [2007] EWHC 971 (Admin).

[72] ibid at 20.

in this chapter: how legally relevant knowledge of the resulting terms is attributed to the operator where no intermediary scrutiny is available.

Hence, this case goes beyond *L'Estrange* v *Graucob*, as it specifically addresses an offer determined by software, thereby drawing a closer parallel to the issue of algorithmic contracts.

In *United Dominions Trust Ltd v Western*, the defendant signed a blank form in the expectation that the seller would insert the agreed figures. The completed document, relied upon by the finance company, contained terms that differed from what the defendant believed had been agreed; although the discrepancy was apparent, it was not immediately challenged.[73] This case established that a contract can be deemed legally binding even if certain aspects or items are left to be finalised by a third party who holds no agency or representative capacity on behalf of the contracting party. Moreover, it set the precedent for a party to be liable, even if the contract has been completed in a manner different from that intended by that party.

There are two ways in which this is relevant to algorithmic contracts. First, it demonstrates that data filled in by a third party devoid of agency or representative capacity can still be binding. Second, it concerns a scenario where one of the contracting parties lacks precise knowledge of the exact terms of the contract at the time of its formation. There are also two key differences with the case of algorithmic contracts. In the latter, there is no direct human involvement, with a tool being used instead. Second, and more importantly, even if there may be some uncertainty surrounding the final outcome, the tool consistently functions within the predefined parameters and objectives set by the human operator, who represents the contracting party. Consequently, given the rationale expounded in *Dominions Trust Ltd* v *Western*, there is a heightened justification for deeming the outcome binding upon the contracting party in the case of algorithmic contracts.

*Quoine Pte Ltd v B2C2 Ltd* arose from algorithmic trading on a cryptocurrency exchange. Following a system incident, trades were executed at an abnormally favourable rate for B2C2, and the platform operator later reversed them, contending that the transactions were void or voidable for unilateral mistake. The court of appeal, however, rejected unilateral mistake on the facts.[74] While the case does confirm as a threshold matter, that contracts formed between deterministic algorithms are valid and binding, this conclusion was reached only incidentally without sustained normative analysis. The dominant thrust of the case is rather on the applicability of the law of mistake to algorithmic context, and the deeper question of enforceability, particularly as regards non-deterministic machine learning systems, is left unresolved.

The court treated the algorithms as 'mere machines' and held that, where unilateral mistake is alleged, the relevant inquiry into knowledge must be anchored in the state of mind of the programmer at the time the relevant part of the software was written, rather than in any form of knowledge attributable to the system at

[73] *United Dominions Trust Ltd v Western* [1976] QB 513.
[74] *Quoine Pte Ltd v B2C2 Ltd* [2020] SGCA (I) 2.

the moment of execution.[75] The practical effect is that unilateral mistake becomes difficult to establish in automated environments: where contracting is delegated to software, the doctrine is constrained by the requirement of human knowledge at a point temporally remote from the transaction.

The scope of *Quoine* must nonetheless be kept in view.[76] The dispute arose within a platform-based trading structure, and the immediate contest was between the trader and the platform operator that reversed the transactions, rather than a bilateral dispute between the contracting counterparties themselves.[77] Moreover, the systems in issue operated by reference to pre-set rules, and the judgment did not engage with the additional attribution difficulties raised by adaptive or learning systems.[78] These qualifications do not detract from the case's significance for present purposes.[79] On the contrary, they underscore the doctrinal consequence identified above: once contractual performance and execution are delegated to software, the law of mistake localises knowledge in human actors at a temporally remote stage, thereby narrowing the circumstances in which defective consent can be established in automated contracting environments.

Taken together, the cases examined in this section demonstrate the capacity of contract law to accommodate machine-mediated contracting without abandoning its core structures. Courts have accepted that contracts may be formed through machines, that offers may be addressed to an open class of counterparties, and that binding obligations may arise notwithstanding the absence of contemporaneous human involvement or full knowledge of detailed terms. At the same time, these decisions reveal a consistent judicial tendency to anchor contractual validity and consent-based remedies in human acts of authorisation and control rather than in the operation of the systems themselves.

What the case law does not yet provide is a fully satisfactory account of how knowledge relevant to doctrines of defective consent – most notably unilateral mistake – is to be attributed where contractual terms are generated and executed at system level. In particular, the localisation of legally relevant knowledge in human actors at stages temporally removed from the transaction leaves uncertain the position where contractual outcomes are produced through processes that cannot be exhaustively specified in advance or fully traced to fixed prior instruction. The judicial treatment of machine-mediated contracting therefore confirms both the adaptability of existing doctrine and the persistence of a structural gap in relation to consent.

[75] ibid [209]–[211].

[76] For its frequent use as a reference point in discussions of contracting through automated systems, see Law Commission, *Smart Legal Contracts: Advice to Government* (Law Com No. 401, 2021); Liu (n 66) 144–46.

[77] *Quoine* (n 74) [32].

[78] ibid [15].

[79] In *Quoine* 'judges (…) struggled to identify both a person to whom knowledge could be attributed and a time at which it was appropriate to do so'. KFK Low and E Mik, 'Lost in Transmission: Unilateral Mistakes in Automated Contracts' (2020) 136 *Law Quarterly Review* 563, 566.

# IV. The Knowledge Dimension of the Proxy Issue: Attribution Under Objective Contract Theory

## A. Exploring Synergies: Objective Contract Theory and the Tools Account

The knowledge dimension of the proxy issue is best approached through the objective theory of contract. On this view, questions of intention, knowledge, and belief are addressed through outward manifestations rather than any inquiry into inner mental states.[80] This provides a doctrinal basis for attributing contractual consequences to the operator who deploys an algorithmic system to contract on their behalf.

At the same time, the mere tools perspective, taken in its simplest form, is an incomplete attribution rule: it identifies the human source of the system's acts but does not explain how knowledge of the existence and content of system-generated agreements becomes legally attributable to that person at the moment of formation.[81] Recent attempts to refine the tools account point in the right direction. Ooi seeks to accommodate algorithmic contracting by extending objective theory through a notion of prior intention to be bound, and Liu develops a related model through the idea of the 'refurbished vending machine'.[82] Their analyses, however, do not supply a complete doctrinal basis for attribution, and they leave unresolved questions, in particular on the acceptance side and in scenarios where system outputs cannot be exhaustively specified in advance.[83]

The remainder of this section therefore proceeds in two steps. IV.B defines the proxy issue in its knowledge dimension and distinguishes it from the decision-making function of the system. IV.C then develops the doctrinal basis on which knowledge generated and received at system level may be attributed to the operator under objective contract principles.

## B. Unpacking the Proxy Issue

The proxy issue concerns attribution. It is the problem of attributing to the operator of an algorithmic system knowledge of: (i) the conclusion of an agreement; and (ii) the content of the terms generated and executed through that system. For analytical clarity, two connected but distinct functions must be separated. The first is the system's role in generating contractual content through

[80] Chopra and White (n 62) 76.

[81] See, eg, 'In other words, the courts would hold that the human trader's generalized and indirect intention to be bound by computer-generated agreements is sufficient to render the agreements legally binding.' Allan and Widdison in Chopra and White (n 14) 34.

[82] See Ooi (n 26) 109–12; Liu (n 66) 143–52.

[83] See Ooi (n 26) 111; Liu (n 66) 153.

a decision-making process. The second is the attribution of knowledge of the resulting offer, acceptance, and terms to the human party who deploys the system. Algorithmic contracting concentrates both functions within the system, which is why existing doctrinal analogies tend to address one while leaving the other under-explained.

This can be seen in recent efforts to refine the tools account. Ooi distinguishes between passive mechanisms, operating as communication devices, and active mechanisms, where the user lacks contemporaneous knowledge of the terms and must instead be taken to have authorised the system in advance.[84] Liu similarly divides the problem between the offer and acceptance perspectives, but the attribution of knowledge remains particularly difficult on the acceptance side, where the contractual content may not be accessible to either party at the moment of formation.[85]

The remainder of this section concentrates on the second function. The question is not how the system generates contractual terms, but how the knowledge embodied in the system's formation acts and outputs can be attributed to the operator within an objective framework of contract formation.

## C. How to Attribute System-Level Knowledge to the Contracting Party

The knowledge dimension of the proxy issue is not resolved by asking whether the operator subjectively understood the system's output at the moment of contract formation. Objective contract doctrine does not require contemporaneous reflective understanding. The question is whether the information constituting the offer, acceptance, and resulting terms lies within the operator's domain, so that knowledge of it is attributable to the operator for the purposes of contract formation and consent-based doctrines.

Two clarifications are important at the outset. First, 'knowledge' in this context concerns two targets. It concerns knowledge of the *fact* of formation (that an offer has been accepted and obligations have crystallised) and knowledge of the *content* of the resulting terms. Second, the proxy issue arises most sharply in automated contracting because these two forms of knowledge are generated and recorded at system level, often before either human party has reviewed the specific outcome.

The doctrinal basis for attribution begins with a distinction between the functions that algorithmic systems may perform. One is the generation of contractual content through a decision-making process. The other is the attribution of knowledge of the resulting offer, acceptance, and terms to the party who deploys the system. These functions may coincide, but they need not. *Software Solutions*

[84] Ooi (n 26) 111.
[85] Liu (n 66) 143–53.

illustrates the separation: the software generates the 'offer' automatically, yet the broker has access to the offer and its content on behalf of the insurer before it is presented to the insured.[86] The proxy issue is therefore not triggered merely by software-generated content. It is triggered where contractual content is generated and executed through interacting systems without any human intermediary having contemporaneous access to the terms.

Within an objective framework, 'knowledge' operates as attribution of information rather than reflective understanding. As Chopra and White put it, 'the knowledge and belief of an entity are revealed not via an examination of its "inner" mental states but rather by a set of visible manifestations of behaviors and attitudes'.[87] The relevant inquiry is therefore not whether the system knows' in a human sense, but whether it reliably acquires and uses information in the ordinary course of its operation to execute its designated purpose.[88] In this sense they could be equated with corporations.[89] Furthermore, such knowledge acquisition is not accidental but rather the outcome of reliable procedures during the normal course of operation of these systems.[90] The purpose of the system is to gather information through parametrised processes and, therefore, the acquisition of knowledge by the system takes place according to rules with the aim of achieving an overarching goal.

The ability of the system to access information and use it effectively in order to fulfil its purpose is determined by the programming of the algorithm, and this supports the point made in the preceding chapter: a contract is effectively established in these cases when the two algorithms converge, accessing and utilising data in a manner akin to the bargaining process observed in face-to-face contracting.[91] It is at this particular moment that the information becomes accessible to the algorithm, which it then utilises to initiate the contractual agreement. Simultaneously, the algorithm verifies whether the information has been transmitted to the other system, providing further justification to conclude that the contract has been formed at that stage.

The expression of consent to an agreement requires knowledge of its content. As already outlined above, in the field of algorithmic contracts, the possession of such an understanding regarding the content of the agreement during the process of contract formation lies primarily with the algorithm itself, and not with the contracting party using it. It is therefore important to know what is meant by 'knowledge' in this context. The knowledge possessed by an algorithm is to be understood as information and not 'a reflective understanding of the proposition in question'.[92] The manner in which the system acquires such knowledge

[86] See comments on *Software Solutions*, above section III, nn 71–72.
[87] Chopra and White (n 62) 76.
[88] ibid 76–77.
[89] ibid 81.
[90] ibid 77.
[91] See ch 5, section IV.
[92] Chopra and White (n 62) 79.

pertains to the realm of the second role of the algorithmic system, namely the decision-making process. This pertains to the internal state of the algorithm.[93]

The case law shows that a party may be bound notwithstanding incomplete knowledge of the detailed terms at the point of acceptance, and that contractual consent may rest on a reasonable appearance of assent rather than subjective understanding.[94] Therefore, the next questions to answer are: what specific knowledge is being addressed when examining the function attributed to the intelligent system in relation to the proxy issue? What do we mean by knowledge? How do we define and conceptualise the term 'knowledge' in this context?

It is accurate to acknowledge that within algorithmic contracts, knowledge can refer not only to knowledge of the content (inner state), but particularly knowledge of the fact of the confluence of the offer and the acceptance. This line of reasoning suggests that the term 'knowledge' pertains more specifically to the awareness of the acceptance of a given proposition, the moment in which the contract becomes binding for both parties. The rationale behind the postal rule can be invoked to substantiate this assertion.[95] Some authors argue on the basis of commercial convenience, on the grounds that the offeror can always demand true notification of acceptance, limit the possibilities of revocation, and finally, because it is easier for the offeror to detect the non-receipt of the acceptance of the offer.[96] Moreover, an additional rationale for this perspective lies in the notion that it is deemed sufficient for the acceptance to have entered the domain of the addressee, even if it has not been attended to.[97] Hence, the use of the dispatch or receipt rule is determined by the possibility of monitoring the success of the communication process[98] and these arguments collectively focus on the acknowledgement of acceptance, specifically where acceptance has taken place, which pertains to the realm of inner states.

The examination of the evolution of the postal rule also provides insights into addressing the final question that was posed earlier: how do we ascribe the knowledge attributed to the system onto the operator? In *Brinkibon Ltd v Stahag Stahl G.m.b.h.*, Lord Fraser of Tullybelton explained that 'once the message has been received on the offeror's telex machine, it is not unreasonable to treat it as delivered to the principal offeror, because it is his responsibility to arrange for prompt

[93] Giovanni Sartor has made noteworthy contributions regarding the issue of attributing cognitive states to artificial intelligent systems. See Sartor, 'Cognitive Automata and the Law: Electronic Contracting and the Intentionality of Software Agents' (n 40) 253–90. Here, the present chapter solely acknowledges the inner state in contrast to the system's externalisation of knowledge, without explicitly acknowledging the system's intentional stance. However, it is important to note that this matter will be further examined and deliberated upon in the subsequent chapter when analysing the decision-making process.

[94] See comments on *L'Estrange v E. Graucob Ltd* above, section III.

[95] For a more exhaustive analysis of the evolution of the postal rule, see section III.A in chapter 5.

[96] Andrew, Beatson and Cartwright (n 36) 50–51.

[97] *Brinkibon Ltd v Stahag Stahl und Stahlwarenhandelsgesellschaft mbH* [1983] 2 AC 34, 42; *Entores v Miles Far East Corporation* [1955] 2 QB 327, 331.

[98] Andrew, Beatson and Cartwright (n 36) 34.

handling of messages within his own office'.[99] On that reasoning, where an operator adopts an algorithmic system as the mode of contracting, outputs and records that enter the system (and are retrievable from it) fall within the operator's sphere in a way analogous to messages received within an office.

At this point, it is necessary to distinguish between epistemic access and normative attribution. The operator's ability to retrieve system outputs and records bears on access to information; the further question is the doctrinal basis on which contract law attributes that information – and its consequences – to the operator because the system was adopted to contract on the operator's behalf.

The same perspective reinforces the objective dimension of consent. *Brinkibon* stresses that receipt-based rules operate where the exchanges are intended to be effectively instantaneous and fall within the parties' chosen mode of communication.[100] In objective contract theory, the operator's conduct in deploying a system as the contracting interface supplies the outward manifestation on which attribution rests.

## V. Conclusion: Knowledge Attribution as a Partial Resolution of the Proxy Issue

Algorithmic contracts have opened up a new dimension in the realm of contract formation. The systems used to form these contracts not only serve as a means of communication between parties but also have the decision-making process delegated to them. Based on the objective theory of contract, formation occurs at the point of convergence between the two interacting systems. The difficulty is that, at that point, the legally relevant information about formation and terms may exist only at system level.

A combined reading of the mere tools theory and the objective theory of contracts offers a limited but workable way of addressing this aspect of the proxy issue without recourse to agency or personality solutions. However, applying these theories to the proxy issue shows that the problem has two distinct facets: first, whether the system can be treated as holding the relevant knowledge; and second, how the system's outputs form and specify the contracting party's legal position, encompassing both the internal and external aspects of the agreement.

Interpreting knowledge, for these purposes, as information rather than reflective understanding provides a workable route through the proxy issue and reinforces the position developed in the preceding chapter. On this account, algorithmic contracts are formed at the point of convergence between interacting systems, regardless of whether the contracting parties have contemporaneous human awareness of that convergence. The mere possibility of accessing the

[99] *Brinkibon Ltd v Stahag Stahl und Stahlwarenhandelsgesellschaft mbH* [1983] 2 AC 34, 43.
[100] ibid 42.

information generated and recorded at system level is sufficient to locate both the moment of formation and the content of the agreement. What remains unresolved is the justificatory question: why that system-level information, once so accessible, should be attributed to the operator as legally relevant knowledge, together with its contractual consequences.

However, objective contract theory cannot resolve all the problems posed by algorithmic contracts. The other task delegated to algorithmic contracts, the specification of the terms of the agreement, and the attribution of knowledge of the meeting of the algorithms to humans require further analysis. These issues are linked to the other problem already specified in the previous chapter on algorithmic subjectivity, and they will be considered in the following chapter.

# 7

# Subjectivity in Algorithmic Contracts: Embracing the Human Element and the Meeting of the Minds

## I. Introduction

In algorithmic contracts, the algorithmic system plays a dual role: firstly, it converts the parameters set by one party, the operator, into an offer, and, secondly, it facilitates communication by conveying the other party's interest in it. These functions have both internal and external components. Internally, the decision-making process requires the human operator to define rules and objectives for the system, while externally, the system relies on external data to achieve the objectives that it has been set. The external component of the communication role requires the system to interact in a public environment with potential interested parties with reciprocal interests, and, internally, the system and operator must communicate with each other, a component which is crucial for knowledge attribution and therefore for consent. Together, these functions enable the 'meeting of the algorithms'.

Chapter six addressed formation and knowledge in this setting. The remaining difficulty is one of attribution. The shift from human-to-human bargaining to machine-to-machine interaction inserts a non-human proxy into the process, and the law remains structured around doctrines directed to human conduct.[1] The question is therefore how the decision-making output of the system is to be treated as the act of the party who deploys it.

Rather than treating algorithmic systems as autonomous agents or legal persons, the analysis proceeds on the basis that their outputs are attributable to the human operator. This chapter examines how subjectivity is preserved in algorithmic contracting despite the delegation of decision-making to software. It develops a theory of the 'meeting of the algorithms' that does not posit any form of algorithmic subjectivity. Instead, the framework operates through the legal attribution of algorithmic outputs to the human operator, allowing the traditional 'meeting of the minds' – as the sole locus of subjectivity – to be maintained.

[1] Y Bathaee, 'The Artificial Intelligence Black Box and the Failure of Intent and Causation' (2018) 31 *Harvard Journal of Law & Technology* 889, 890–91.

This chapter explains why the apparent 'meeting of the algorithms' does not displace the requirement of human assent and develops an attribution-based account of how system-level outcomes can be treated as the operator's contractual will.

## II. The Under-Explored 'Meeting of the Algorithms'

In algorithmic contracts, the decision-making process culminates with the 'meeting of the algorithms'. That system-level convergence can be sufficient for the objective account of formation: it identifies when the relevant outputs align and obligations crystallise. What is more often left implicit is how that account connects to the traditional requirement of a 'meeting of the minds', particularly once the analysis turns from formation to consent-sensitive doctrine.[2] The tension is familiar: the outward manifestations of agreement may be present, even where 'the direct operation of human choice is not'.[3]

The general rule is that the existence and content of an agreement are determined by the parties' objectively ascertained intention; algorithmic contracting tests that rule because the legally relevant acts are generated and executed at system level rather than by a human mind at the point of formation. The issue is therefore not whether the objective approach survives, but how it must be applied where the contracting party's contribution consists in deploying a system to decide and communicate on its behalf.

In this chapter, 'meeting of the minds' is used in two distinct senses that must be kept separate. Firstly, in English law's objective framework, it operates as doctrinal shorthand for agreement/assent, assessed by outward manifestations that can be generated through systems. Secondly, subjectivity matters only indirectly, as it re-enters through vitiating doctrines (mistake, misrepresentation, undue influence, unconscionability) that can defeat enforcement even where objective agreement is present. The task of attribution is to keep those doctrines coherent when execution is system-level: the system's outputs are treated as the operator's acts, while consent-defects are assessed by reference to the human parties' positions and what reliance is reasonable.

The 'meeting of the minds' is sometimes invoked merely to mark the point at which offer and acceptance converge, without any sustained attention to its subjective dimension.[4] The objective test has proven useful in identifying the existence of an agreement, but the true intention of the contracting parties and the presence of

[2] M Rizzi and N Skead, 'Algorithmic Contracts and the Equitable Doctrine of Undue Influence: Adapting Old Rules to a New Legal Landscape' (2020) 14 *Journal of Equity* 301, 312–13. See also A Beckers and G Teubner, *Three Liability Regimes for Artificial Intelligence. Algorithmic Actants, Hybrids, Crowds* (Hart Publishing, 2021).

[3] JC Dodd and JA Hernandez, 'Contracting in Cyberspace' (1998) 1 *Computer Law Review and Technology Journal*.

[4] A Rawls, 'Contract Formation in an Internet Age' [2009] *Columbia Science and Technology Law Review* 200, 217.

consent cannot be disregarded. Issues such as misrepresentation, unconscionability, and mistakes can still arise in algorithmic contracts.[5] Moreover, certain vices of consent may result from system malfunctions and can only be understood by examining the intentions, objectives, and expectations of the human party operating behind the system.[6]

Focusing solely on the appearance of the outcome from the perspective of a reasonable addressee, while disregarding the decision-making process, would amount to 'a *reductio ad absurdum* of the fundamental principle of *consensus ad idem* under contract law'.[7] English contract law itself resists such reductionism. Although the objective test remains the default, the courts have long accepted that it admits of qualification where the circumstances require closer scrutiny of the parties' actual understanding.[8] As Aikens J observed, in such cases the court may depart from a purely objective analysis and admit evidence that both parties subjectively intended to agree on particular terms.[9] The persistence of this subjective inquiry – most clearly in cases concerned with contract avoidance – confirms that subjectivity continues to play a necessary, if bounded, role within the law of contract.[10]

Classical accounts of consent already recognise the tension between subjective assent and the law's reliance on outward manifestations; modern contract doctrine resolves that tension by prioritising legally attributable appearances over inner states.[11] The 'meeting of the minds' is a requirement of subjective *consensus ad idem* – an actual agreement on the same terms.[12] The difficulty in algorithmic contracting is not the concept, but identifying where that assent is located when terms are generated at system level.

[5] A clear example of this, specifically in relation to misrepresentation, is the recent case *Moffatt v Air Canada*, 2024 BCCRT 149 (CanLII). As Perillo stated some argue that '[d]uress, fraud and mistake vitiated the will and contaminated the appearance of consent'. See JM Perillo, 'The Origins of the Objective Theory of Contract Formation and Interpretation' (2001) 69 *Fordham Law Review* 427, 459. For in-depth analysis of different contract defences in relation to contracts generated by software, code contracts or algorithmic contracts see, eg, Rizzi and Skead (n 2) 301–26; V Ooi, 'Contracts Formed by Software: An Approach Form the Law of Mistake' (2022) 2 *Journal of Business Law* 97, 97–117; A Savelyev, 'Contract Law 2.0: "Smart" Contracts As the Beginning of the End of Classic Contract Law' (2017) 26 *Information & Communication Technology Law* 116.

[6] C Poncibò, 'Remedies for Artificial Intelligence' in M Ebers, C Poncibò and M Zou (eds), *Contracting and Contract Law in the Age of Artificial Intelligence* (Hart Publishing, 2022) 201 205. Frattone distinguishes between *automation mistakes* – errors arising within programmed parameters – and *autonomy mistakes*, which occur when an algorithm's behaviour evolves through machine learning beyond what the programmer could reasonably foresee. See C Frattone, 'Algorithmic Mistakes in Machine-Made Contracts: The Legal Consequences of Errors in Automated Contract Formation' (2023) 28 *Uniform Law Review* 407.

[7] M Ebers, 'Artificial Intelligence, Contracting and Contract Law: An Introduction' in M Ebers, C Poncibò and M Zou (eds), *Contracting and Contract Law in the Age of Artificial Intelligence* (Hart Publishing, 2022) 19, 31.

[8] J Cartwright, *Contract Law* (Hart Publishing, 2016) 99.

[9] *Statoil ASA v Louis Dreyfus Energy Services LP* [2008] EWHC 2257 (Comm) at [87].

[10] Perillo (n 5) 467.

[11] B Nicholas, *An Introduction to Roman Law* (Oxford University Press, 2008) 175–76.

[12] D McLauchlan, 'Contract Formation and Subjective Intention' (2017) 34 *Journal of Contract Law* 41, 47.

As early as 2001, Ian Kerr foresaw the rise of intelligent systems that would depersonalise negotiation and identified a central difficulty for contract doctrine: how a meeting of the minds can be established where bargaining is delegated to software.[13] The essence of contractual doctrine lies in the mutual understanding between parties, generally referred to as the 'meeting of the minds' or *consensus ad idem*. This traditional concept places the emphasis on the subjective element of mutual assent, implying a convergence of intentions between contracting parties. Moreover, the meeting of the minds is not only a mutual agreement but also underscores the voluntary nature of contractual obligations,[14] highlighting the importance of parties entering into agreements of their own free will.

Any adequate account of algorithmic contracting must confront the subjectivity that contract law presupposes. The question is not merely whether contractual outcomes can be generated at system level, but whether the processes that generate them can be reconciled with the human elements of intention, assent, and voluntariness that underpin consent-based doctrines. If algorithms cannot themselves form intent or participate in a shared understanding, the analysis must explain where – if anywhere – subjective assent is located when contracting is mediated by machine-to-machine interaction. At the same time, reliance on algorithmic systems may reconfigure how human volition is expressed in practice, producing what may be described as 'technologically mediated subjectivity'.[15]

The shift from the 'meeting of the minds' to the 'meeting of the algorithms' brings the problem of consent into sharper relief. It may appear that 'the human element has apparently disappeared completely and is replaced by algorithms that interact with other algorithms';[16] but that disappearance is only apparent. For contract law, the point is that system-level convergence does not displace the human source of contractual commitment: the human mind remains central to the process, shaping outcomes by defining the system's ultimate goal.

The term 'meeting of the algorithms' describes a process in which outcomes, initially defined in broad terms by the parties operating algorithmic systems, undergo convergence. This convergence is achieved through the functioning of algorithms that parametrise, refine, and specify the outcomes based on an analysis of external data. The operator sets the overarching objective, guiding the

[13] IR Kerr, 'Ensuring the Success of Contract Formation in Agent-Mediated Electronic Commerce' (2001) 1 *Electronic Commerce Research* 183, 190.

[14] ibid.

[15] 'Technologically mediated subjectivity' refers to the idea that human experiences, actions, and identity are profoundly influenced and shaped by technology, which plays a fundamental role in mediating various aspects of human existence. The term implies that our interactions with technology go beyond mere tool usage; instead, technology is an integral part of our subjective experience, influencing how we perceive and engage with the world. P-P Verbeek, 'Subject to Technology: On Autonomic Computing and Human Autonomy' in M Hildebrandt and A Rouvroy (eds), *Law, Human Agency and Autonomic Computing: The Philosophy of Law Meets the Philosophy of Technology* (Taylor & Francis Group, 2011) 27, 27.

[16] MacKenzie and Lange in C Borch and A-C Lange, 'High-Frequency Trader Subjectivity: Emotional Attachment and Discipline in an Era of Algorithms' (2017) 15 *Socio-Economic Review* 283, 284.

algorithms to produce a more precise and tailored result suited to the specific circumstances. Ideally, the convergence of these algorithmic instructions should result in a perfect alignment of the parties' intentions, culminating in the formation of an irrevocable agreement.

Contract defences cannot be sidelined merely because execution occurs at system level. Even where no human is contemporaneously involved, algorithms operate within the boundaries of pre-programmed instructions and parameters, so the relevant human choices have not disappeared but have been displaced upstream. This underscores why the disappearance of the human element is not absolute. This remains applicable irrespective of whether the algorithms in question are deterministic or nondeterministic. Moreover, algorithmic operations cannot be equated with human mental processes,[17] underscoring the fundamental distinction between algorithmic mechanisms and human cognition.

The notions of subjective and objective standards should not be perceived as conflicting, but rather as interconnected and mutually reinforcing standards.[18] Faced with the subjectivity-objectivity dichotomy, two approaches emerge: advocating for a strictly objective perspective or developing rationales for a blended objective-subjective framework.[19] As Lerouge observes, 'the notion of assent appears to be the price we most pay to maintain the coherence of contract law'.[20] Subjectivity plays a critical role in defining the boundary that determines whether a contract exists.

Notably, within the structure of contractual doctrine, the objective theory of contract inherently incorporates a subjective dimension. In this context, the cognitive knowledge and mutual conviction of the contracting parties gain particular importance.[21] Moreover, the objective theory serves as a rule designed to address specific cases, situated within a broader framework whose fundamental organising principle is the actual mutual assent of the parties.[22] That is why contract doctrine continues to treat the parties' actual understanding as legally relevant in defined contexts – most clearly where vitiating factors such as mistake, misrepresentation, or undue influence are at issue. The objective test therefore operates as a rule of decision within a wider structure that continues to presuppose genuine consent.

The persistence of this subjective dimension does not entail a return to a psychological account of assent at the moment of formation. Rather, it reflects the structure of contract doctrine itself, which combines an objective test for

[17] G Teubner, 'Digitale Rechtssubjekte? Zum Privatrechtlichen Status Autonomer Softwareagenten / Digital Personhood? The Status of Autonomous Software Agents in Private Law' [2018] *Ancilla Iuris* 35, 48.

[18] See N Sage, 'Reconciling Contract Law's Objective and Subjective Standards' (2023) 86 *Modern Law Review* 1422, 1422–46.

[19] ibid 1422–23.

[20] J-F Lerouge, 'The Use of Electronic Agents Questioned Under Contractual Law: Suggested Solutions on a European and American Level' (1999) 18 *John Marshall Journal of Computer & Information Law* 403, 433.

[21] Ooi (n 5) 109.

[22] LM Solan, 'Contract as Agreement' (2007) 83 *Notre Dame Law Review* 353, 357.

the existence of agreement with a limited set of consent-sensitive doctrines that may defeat enforcement notwithstanding outward manifestations of assent. In that structure, subjectivity is not a freestanding requirement of formation, but a constraint that operates selectively and ex post, policing the legitimacy of reliance where enforcement would be inconsistent with the parties' position as properly understood. This dual structure – objective agreement qualified by targeted doctrines of vitiation – has long enabled contract law to accommodate mediated and technologically displaced forms of contracting without collapsing into an inquiry into inner mental states.

In algorithmic contracting, the continued relevance of such vitiating doctrines must be understood with care. The absence of contemporaneous human awareness of the terms at the moment of system-level formation does not, without more, constitute a mistake capable of vitiating consent. Where a party has authorised an algorithmic system to generate and conclude contracts within a defined space of objectives, parameters, and constraints, the system's outputs ordinarily fall within the scope of that authorisation and are attributable to the operator as manifestations of assent. Mistake doctrine therefore operates only residually, as a corrective in cases where the output cannot reasonably be treated as an implementation of the authorised decision-making process – most notably where the counterparty could not reasonably rely on the system's communication as expressing genuine assent. Properly confined in this way, mistake does not substitute for consent in algorithmic contracts but remains a limited safety valve that preserves coherence between system-level formation and party-level responsibility.

Having unpacked the proxy issue and previously addressed the question of knowledge, the remaining key question concerns how, from a contract law perspective, to account for the fact that in algorithmic contracts there is a 'substitution of the judgement of the human for the program output of the machine'.[23] Existing attempts to resolve this problem through the objective theory of contract are limited. The objective theory is concerned with the legal significance of manifested outcomes, not with the internal process by which those outcomes are generated.[24] As a result, it offers only a partial response to situations in which the determination of contractual terms is delegated to an algorithmic system.

This chapter examines the delegation of the decision-making process to algorithms, departing from agency theories and the attribution of legal personality to autonomous software – approaches that have been demonstrated to be unworkable. It turns instead to the 'meeting of the algorithms' and tests it against the classical framework of offer and acceptance. The analysis asks whether, and on what terms, algorithmic interactions can satisfy the agreement requirement and generate binding obligations within orthodox contract doctrine.

[23] LH Scholz, 'Algorithms and Contract Law' in W Barfield (ed), *The Cambridge Handbook of The Law of Algorithms* (Cambridge University Press, 2020) 141, 145.

[24] E Mik, 'AI in Negotiating and Entering into Contracts' in LA Di Matteo, C Poncibò and M Cannarsa (eds), *The Cambridge Handbook of Artificial Intelligence* (Cambridge University Press, 2022) 45, 50.

Building on that account of formation, the analysis turns to attribution: on what basis are the outcomes of delegated algorithmic decision-making treated as the acts of the operator? The discussion develops a parallel with the earlier argument on knowledge attribution and asks how far contract law can treat system-level outputs as legally attributable to the deploying party. The question, in its strongest form, is whether – and in what sense – the 'meeting of the algorithms' can satisfy the requirements normally captured by the 'meeting of the minds'.

# III. Analysing the Meeting of the Algorithms from an Offer and Acceptance Perspective

## A. Reassessing Offer and Acceptance in the Context of Algorithmic Contracts

From a traditional contract law perspective, '[t]o determine whether an agreement has actually been concluded, it is normally necessary to inquire whether in the negotiations which have taken place between the parties there has been a definite offer by one party, and an equally definite acceptance of that offer by the other'.[25] The normal analytical method used to verify the existence of such an agreement involves examining the concurrence of the offer and the acceptance. This method aligns closely with the objective theory of contract, as it aims to avoid a subjective assessment of what each party really intended subjectively. Instead, it adopts an objective analysis of the presented offer and the consequent acceptance. This approach steers clear of a more liberal approach and focuses on determining whether the parties, from an objective standpoint, have reached an agreement.[26]

This particular approach focuses on the chronological sequence of the contractual intentions expressed by the parties.[27] The justification for this temporal sequence lies in the fact that it facilitates the possibility of determining the place and time of the formation of the contract.[28] But the classical offer-acceptance approach had been challenged long before the emergence of algorithmic contracts. In the 1970s, Lord Denning voiced his dissent, attributing the approach's persistence to the inertia of textbook authors.[29] In a paradigm-shifting approach, he advocated for a more comprehensive view of the contracting process, challenging the

[25] A Burrows, J Cartwright and J Beatson, *Anson's Law of Contract* (Oxford University Press, 2020) 31–32.

[26] R Taylor and D Taylor, *Contract Law Directions* (Oxford University Press, 2023) 22.

[27] P Owsia, 'The Notion and Function of Offer and Acceptance Under French and English Law' (1992) 66(4) *Tulane Law Review* 871, 890.

[28] Atiyah in ibid 892.

[29] See *Port Sudan Cotton Co v Chettiar* [1977] Lloyd's Rep 5; *Gibson v Manchester City Council* [1978] 1 WLR 520 [523].

emphasis that the classical perspective places on sequential events.[30] The law's concern is not with preserving a sequence for its own sake, but with identifying whether the parties are legally committed on ascertainable terms. This perspective highlights the lack of genuine scrutiny concerning offer and acceptance in the traditional model and suggests that the courts should not focus on determining whether a contract exists.[31] Instead, the inquiry should centre on '[w]hat enforceable terms, if any, are there between the parties?'.[32]

Algorithmic contracting brings the limits of sequential analysis into view. Where software systems interact in synchronous, bidirectional exchanges, it may be artificial to insist on a clear temporal ordering of offer and acceptance. When algorithms interact, identifying a clear communication sequence becomes increasingly challenging. The interaction more closely resembles the category of contracting in which simultaneity is assumed – face-to-face or telephone dealings – where courts have accepted that an offer-and-acceptance analysis may be unhelpful.[33] In *Apple Corps v Apple Inc*, Mann J, drawing on Lord Diplock's approach in *Gibson v Manchester City Council*, treated offer and acceptance as an inappropriate frame for analysing the formation question in the circumstances.[34] The point is not that offer and acceptance cease to matter, but that the law can recognise agreement even where the conventional sequence is not readily observable. This reasoning is equally valid for algorithmic contracts, where simultaneity and mutual alignment often render the sequential framework impractical.

Still, some scholars have attempted to explain the phenomenon of algorithmic contracts through the lens of offer and acceptance. It has been argued that identifying an offer from the offeror's perspective is not particularly challenging, even if the party is unaware of the offer's existence or its terms. This perspective classifies such an offer as a unilateral offer, as it is not specifically directed to any identifiable offeree. To address challenges regarding unilateral offers, including issues of attribution and certainty of terms, reliance has been placed on the mere tools theory to resolve the attribution problem and on principles established in *United Dominions*, which support the binding nature of offers made by third parties.[35]

However, greater challenges arise when analysing the issue from the perspective of the offeree, particularly due to the requirement that the offeree must be aware of the specific offer to accept it. To address this, a proposal involves creating an acceptance sequence by enabling the offeror's software to interact with the relevant code containing the offer.[36] Yet, this would effectively result in a ratification process.

[30] *Port Sudan Cotton Co v Chettiar* [1977] Lloyd's Rep 5 [10].
[31] SJ Bayern, 'Offer and Acceptance in Modern Contract Law: A Needless Concept' (2015) 103 *California Law Review* 67, 74.
[32] ibid.
[33] ibid 75.
[34] *Apple Corps Limited v Apple Computer, Inc* [2004] EWHC 768 (Ch) [42].
[35] N Liu, 'The "Contracting Problem" Revisited: Explaining the Formation of Algorithmic Contracts under the Common Law' in Z Slakoper and I Tot (eds), *Digital Technologies and the Law of Obligations* (Routledge, 2022) 133, 146–47.
[36] ibid 147–52.

This approach reveals significant limitations, particularly in cases involving simultaneous communications where the notion of sequentiality is both illusory and unnecessary. This does not imply that the accepting party lacks knowledge of the offer. On the contrary, the accepting party possesses the same level of knowledge as they would in face-to-face negotiations. However, in algorithmic contracts, the system's knowledge must be attributed to the operator using the same legal fiction that attributes knowledge of the offer to the offeror.

Two distinct types of knowledge arise in algorithmic contracts: knowledge of the fact of the agreement and knowledge of the precise terms of the offer, both happening in the realm of the system at the contract formation stage. Each algorithmic system possesses knowledge of the agreement when the two algorithms meet, and this knowledge becomes accessible to each party within their respective systems, much like mail waiting in a mailbox.

The rapid proliferation of technologies capable of emulating face-to-face interactions has brought about an awareness that the classic paradigm of offer and acceptance needs to be reassessed.[37] In the field of algorithmic contracts, this conventional framework has become redundant. The dynamics of algorithmic decision-making and contract formation require a re-evaluation of established legal doctrines, and a new perspective will be provided in the coming pages.

## B. Reframing Offer and Acceptance for System-Level Convergence

Lord Denning has not been the only voice to question the conventional offer and acceptance paradigm. In a forward-looking article published in 1996, Tom Allen and Robin Widdison envisioned the prospect of autonomous software-generated agreements in times to come.[38] Their analysis introduced the concept of unilateral contracts in the context of such agreements, arguing that these offers are not addressed to a specific individual but to a general audience, akin to the principles established in *Carlill v Carbolic Smoke Ball Co*. They further implied that such an offer could become irrevocable where the system user commits in advance to be legally bound by transactions concluded by the software.[39] The point matters because it exposes a doctrinal ambiguity: an offer made to the public is not, without more, a unilateral contract; the classification turns on whether the offer is structured as a promise to be bound upon performance, and on what counts as 'performance' in a system-mediated exchange.

Building on Allen and Widdison, later commentary has treated the spread of mechanised contracting – from vending and ticket machines to online interfaces – as

[37] Rawls (n 4) 209.
[38] T Allen and R Widdison, 'Can Computers Make Contracts?' (1996) 9 *Harvard Journal of Law & Technology* 25, 25.
[39] ibid 49.

evidence that unilateral contracting has become routine.[40] Drawing on the validity of offers made to the general public, as established in *Carlill v. Carbolic Smoke Ball Co.*, this perspective classifies operations conducted through vending or ticket machines as unilateral contracts. These older mechanisms are equated with modern systems involved in contract formation, despite an absence of detailed analysis regarding the differences between them.[41] This view concludes that the recognition of a general intent to be bound by such agreements is historically rooted in common law.[42] While this analysis provides an interesting perspective, it appears to lack depth and accuracy.

The analysis appears superficial because the complexity of algorithmic contracts far surpasses that of vending machines or car park ticket dispensers. Data analysis and management play integral roles in these advanced contractual practices.[43] In algorithmic contracts, data analysis and management are integral to the contractual process, introducing a level of sophistication absent in older mechanisms. As previously discussed in the context of the proxy issue, there is significantly greater uncertainty in the provisions of the offer based on the instructions of the algorithm operator compared to parking fees determined algorithmically,[44] which are limited to calculations based on an hourly rate and the duration of stay. The latter system is deterministic, whereas algorithmic contracts often operate in a non-deterministic framework.[45] Moreover, in the case of the car park ticket machine, the identification of the contracting party, introducing an extra element of indeterminacy, is not contingent upon the predefined instructions of the algorithm, but rather on the volition of the individual selecting the parking facility. A comparable critique applies to vending machines, further emphasising the limitations of drawing parallels between such mechanisms and the complexities of algorithmic contracts.

The characterisation of these contracts as unilateral is also inaccurate. A unilateral contract is a type of contract in which one party makes a promise in exchange for a specific action or performance by another party. In unilateral contracts, one party is obligated to perform if the other party completes the specified action, with

[40] Ooi (n 5) 110. While Ooi speaks of 'contracts formed by software', these are one and the same with algorithmic contracts, as elucidated in the analysis contained in ch 2, section III.

[41] ibid 111.

[42] ibid 115.

[43] S Martinelli and C Rossi Chauvenet, 'From Document to Data: Revolution of Contract through Legal Technologies' in M Ebers, C Poncibò and M Zou (eds), *Contracting and Contract Law in the Age of Artificial Intelligence* (Hart Publishing, 2022) 81, 96.

[44] It is worth noting that not every algorithm is based on artificial intelligence. An algorithm is a step-by-step set of instructions in a formal language designed to accomplish a specific task or to solve a particular problem. While artificial intelligence algorithms leverage machine learning and non-deterministic approaches, algorithms in a broader sense can encompass deterministic and ruled-based procedures across various computational domains.

[45] Artificial intelligence systems, in their current conception, are non-deterministic due to their reliance on machine learning tools, departing from the if-then approach. Determinism is limited to the training phase of the systems, and non-determinism and stochasticity come into play when the algorithm operates in real-world scenarios. For this distinction see section IV.B.ii in ch 3.

the obligation being one-sided.[46] The contract is not formed until the action is completed.[47] The party making the promise is the offeror, and the party performing the action is the offeree. In contrast, a general offer, on the other hand, is an offer made to the public at large, often in the form of advertisements, circulars, or announcements. It is an offer that is intended to be open for acceptance by anyone who meets the stated conditions. Unlike unilateral contracts, general offers typically involve a promise in exchange for a promise (rather than a promise for an action). Despite drawing on Allen and Widdison's work, this analysis disregards their scepticism about the relevance of unilateral contract doctrine to contracts formed through autonomous software.[48] Characterising this contract type as unilateral is an attempt to move away from the conventional framework of offer and acceptance, but it lacks a genuine and substantive legal rationale.

Having outlined the reasons for refraining from categorising algorithmic contracts as unilateral agreements, it is more appropriate to consider them as bilateral contracts initiated by a general offer that is subsequently refined by the algorithm. A contract is bilateral because both parties are obligated to do something or refrain from doing something in the future when the contract is formed. This creates an ongoing responsibility for each party. Building on prior analysis, some interpretations diverge on the nature of these contracts. For instance, it has been argued that certain algorithmic contracts undergo a transition from being unilateral to bilateral in nature. This perspective suggests that while the initial stages of contract formation may resemble unilateral agreements, the evolving interaction between the algorithms results in bilateral obligations, redefining the nature of the agreement.[49] However, this characterisation is problematic. These contracts are not unilateral at any stage; they begin with a general offer directed at the public, which does not inherently make them unilateral.

In the limited body of case law addressing contracts generated by software,[50] such as *Quoine* or *Software Solutions*, or other cases referred to in these discussions, such as *Thornton*, there is no explicit categorisation of these contractual relations as unilateral in any way. Notably, while some scholars may argue for such a classification,[51] there is no explicit recognition of this in the judgements of these cases. The theory of unilateral contracts, though occasionally referenced, is not widely accepted as a valid framework for understanding the formation of

[46] Andrew, Cartwright and Beatson (n 25) 32.

[47] This is without prejudice to the fact that, once execution has begun, it becomes binding on the offeror. See *Dahlia v Four Millbank Nominees* [1978] Ch 231.

[48] Allen and Widdison (n 38) 49.

[49] Liu (n 35) 149.

[50] These contracts are not referred to here as algorithmic contracts deliberately because they depart from the narrow definition of algorithmic contracts employed in this work. An algorithmic contract is defined here as a contractual agreement wherein both involved parties engage in decision-making processes operating an algorithmic system rooted in artificial intelligence. See ch 1, section II.A.

[51] Kerr (n 13) 188. S Chopra and LF White, 'Artificial Agents and the Contracting Problem: A Solution via an Agency Analysis' (2009) 2009 *University of Illinois Journal of Law, Technology & Policy* 363, 372–74.

algorithmic contracts. This is due to the inability of certain mechanisms, such as vending machines, to alter the terms of an offer, as they lack the intelligence and autonomy inherent in software-generated contracts.[52] Similarly, systems such as websites or parking machines are seen as merely communicating pre-existing conditions rather than independently determining terms.[53]

Before applying the doctrine of unilateral contracts to the realm of algorithmic contracts, it is necessary to examine whether all contracts executed through mechanical or electronic means inherently exhibit a unilateral nature. This assumption is debatable. While contracts concluded through vending machines may align with the concept of unilateral contracts, others, such as those governing vehicle deposits in car parks or the contract between Quoine and B2C2, do not necessarily conform to this framework.[54] Several counterarguments substantiate this position. For instance, bilateral contracts involve two enforceable promises, allowing either party to breach the agreement, whereas unilateral contracts entail only one enforceable obligation.[55] Furthermore, a unilateral contract is characterised as a promise rather than a mutual agreement.[56] In the context of vending machine contracts specifically, the offer should be interpreted as a standing or firm offer rather than a mere promise. This distinction is crucial when analysing the nature of such agreements.

*Thornton* has been cited by some scholars as a case supporting the view that certain contracts, particularly those involving automated mechanisms, are unilateral in nature.[57] Although the primary issue in *Thornton v Shoe Lane Parking Ltd* concerns the inclusion of disclaimers in the contract, the case also serves as a precedent for situations where a machine acts in place of a human for one of the contracting parties. However, contrary to the claims of many scholars, the contractual relationship between Mr Thornton and Shoe Lane Parking Ltd is better understood as bilateral. This interpretation arises from the reciprocal obligations borne by both parties. Specifically, Mr Thornton is required to pay for the parking facility's use, while the car park owner is obligated to store the vehicle through mechanical means. These mutual obligations, each enforceable and subject to breach, align more closely with the characteristics of a bilateral contract.[58]

A similar conclusion can be drawn from an analysis of *Quoine* or *Software solutions*. In *Quoine*, B2C2 entered into an agreement with Quoine that enabled it to execute cryptocurrency transactions with various counterparties through Quoine's

[52] Kerr (n 13) 188.

[53] Chopra and White (n 51) 373.

[54] As noted above, *Thornton* is cited by Kerr, Chopra and White and Ooi in their analyses of the unilateral nature of machine- or software-driven contracts. See Chopra and White (n 51) 373. See also Ooi (n 5) 99.

[55] SJ Stoljar, 'The False Distinction between Bilateral and Unilateral Contracts' (1955) 64 *Yale Law Journal* 515, 516–17.

[56] T Cheong, 'A Promising Idea: Reconceptualising The Formation of Unilateral Contracts' (2014) *Oxford University Undergraduate Law Journal* 1.

[57] See Ooi (n 5) 99.

[58] Although the bilateral nature of the relation is not expressly stated, Lord Denning describes the obligations of each of the parties. See *Thornton* v *Shoe Lane Parking Ltd* [1971] 2 QB 163 at 167.

automated cryptocurrency trading platform.[59] Despite its nature as a contract of adhesion, the contractual relationship between Quoine and B2C2 is fundamentally bilateral, establishing mutual rights and obligations upon its formation. This classification remains valid even though there may be a temporal disjunction between the contract's formation and the subsequent execution of payment commissions or provision of services, as governed by the algorithm embedded within the platform. The bilateral nature of this relationship has significant implications for the parties, particularly in relation to the potential revocation of the offer.

However, the potential revocation of the offer functions differently in the context of algorithmic contracts. Specifically, algorithmic contracts can be likened to other telematic contracts, where 'the interval between sending and delivering is so short that the offer and acceptance are separated by a negligible fraction of time, thus making the revocation almost impossible'.[60]

In *Software Solutions*, although '[t]he premium calculated by SSP is a guaranteed price binding on the insurer',[61] it is essential to recognise that the contractual relationship between SSP and the insurer, as well as between the insurer and the client, remains bilateral. There are enforceable obligations for each party. The software company is obliged to provide the service of generating offers, while the insurance company is obliged to remunerate this service. Simultaneously, the insurance company is obliged to provide insurance cover to the customer, and the insured is obliged to pay the insurance premium determined by the automatically generated offer.

From the foregoing analysis, it becomes evident that unilateral contracts do not provide a suitable legal framework for understanding the establishment of algorithmic contracts. Instead, algorithmic contracts are more accurately characterised as bilateral agreements initiated by a general offer defined or specified by an algorithm. Transactions executed by machines often involve general or open offers,[62] because they are not made to a specific person, which is unquestionably compliant with English contract law.[63] Despite the fact that in *Carlill v Carbolic Smoke Ball Company* a general offer and a unilateral contract concur at the same time, not every unilateral contract contains an offer to the general public, nor does every general offer result in a unilateral contract. The distinction of these concepts, though occasionally blurred, is crucial. For example, an employer's promise of rewards or bonuses to a salesperson for achieving specific sales targets exemplifies a unilateral contract directed at a specific individual rather than a general audience.[64] In contrast, the scenario involving a car park is an example of a bilateral contract initiated by a general offer.

[59] *Quoine Pte Ltd v B2C2 Ltd* [2020] 2 SLR 20 at [1].

[60] AM Gambino and A Stazi, 'Contract Automation from Telematic Agreements to Smart Contracts Essays' (2021) 7 *The Italian Law Journal* 97, 103.

[61] *R (on the application of Software Solutions Partner Ltd) v Revenue and Customs Commissioners* [2007] EWHC 971 (Admin) at 16.

[62] Andrew, Cartwright and Beatson (n 25) 37.

[63] ibid 39.

[64] See, eg, *Attrill v Dresdner Kleinwort Ltd* [2013] EWCA Civ 394 in which an announcement of a bonus made by the CEO of Dresdner Bank at a townhall meeting was considered to be a unilateral contract.

A foundational principle in contract law asserts that two identical counteroffers do not result in the formation of a contract.[65] In the context of interactions between algorithms, this principle warrants reconsideration. When two algorithms interact, it can be argued that their actions constitute a process of intersecting offers within a digital framework. Rather than viewing this as a mere exchange of offers, it can be understood as the convergence of conflicting yet reciprocal interests. For instance, consider one party aiming to sell a product at a specific price per unit and another party intending to buy the same product at a similar price. The algorithms, pre-programmed to adjust prices to prevailing market conditions by accessing relevant data, facilitate the alignment of these interests. At the point where these interests converge, there is no definitive 'acceptance' of the other party's offer in the traditional sense of contract law. Consequently, no contract is formed under a strict interpretation of acceptance. This scenario aligns more closely with the concept of a cross-offer, wherein both parties simultaneously present offers without explicitly acknowledging or accepting the other's terms. Given this, the traditional view that cross-offers cannot result in a contract merits reexamination.

The absence of substantive grounds for the non-recognition of cross-offers as enforceable contracts is notable. The only authority cited in the scarce literature on the subject is *Tinn v Hoffman & Co*.[66] The need for prior communication of the offer for its subsequent acceptance is stated as a reason why two identical cross offers are not admissible as a method for the formation of a contract.[67] The lack of consideration in these agreements is also noted as a cause for concern.[68]

In *Tinn v Hoffman & Co*, the defendant, Mr Hoffman, wrote to the plaintiff, Mr Tinn, offering to sell him a specific quantity of iron at a certain price per tonne. On the same day, and without knowledge of this offer, Mr Tinn also wrote to Mr Hoffman, offering to buy the iron on similar terms. The court held no contract existed. The reason for finding the non-existence of an enforceable contract could be summarised in this argument of Justice Blackburn: '[in the case of a] promise or offer made on each side in ignorance of the promise or offer made on the other side, neither of them can be construed as an acceptance of the other'.[69] The underlying rationale for the non-enforceability of cross-offers primarily concerns the inherent risk associated with delays in communications. However, the simultaneity and immediacy of algorithmic contracts prevent such delays.

[65] See, eg, Andrew, Cartwright and Beatson (n 25) 41; E McKendrick, *Contract Law: Text, Cases and Materials* (Oxford University Press, 2022) 112; PS Davies, *JC Smith's The Law of Contract* (Oxford University Press, 2021) 26.

[66] *Tinn v Hoffman & Co.*, (1873) 29 LT 271.

[67] Andrew, Cartwright and Beatson (n 25) 41; McKendrick (n 65) 112.

[68] Bayern (n 31) 85. The consideration requirement is not being examined in this study: it is identified as a future avenue for research in ch 8.

[69] *Tinn v Hoffman & Co.*, (1873) 29 LT 271 [279].

*Apple Corps Ltd v Appel Computer Inc*[70] saw the revival of Lord Denning's revolutionary approach to avoid analysis from the perspective of offer and acceptance.[71] In this case, the ultimate conclusion reached concerned the potential for the contract to be formed in two places simultaneously,[72] but the judgment makes a point which is relevant for the reconsideration of the admissibility of cross offers. Justice Mann stated:

> The parties had, by a long process of negotiation, arrived at agreed forms of agreement which were not to be made binding until both parties indicated that they were. If both parties had met in order to sign and complete in the same place, it might well have been extremely difficult to find anything amounting to an offer and acceptance.[73]

For Justice Mann, simultaneous and reciprocal acceptance is possible. Following this statement, for algorithmic contracts, the solution may involve the fiction of considering that, as in *Apple*, there is reciprocal and simultaneous acceptance by both parties when the two algorithms meet. If the risk in cross offers concerns the risk of assent not reaching the knowledge of the other party, this does not occur in algorithmic contracts in which, as was shown in the previous chapter, knowledge can be assumed when this is in the system's possession.

Rather than referring to 'cross-offers', the term 'concurrent offers' more aptly describes those already determined by the algorithms. This terminology captures the unique nature of algorithmic interactions, where the traditional sequential model of offer and acceptance may not apply. In critiques of the offer-and-acceptance framework, it has been argued that contracts formed through simultaneous communication processes, such as face-to-face interactions, allow for assent to occur concurrently rather than sequentially.[74] This reasoning is equally applicable to algorithmic contracts, where interactions often mirror the dynamics of simultaneous, real-time exchanges.

In algorithmic transactions, communication between algorithms is synchronous, instantaneous, and bi-directional, and as such, assent is concurrent. Assent could also be said to be interrelated: in this sense, although in reference to the field of smart contracts, it has been suggested that a bilateral or multilateral contract could be approximated through the creation of two or more interrelated unilateral contracts.[75]

Applying Justice Mann's reasoning in the *Apple* case to algorithmic contracts, the concept of simultaneous and reciprocal acceptance becomes not only feasible but also practical. Consider the example of one party seeking to sell a product at a

[70] *Apple Corps Ltd v Apple Computer Inc* [2004] EWHC 768 (Ch).
[71] R Stone, 'Forming Contracts without Offer and Acceptance, Lord Denning and the Harmonisation of English Contract Law' (2012)(4) *Web Journal of Current Legal Issues* core.ac.uk/download/pdf/9553724.pdf accessed 2 May 2024.
[72] Although the place of formation of algorithmic contracts is not the subject of analysis in this thesis, the *Apple* case could serve as a starting point for an analysis of this issue.
[73] *Apple Corps Ltd v Apple Computer Inc* [2004] EWHC 768 (Ch) [42].
[74] Bayern (n 31) 81.
[75] K Werbach and N Cornell, 'Contracts Ex Machina' [2017] *Duke Law Journal* 343.

specific price per unit and another wishing to purchase it under similar conditions. The algorithms, having already adjusted the price through parametrisation and analysis of market data, engage in communication or interaction. In this scenario, we can employ the legal fiction that both offers are mutually and simultaneously accepted, as each is effectively brought to the knowledge of the other party at the same moment.[76] This interaction mirrors the dynamics of two individuals agreeing to a contract in person.

With algorithmic contracts, this reasoning brings the concept of contract formation full circle. The sequential analysis of offer and acceptance, developed to provide legal certainty in contexts lacking simultaneity and to mitigate risks arising from delays, becomes unnecessary in the algorithmic context. The instantaneous nature of algorithmic interactions eliminates the temporal gaps that necessitated sequential analysis, allowing for a more straightforward application of mutual assent.

The proposal advanced here is that algorithmic contracts should be understood as bilateral contracts, initiated by a general offer defined or specified by the algorithm in accordance with the instructions received (the parameters) and the market situation (the data); this offer becomes binding when it meets with another competing or interrelated offer, at which time there is a reciprocal acceptance of the offers or interests of both parties. This interaction constitutes the 'meeting of the algorithms'. But this 'meeting' represents a convergence of interests occurring at the systems level.

## IV. Attributing the 'Meeting of Algorithms' to the Operator's Assent

The previous chapters have unpacked the complexities arising from the proxy issue and provided a comprehensive legal argument to deal with these complexities from a contract law perspective. A key question remains: how is the parties' will embedded in the contract created by the algorithms? In other words, how can the decision-making processes performed by algorithms be attributed to their human operators? How can the meeting of the algorithms be reconciled with the meeting of the minds? 'The real problem, therefore, is that of mutual understanding between AI systems and the human contractual party so that the expectations of the latter correspond to the results of the contractual activity conducted by the machine.'[77]

Up to this point, the algorithmic system has acted as a means of communication between the parties. In this context, the bidirectionality and simultaneity

[76] In this regard, it is worth recalling the proposal made in the preceding chapter in that the knowledge of the agreement can be imputed to the operator of the algorithmic system from the moment access or control over it is presumed, applying the same rule established for emails.

[77] Poncibò (n 6) 205.

of communications undertaken to form a contract create a process analogous to face-to-face communications. The formation of the contract occurs at the moment when the algorithmic systems complete their operations. The challenge of attributing knowledge of the agreement, including its specific terms, to the operator has been addressed by adapting the rule of availability and accessibility of information for the system operator. This approach mirrors the principles developed for contracting via email, ensuring that operators are deemed aware of the agreement when the relevant information is available and accessible to them.

Moreover, regardless of the legal definitions of contract, a contract is nothing more than the shared intention of two parties to achieve a goal.[78] Shared intentionality, however, is a distinctly human capability.[79] AI systems lack the capacity to form intentions, including the intention to enter into a contract.

To address this final and definitive question, this section will examine both the system perspective and the operator perspective, aiming to identify solutions that bridge the gap between the algorithmic system and its human operator.

## A. Attribution as the Party's Act: Authorisation, Scope, and Goal-Constraint

This subsection adopts a system perspective on the enabling factors that connect the 'meeting of the algorithms' to the 'meeting of the minds'. The next subsection addresses the same question from the perspective of the human party to the contract.

How can the meeting of the algorithms be equated with the traditional meeting of the human minds? Bridging this gap is significant because, under the objective theory of contract, the focus remains on the manifestation of assent by a person rather than the electronic agent. When an individual uses an electronic agent for contract formation, their conduct is deemed to express assent. The relevant manifestation of assent is that of the person directing the agent, not the agent itself,[80] thus preserving the human-centric foundation of contractual obligations.

Ian Kerr's analysis of the use of software to automate e-commerce transactions provides an excellent starting point for an examination of this matter.[81] The first of the recommendations he makes for the success of what he calls 'contracting agents'

[78] J Linarelli, 'Artificial Intelligence and Contracts Formation: Back to Contract as Bargain?' (2023) *Emerging Issues at the Intersection of Commercial Law and Technologies* 14 ssrn.com/abstract=4363410 accessed 2 May 2024.

[79] J Linarelli, 'A Philosophy of Contract Law for Artificial Intelligence: Shared Intentionality' in M Ebers, C Poncibò and M Zou (eds), *Contracting and Contract Law in the Age of Artificial Intelligence* (Hart Publishing, 2022) 59, 77.

[80] EM Weitzenboeck, 'Electronic Agents and the Formation of Contracts' (2001) 9 *International Journal of Law and Information Technology* 204, 222.

[81] Kerr (n 13) 183–202.

in contract formation seems to conflict directly with this technology's characteristics: '[e]nsure that the electronic agent manifests the originator's assent'.[82] Is this possible? This raises the question: is such assurance possible? The answer likely resides in the inherent inflexibility of algorithms, which can serve as a mechanism to reliably express the operator's intention.

However, to date, the usual response to this question has been a negative one. It has been argued that formation theory raises doubts about whether algorithmic contracts are properly formed under the law,[83] primarily due to the challenges in affirming that black-box algorithmic systems can adequately express the consent of the party involved.[84] Nondeterministic algorithms, particularly those incorporating unsupervised machine learning, are often excluded from such analyses due to their inherent unpredictability.[85] Similarly, it has been suggested that the provision of valid consent becomes problematic when dealing with machine learning systems operating outside the framework of deterministic algorithms.[86] Some of those who argue for providing AI systems with legal personality speak of such systems' potential ability to 'pursue goals autonomously', albeit within the scope of the 'top-level goals' defined by the operator.[87]

The inflexibility of algorithms is, in fact, definitive: algorithms always act in conformity with the top-level goals defined by their operator. These goals represent the operator's consent. But can an algorithm truly adhere to the goals it has been programmed to achieve? The answer is 'yes', and this is due to the inherent nature of algorithms. Their inflexibility ensures that they embody the consent of their users. That inflexibility is the feature of algorithms that is the key to understanding their impact on contract formation, as it inherently reflects the operator's consent and intent.

Scholarly debate on this issue has primarily emphasised the complexities and risks associated with autonomous algorithmic systems while overlooking their fundamental inflexibility,[88] and it is this characteristic that can serve as the basis for the attribution of the algorithmic decision-making process to the operator. Yet in the field of contract automation, there is debate among authors

[82] ibid 197.

[83] LH Scholz, 'Algorithmic Contracts' [2017] *Stanford Technology Law Review* 128, 158.

[84] See, eg, ibid 128–69. Bathaee (n 1) 889.

[85] Liu (n 35) 135.

[86] M Ebers, 'Artificial Intelligence, Contracting and Contract Law: An Introduction' in M Ebers, C Poncibò and M Zou (eds), *Contracting and Contract Law in the Age of Artificial Intelligence* (Hart Publishing, 2022) 19, 30.

[87] C Novelli, G Bongiovanni and G Sartor, 'A Conceptual Framework for Legal Personality and Its Application to AI' (2022) 13 *Jurisprudence* 194, 198.

[88] For example, Lauren Scholz refers to the difficulty derived from the unpredictability of black-box algorithms, considering them unlikely to be enforceable. Scholz (n 83) 149–57; Teubner refers to liability gaps. See Teubner (n 17) 38–40; Vicent Ooi highlights the lack of a rule of attribution in the common law similar to that seen in the ECC or Directive 2000/31/EC. See Ooi (n 5) 15; Liu places the emphasis on the lack of knowledge of the offeree of the specific offer at the moment of the contract formation. See Liu (n 35) 147–52.

about the perceived inflexibility trade-off.[89] While some scholars argue that the rigidity of automated contracts creates limitations,[90] they also argue that this same inflexibility can be advantageous, bringing objectivity and predictability to the process.[91]

AI systems no longer merely execute pre-programmed instructions but arrive at dynamic solutions based on data patterns.[92] 'The revolution is the application of data analysis (…) in contracting practices.'[93] Regarding black-box algorithms, articulating the precise data patterns discerned by a machine-learning algorithm may pose challenges.[94] Nevertheless, the ultimate objective, top-level goal, top-goal,[95] or overarching goal,[96] remains inflexible. To put it another way, the fact that they are black-box algorithms is irrelevant: it may be impossible to know how an AI system that has absorbed massive amounts of data makes its decisions, but this does not mean that it departs from the purpose for which it was programmed. For example, if the objective of an AI system for stock trading is to maximise profit, this objective does not change even if one cannot get to know the decision-making process behind the system.[97] The fact that 'the way in which such top-goals are pursued by the agents – including the choice of lower-level instrumental goals – is responsive to the physical and social environment in which the agents act'[98] does not alter the top-level goal. Hence, that purpose, objective, end, or intention, still belongs to the sphere of the system operator, and, therefore, the outcomes generated by the algorithm are attributable to the operator. This attribution is grounded in the fact that critical decisions – such as selecting which algorithms to deploy, determining the feedback to provide, and deciding on the data used to train them – are, at present, entirely human choices.[99]

Learning algorithms are best understood as general templates with adjustable parameters. These parameters are fine-tuned by the algorithm itself based on a

[89] JM Sklaroff, 'Smart Contracts and the Cost of Inflexibility' (2017) 166 *University of Pennsylvania Law Review* 263, 263–303.

[90] Helen Eenmaa-Dimitrieva and Maria José Schmidt-Kessen, after citing Eliza Mik, state that '[c]oding of contracts precludes contractual parties to adopt clauses that allow for desirable and necessary flexibility that allow for adaptations of contracts to unforeseeable future scenarios'. See H Eenmaa-Dimitrieva and MJ Schmidt-Kessen, 'Creating Markets in No-Trust Environments: The Law and Economics of Smart Contracts' (2019) 35 *The Computer Law and Security Report* 69, 75.

[91] M Schmidt-Kessen, H Eenmaa and M Mitre, 'Machines That Make and Keep Promises – Lessons for Contract Automation from Algorithmic Trading on Financial Markets' (2022) 46 *Computer Law & Security Review* 105717, 105717.

[92] Bathaee (n 1) 891.

[93] Martinelli and Rossi (n 43) 76.

[94] T Bucher, *If… Then: Algorithmic Power and Politics* (Oxford University Press, 2018) 57.

[95] The term is borrowed from Novelli, Bongiovanni and Sartor (n 87) 198.

[96] The term is borrowed form Bathaee (n 1) 907.

[97] The potential liabilities that could be incurred due to non-compliance with other regulations, such as competition law, financial market regulations or even criminal liability, as Bathaee points out, are not assessed at this point. See ibid.

[98] Novelli, Bongiovanni and Sartor (n 87) 197.

[99] I Rahwan et al, 'Machine Behaviour' (2019) 568 *Nature* 477, 480.

performance criterion defined by the data it processes.[100] This design highlights the inherent inflexibility of algorithms, even in systems characterised as autonomous. As noted in discussions distinguishing automation from autonomy, even systems that utilise non-deterministic software, exhibit emergent properties, or engage in learning behaviours remain designed, programmed, and ultimately controlled by human operators in some capacity.[101]

Autonomy in computational entities is distinct from human autonomy, and the two should not be conflated when analysing contract formation under English law.[102] The systems relevant here are Narrow AI: task-specific tools trained and deployed for designated contracting functions. Crucially, the system's performance criteria and operational constraints are set by humans through choices about parameterisation, weighting, and data design.[103] Accordingly, the system's outputs fall within a human-defined scope of authorisation, supporting attribution to the operator as the contracting party.

Prominent scholars reinforce this notion. In examining the legal status of autonomous software agents, it has been observed that AI systems do not act in their own self-interest but rather in the interests of their users.[104] Similarly, analyses of the intentional stance of AI systems emphasise that their purposes are assigned by humans.[105] This attribution will continue to apply 'until and unless they learn to determine their own ends and purposes and the will to propel themselves in their pursuit'.[106]

However, algorithms are general and abstract to reach an end, but their programming includes at the same time the guidelines with which, through the

[100] A Tamò-Larrieux, 'Decision-Making by Machines: Is the "Law of Everything" Enough?' (2021) 41 *Computer Law & Security Review* 105541, 3 www.sciencedirect.com/science/article/abs/pii/S0267364921000145 last accessed.

[101] E Mik, 'AI as a Legal Person?' in JA Lee, RM Hilty and KC Liu (eds), *Artificial Intelligence and Intellectual Property* (Oxford University Press, 2021) 419, 424.

[102] DG Johnson and M Verdicchio, 'AI Anxiety' (2017) 68 *Journal of the Association for Information Science and Technology* 2267, 2268.

[103] Autonomy in software denotes functional independence in executing tasks within objectives and constraints set by humans; it is not autonomy in the sense of self-authored ends. These systems are Narrow AI, deployed for specific tasks rather than general-purpose agency. For a technical characterisation of algorithms in this context, Adam Wellstead, Tanya Heikkila and Matthew Wood define algorithms as 'computational sets of rules that computer programmers input into technologies to "design in" particular patterns of decision-making, which generate outputs the technologies are designed to solve'. A Wellstead, T Heikkila and M Wood, 'Fourth Industrial Revolution and Algorithms: New Challenges for Policy Design' in B Guy Peters and G Fontaine (eds), *Fourth Industrial Revolution and Algorithms: New Challenges for Policy Design* (Edward Elgar, 2022) 194. The doctrinal relevance is that parameterisation, weighting, and data design are human choices that help define the scope of what the operator has authorised the system to do.

[104] Teubner (n 17) 43.

[105] G Sartor, 'Cognitive Automata and the Law: Electronic Contracting and the Intentionality of Software Agents' (2009) 17 *Artificial Intelligence and Law* 253, 265.

[106] Lipshaw makes this statement when referring to algorithmic systems as tools for decision-making. See JM Lipshaw, 'Lawyering Somewhere between Computation and Will to Act' in LA Di Matteo and others (eds), *The Cambridge Handbook of Lawyering in the Digital Age* (Cambridge University Press, 2021) 327, 338.

use of dynamic solutions such as data analysis of the market conditions, they are instructed to reach their overarching or top-level goals. Although the decision-making processes of machine-learning algorithms, particularly those using deep learning, can be opaque or difficult to explain, this lack of transparency does not undermine their fundamental purpose. These systems remain firmly tied to the objectives for which they were designed. Their inflexibility – the adherence to the overarching goal – strengthens the argument that their outcomes can be attributed to the operator. Even in highly autonomous systems, the overall objective remains constant, with adaptability limited to the refinement and updating of decision parameters through data analysis.[107] As emphasised, '[e]ven the most autonomous system has not created or programmed itself',[108] underscoring the direct connection between the system's results and the human decisions behind its design and programming. In conclusion, the lack of flexibility – defined as the inability of an algorithmic system to deviate from the purpose for which it was programmed – supports the assertion that the algorithm's programming, or more precisely, its parameterisation, encapsulates the intention and, ultimately, the consent of its operator.[109]

Programming an AI system revolves around achieving specific goals set by its operators and defining the means permitted for the machine or program to accomplish those goals.[110] Contrary to the perception that autonomous systems replicate human intelligence, they are typically designed to address specific problems or optimise pre-defined tasks that may be too complex, hazardous, or time-sensitive for direct human intervention.[111] As noted, while these systems operate within creator-imposed objectives and conditions, they process and understand details that may remain unknown to their operators.[112] This characteristic strengthens the argument that the outcome of the system's actions remains attributable to the human operator, as the system's inflexibility ensures alignment with its programmed goals. It is important to emphasise that '[t]he

[107] M Gal, 'Algorithmic Challenges to Autonomous Choice' (2018) 1 *Michigan Technology Law Review* 59, 63.

[108] E Mik, 'AI as Legal Person?' in JA Lee, RM Hilty and KC Liu (eds), *Artificial Intelligence and Intellectual Property* (Oxford University Press, 2021) 419, 424.

[109] In algorithmic contracts, consent is effectively programmed—broadly defined but inherently inflexible. A useful analogy is that of a vending machine, albeit a highly sophisticated one. Unlike a traditional vending machine that dispenses pre-packaged soft drinks, an AI system combines ingredients based on specific user inputs and dynamically adjusts pricing using various parameters, such as raw material costs and availability. Despite the complexity and diversity of possibilities, the range of outcomes remains finite and predefined by the programming. This inflexibility means that: '[w]hile it might indeed be difficult to explain what patterns in the data are being caught by the model of a machine learning algorithm (…) the general principles and operational logics of these systems are very-well known. That's why they are used in the first place'. Bucher (n 99) 57. A further analogy points in the same direction: Lord Sales compares coding algorithms to laws, noting that '[a] coding algorithm, like laws, is a rule established in advance to govern a future situation'. Lord Sales, 'Algorithms, Artificial Intelligence and the Law' (2021) 105 *Judicature* 23, 26.

[110] Bathaee (n 1) 906.

[111] Mik (n 108) 425.

[112] Scholz (n 83) 134.

operations of the algorithms cannot in any way be equated with the mental operations of humans'.[113] They are merely operations, not independent cognitive processes. From a systems perspective, the decision-making process is best understood as a procedural mechanism rather than a function involving autonomous cognition.

## B. Delegation and Responsibility: Contractual Freedom and Its Limits

Where the preceding subsection approached attribution from a system perspective, this subsection shifts the focus to the human party to the contract. It examines the enabling factors through which the deployment of an algorithmic system can be attributed to a contracting party as an exercise of that party's will, rather than as an autonomous act of the system itself. The emphasis therefore moves from the internal operation of the system to the human decisions.

The principle of contractual freedom provides a fundamental justification for operators' decisions to enter into algorithmic contracts. This principle aligns with the voluntary nature of contracts, as emphasised by the concept of the meeting of the minds,[114] which underscores the parties' willingness to be bound by their agreement.

However, the paternalistic underpinning of contract law compels us to search for additional justifications that extend beyond the mere alignment with the preferences of the contracting party.[115] While Lord Green's assertion that 'parties become bound by contract when, and in the manner in which, they intend and contemplate becoming bound'[116] may be read as a strong statement of contractual autonomy, delegation of contracting decisions to an algorithm tests whether autonomy alone can carry the full justificatory load. One of the most frequently cited arguments by scholars addressing this issue involves adopting a broader view of the concept of intention.[117] It has been suggested that employing a clear-box algorithm to negotiate a contract may suffice to demonstrate an intent to be bound within a reasonably defined range of outcomes.[118]

[113] Teubner (n 17) 48.
[114] Kerr (n 13) 190.
[115] For a more in-depth analysis of paternalism and its limits to the principle of freedom of contract in contract law see P Cserne, 'Paternalism and Contract Law' in K Grill and J Hanna (eds), *The Routledge Handbook of the Philosophy of Paternalism*, 1st edn (Routledge, 2018) 293 293–310; WH van Boom and Anthony Ogus, 'Introducing, Defining and Balancing "Autonomy v. Paternalism"' (2010) 3 *Erasmus Law Review* 1, 1–5.
[116] Lord Greene MR in *Eccles v Bryant* [1948] Ch 93.
[117] See, eg, E Mik, 'From Automation to Autonomy: Some non-existing problems in Contract Law' (2020) 26 *Modern Law Review* 205; M Ebers, 'Artificial Intelligence, Contracting and Contract Law: An Introduction' in M Ebers, C Poncibò and M Zou (eds), *Contracting and Contract Law in the Age of Artificial Intelligence* (Hart Publishing, 2022) 29.
[118] Scholz (n 83) 136.

Despite the close conceptual proximity between the constructs of intent and agreement,[119] it is imperative to recognise that they constitute distinct prerequisites for establishing the validity of a contractual formation. However, many of the academic attempts to resolve the problem of the attribution of the outcome of the decision-making process from the system to the human operator tend to conflate the two, giving more weight to the intent and ignoring the agreement.[120] From the perspective of the objective theory of contractual intent, the formation of a contract does not rely on the subjective assent of the parties but rather on an unequivocal expression of the intent to enter into a contract, without the need for explicit reference to a specific contract.[121] But the concept of the 'meeting of the minds' pertains not to intention per se, but rather to the substance of the agreement. It encompasses a shared understanding between the parties concerning the nature and extent of the rights and responsibilities associated with the exchange of promises.[122] The agreement, based on the concept of the meeting of the minds, remains a factor yet to be identified in algorithmic contracts.

The justification for algorithmic contracts can be further understood by examining the principle of contractual freedom, which encompasses multiple dimensions. Firstly, contractual freedom represents the autonomy to decide whether to enter into a contractual agreement and to do so on terms chosen by the contracting party. This autonomy highlights the connection between contractual freedom and the concept of will.[123] Secondly, it refers to the principle that there should be no imposition of obligations or liabilities in the absence of consent properly incorporated into a valid contract.[124] When examined from both an affirmative and a negative perspective, the concept of contractual freedom demonstrates a stronger correlation with the notion of agreement than with that of intention. It is intrinsically intertwined with the decision-making process and the mutual understanding of the parties involved. Thus, the concept of contractual freedom provides a strong foundational basis for developing a theory of attribution in the context of AI system operators.

The freedom to contract therefore implies autonomy. In the pursuit of advancing this theory, we must answer the following questions: what does this autonomy encompass? Does it also include how the party wants the decision-making process to be carried out? Does the 'choice paradox' have a place in the freedom of contract?[125] Is this admissible within the framework of contractual freedom and contract law in a broader context?

[119] Liu (n 35) 139.

[120] For example, Vincent Ooi, identifies attribution rules with the intention to be bound. Ooi (n 5) 98.

[121] This is the perspective adopted by Chopra and White to resolve what they call 'the contractual problem'. See Chopra and White (n 51) 374.

[122] Kerr (n 13) 190.

[123] Davies (n 65) 6.

[124] Andrew, Cartwright and Beatson (n 25) 4.

[125] Michel Gal refers to the 'choice paradox' as 'the fact that the decision to turn over one's choices to an algorithm is, itself, an act of choice'. Gal (n 107) 63.

Freedom of contract is a concrete expression of the principle of private autonomy.[126] Autonomy, broadly defined, is the fundamental right of individuals to shape their own future through voluntary actions and decisions. Within the realm of private law, this principle is closely tied to freedom of contract.[127] This autonomy would enable individuals, in the unfettered exercise of their contractual freedom, to determine the means by which they decide or define the substance of their obligations. The answer to the second, third and fourth questions would be straightforward and simple if we borrow Friedman's words: '[i]f we take autonomy seriously as a principle for ordering human affairs, (…) people must abide by the consequences of their choices'.[128] Introducing the theory of attributing cognitive states to these entities adds depth to the discussion, suggesting that '[t]he rights and obligations issuing from the contract will fall upon the user, not because he wanted these rights and obligations, but because he has chosen to delegate to his SA [software agent] the formation of contracts in his name'.[129] The choice paradox illustrates that opting to let an algorithm make decisions is, in itself, a deliberate choice and an exercise of contractual freedom, carrying its own consequences: individuals are compelled to adhere to the repercussions stemming from their decision-making actions. It is a decision-making action to delegate the decision-making process. The 'substitution of human judgement by the program output of a machine' is chosen.[130]

Human agency is paramount in the development, deployment, and operation of algorithms. From their design and programming to decisions about usage, timing, and purpose, humans play a central role. Furthermore, the programming of algorithms with data reflects human influence in their selection, organisation, and content.[131] To summarise, the concept of contractual freedom, which pertains to the ability of each party to determine the content of their offer according to their preferences, remains unrestricted by the paternalistic boundaries imposed by contract law. It is fundamentally the principle of contractual freedom, in conjunction with the broader principle of party autonomy, that furnishes the solution to the challenge of integrating the meeting of the algorithm with the meeting of the minds. In essence, this means that the parties involved have the autonomy to shape their contractual arrangements according to their own terms and preferences, aligning the algorithmic process with the traditional notion of mutual understanding and consent in contract formation.

[126] TMJ Mollers, 'Working with Legal Principles – Demonstrated Using Private Autonomy and Freedom of Contract as Examples' (2018) 14 *European Review of Contract Law* 101, 113.

[127] van Boom and Ogus (n 115) 1.

[128] C Fried, *Contract as Promise: A Theory of Contractual Obligation* (Oxford University Press, 2015) 113.

[129] Sartor (n 105) 280.

[130] Balkin in Scholz (n 24) 145.

[131] JM Balkin, '2016 Sidley Austin Distinguished Lecture on Big Data Law and Robotics: The Three Laws of Robotics in the Age of Big Data' (2017) 78 *Ohio State Law Journal* 1217, 1223.

## C. English-law Constraints on Attribution and Delegation: Certainty and Mistakes

Up to this point, the algorithmic system has been analysed as a medium through which contractual communications are exchanged.[132] As shown in chapters five and six, contract formation occurs when the system completes the relevant operations, and the operator's knowledge of the resulting terms is addressed through an adapted availability-and-accessibility approach, drawing on principles developed for email contracting. This chapter has developed the account of attribution and delegation-based responsibility. The remaining question is what English-law doctrines may nevertheless defeat enforcement.

This section addresses the principal English-law constraints that may defeat enforcement even where attribution to the operator and delegation-based responsibility are accepted. It begins with certainty and 'agreements to agree', because algorithmic contracting is often said to generate indeterminate obligations at the point when the parties decide to rely on an automated system. Questions of mistake are considered separately below.

A recurring objection is that algorithmic contracting produces incomplete arrangements akin to 'agreements to agree'. Scholz raises this concern in discussing whether algorithmic contracts might be characterised as incomplete contractual arrangements.[133] However, the doctrines on uncertain, incomplete agreements or agreements to agree do not apply to algorithmic contracts, because algorithmic contracts differ fundamentally from these categories. In uncertain or incomplete agreements, the terms remain undefined even after the parties reach an agreement.[134] In contrast, in algorithmic contracts, any uncertainty exists prior to contract formation – at the ex ante stage. Once the system generates the offer, the precise terms have already been established by the algorithm. These terms are clearly defined and presented as part of the offer made to the potential counterparty.

Consequently, where an algorithmic system generates an offer with determinate terms that are presented to the counterparty, the certainty requirement is, in principle, satisfied because the terms are specified and ascertainable at the point of acceptance. The key point is that the terms are fixed by the system before the counterparty decides whether to contract, even if the operator could not predict ex ante which terms would be produced. On that basis, algorithmic contracts are not properly analysed as uncertain agreements or 'agreements to agree'.

The central point is that, in algorithmic contracting, any indeterminacy typically concerns the ex ante decision to rely on an automated evaluation process, rather than the determinacy of the contractual terms presented to the counterparty. Once the system specifies the terms in the offer, those terms are certain

[132] See ch 5, section IV.
[133] Scholz (n 83) 141–42.
[134] See, eg, *Hillas and Co v Arcos Ltd* (1932) 147 LT 503; *Teekay Tankers v STX Offshore & Shipbuilding* [2017] EWHC 253 (Comm); *Wells v Devani* [2019] UKSC 4.

and ascertainable, even if the operator could not foresee precisely which terms the system would generate. The relevant 'uncertainty' is therefore upstream, at the stage of delegating evaluation and selection to the system before an offer is made. Conceptually, this is not unlike a party choosing a decision procedure (including one involving chance) to settle what terms it will offer, although the claimed advantage of algorithmic decision-making is that the procedure is not arbitrary but data-driven and presented as objective.[135]

Algorithmic contracting introduces two analytically distinct sources of unintended outcomes. Some are automation mistakes – coding errors or technical malfunctions (for example, network failures) within deterministic processes; others are autonomy mistakes – misalignments between the parties' reasonable expectations and the outcome even where no technical error has occurred. Frattone distinguishes these categories and stresses that autonomy mistakes do not imply independent 'ends' in the system, but rather that 'what you ask for is what you get', even when the system's strategy is counter intuitive.[136]

The doctrinal point is that not every surprising or disadvantageous output can be re-described as a 'mistake' capable of defeating enforcement. Relief should be exceptional and targeted to cases where the counterparty is effectively taking advantage of an output that is recognisable as an error in the communication of a term. On this view, the user of the system ordinarily bears the risk of the system's performance, but English-law mistake doctrine can operate as a gatekeeper where it would be unreasonable for the other party to rely on the output as a genuine manifestation of assent – particularly where the malfunction is obvious. This 'no snap-up of an obvious error' logic is captured in the unilateral mistake analysis: if a reasonable counterparty would know an offer contains a mistake undermining consent, there is no objective consent to that term.[137]

A judicial illustration of how this 'recognisable error' inquiry can be framed in an automated setting is provided by *Quoine*. The Singapore Court of Appeal (International) rejected as 'wholly artificial' the attempt to reconstruct a hypothetical human 'meeting on the exchange floor' where the parties had chosen automated contracting with no human element at the point of execution.[138] Mance IJ (dissenting) nevertheless framed the mistake inquiry by asking whether a reasonable trader, with knowledge of the circumstances, would have recognised the trades as the product of a fundamental error.[139]

Paterson and Bant highlight the attempt to assimilate an algorithm to a worker or employee and criticise that move as 'artificial', precisely because 'the operations

[135] Scholz (n 24) 142.
[136] Frattone (n 6) 413–14.
[137] M Oliver, 'Contracting by Artificial Intelligence: Open Offers, Unilateral Mistakes, and Why Algorithms Are Not Agents' (2021) 2(1) *Australian National University Journal of Law and Technology* 45, 85–86.
[138] *Quoine (n 59)* [97].
[139] Ibid [195].

of an algorithmic system can[not] be substituted with those of a person'.[140] The value of this debate for English law is to clarify the structure of the inquiry: whether the counterparty could reasonably treat the system's output as the operator's objective assent, or whether the output was sufficiently and recognisably erroneous that enforcement would reward opportunism. A harder case is where the system is configured not merely to produce an erroneous output, but to capitalise on predictable counterparty mistakes; in that setting, the issue is no longer a mere 'snap-up' but the deliberate engineering of advantage-taking through automated design.[141]

This mistake-based 'gatekeeping' function also fits the broader attribution story: parties may, in general, choose to accept contracts entered by the software they have selected within pre-set parameters, but mistake doctrine supplies a limited corrective where a software-specific failure produces an unintended term and the counterparty's reliance is unreasonable.[142] That combination – general enforceability plus a narrow 'obvious error' gatekeeper – aims to preserve commercial certainty without allowing the automated setting to become a licence for exploitation.[143]

## V. Conclusion: from Algorithmic Interaction to Enforceable Assent

In algorithmic contracts, as opposed to the binary choice of heads or tails in a simple coin toss, the available options can be infinitely diverse, a characteristic that carries consequences. Instead of chance, it is data analysis that comes into play. But whether it happens due to chance or data analysis, 'the option of entrusting contracts to AI (...) entails the consequence of a loss of predictability and control over these processes'.[144] It has been cautioned that algorithms possess the capacity to influence decision-making by employing parameters that can extend beyond human control and understanding.[145] This raises the question of whether algorithmic contracts jeopardise autonomy. Are algorithmic contracts autonomy-endangering

[140] JM Paterson and E Bant, 'Automated Mistakes: Vitiated Consent and State of Mind Culpability in Algorithmic Contracting' in E Bant (ed), *The Culpable Corporate Mind*, 1st edn (Hart Publishing, 2023) 268.
[141] *Quoine* (n 59) [99], [103]–[104]; Frattone (n 6) 416; Paterson and Bant (n 141) 271.
[142] The term 'gatekeeper' is borrowed from Mark B Wessman, who describes the doctrine of consideration as a 'gatekeeper' device controlling access to contractual enforcement: MB Wessman, 'Should We Fire the Gatekeeper? An Examination of the Doctrine of Consideration' (1993) 48 *University of Miami Law Review* 45.
[143] Ooi (n 5) 19 arguing that, in 'Software-Specific Cases', mistake can be used with an extended objective approach to 'promote commercial certainty' while allocating risk to the software-user 'except where it would [be] unreasonable (…) to take advantage of a clear mistake'.
[144] Poncibò (n 6) 216.
[145] Gal (n 112) 104.

agreements?[146] The contention here is that they do not. The argument asserts that the choice paradox aligns with and harmonises with the fundamental principles of contract law, particularly freedom of contract and private autonomy. Rather than undermining autonomy, algorithmic contracts operate within the framework of these principles, preserving the individual's ability to make choices while leveraging the efficiency of algorithmic systems. The chapter's central claim is that, under English law, delegating contractual decision-making to an AI system can be treated as an exercise of private autonomy that supports attribution and presumptive enforceability, subject to limited doctrinal constraints.

This chapter wraps up the discussion by introducing the subjective element into the analysis of algorithmic contracts. While traditional objective contract theory traditionally focuses solely on the outcome of the decision-making process, a comprehensive examination of algorithmic contracts has required a meticulous consideration of the process itself. This requires sustained attention to the delegated process in a way that standard accounts of contracting typically do not foreground, as decision-making was typically directly attributable to the human agent, who carried it out personally or through a representative. However, one of the distinctive aspects of algorithmic contracts lies in the delegation of the decision-making process to the artificial intelligence system, which constitutes one of the two fundamental purposes in the contracting process through algorithms.

The technical perspective on reconciling the 'meeting of the algorithms' with the 'meeting of the minds' underscores the crucial role played by algorithmic inflexibility in addressing concerns surrounding the perceived unpredictability of algorithms. Algorithms, by design, adhere rigorously to predefined rules and instructions, resulting in a lack of deviation on their part from their programmed behaviour. The relevant stabilising feature is not that outputs are predictable, but that the system's objectives and constraints remain operator-set, which supports attribution even where the internal path to the output is opaque. Consequently, the consistent and rule-bound nature of algorithms contributes to establishing a sense of reliability and control, even in the face of assertions regarding the inherent unpredictability of algorithms. It is worth noting that algorithms do not themselves set an overarching goal; rather, this goal is invariably established by their operator. '[W]hat is erased is not so much the human, but *how* humans make judgements and decisions.'[147]

[146] The term autonomy-endangering agreements, borrowed from Stephen A Smith, refers to arrangements that threaten an individual's autonomy by significantly restricting their range of choices. SA Smith, 'Future Freedom and Freedom of Contract' (1996) 59 *Modern Law Review* 167, 167–87.
[147] MI Ganesh, 'The Ironies of Autonomy' (2020) 7 *Humanities and Social Sciences Communications* 1, 4.

# 8

# Conceptual Synthesis

## I. Introduction

Algorithmic contracts as analysed in this book are not a special type of contracts.[1] They remain subject to ordinary principles of contract law. Their distinctiveness lies in how contractual outcomes are produced: the formation process is mediated by algorithmic systems, including artificial intelligence, that perform functions previously carried out through human communication and decision-making. In Calo's sense, this makes such contracting 'exceptional' insofar as it places pressure on settled concepts and requires adaptation in their application.[2] The need for a shift in focus has been brought about by a transition from automation to autonomy within the domain of algorithmic contracts: contemporary systems can generate and refine contractual offers and terms by processing external data in real time, without direct human involvement at the point of formation. The central claim developed across the book is that these practices can still satisfy the requirement of consent, but only if contract doctrine is applied with: (i) a clear account of when formation occurs at system level, and (ii) how the resulting agreement and its terms are attributable to the human operators behind the systems.

This final chapter consolidates that account. It presents the framework as a unified explanation of when algorithmic contracts are formed, how knowledge of formation and terms can be attributed to the operator, and how system-level convergence can be translated into legally meaningful consent. It then tests the framework comparatively across common law and civil law approaches to consent, sketches its relevance beyond the specific class of algorithmic contracts examined in this book, and identifies the limits of the enquiry and the most important directions for future work.

[1] Contracts are usually classified in terms of their subject matter rather than the way they are formed. See DL Kidd Jr and WH Daughtrey Jr, 'Adapting Contract Law to Accommodate Electronic Contracts' (2000) 26 *Rutgers Computer & Technology Law Journal* 215, 269.

[2] See R Calo in CL Reyes, 'A Unified Theory of Code-Connected Contracts' (2021) 46 *Journal of Corporation Law* 981, 998.

## II. From Deconstruction to Reconstruction: A Unified Account of Formation and Consent

An algorithmic contract is a contractual agreement where both involved parties engage in decision-making processes operating an algorithmic system rooted in artificial intelligence.[3] This book focuses on this particular case type: agreements formed through interacting algorithmic systems on both sides of the transaction. The analysis does not assume that algorithmic contracting is limited to such settings but uses them as the clearest site in which system-level formation and the attribution of consent come apart.

'[W]hat is new and different about algorithmic contracts is [that,] in the process of forming an algorithmic contract, computer programs step into decision-making roles previously performed by humans.'[4] Within that formation process, the system performs two analytically separable functions. First, it operates as a means of communication between contracting parties. Second, it operates as a mechanism for decision-making, generating offers and acceptances (or their functional equivalents) in pursuit of specified objectives.

Each function has both an internal and an external dimension, the former concerning the interactions between the system and its human operator, and the latter between the system and the environment within which it operates. This process of deconstructing algorithmic contracts has revealed significant interdependence among the diverse roles and functions involved, necessitating the adoption of a holistic view.

The external communication function can be described in two stages: first, the system dynamically communicates the offer to the potentially public environment, and second, it enters into a relationship with the system that presents the corresponding matching offer (or acceptance), at which point a binding agreement can be said to be formed. The content of what is communicated is often dynamic, in the sense that it is generated or refined in light of the data available in the relevant environment at the relevant time. The internal function of the communication role is relevant to the extent that how interactions between the system and the human operator take place determines whether the attribution of knowledge to the latter can be justified.

The decision-making function also divides into internal and external dimensions. Internally, the operator formulates objectives, parameters, constraints, and escalation rules that define the space within which the system is authorised to act. Externally, the system processes data from its environment to pursue those objectives and to generate contractual outputs. This structure clarifies why algorithmic

[3] This definition is consistently employed in this book to provide a narrower conceptualisation of the term algorithmic contract as articulated by Lauren Scholz. See ch 1, section II.A

[4] LH Scholz, 'Algorithms and Contract Law' in W Barfield (ed), *The Cambridge Handbook of The Law of Algorithms* (Cambridge University Press, 2020) 141, 141.

contracting raises questions that cannot be resolved by focusing on 'communication' or 'decision-making' alone: the formation event occurs externally at system level, but the legal significance of that event depends on internal attribution to an operator.

The deconstruction of roles and functions within the AI systems behind algorithmic contracts yields three linked questions that must be answered to show the compatibility of algorithmic contracting with contract law. The first is temporal: when, precisely, does formation occur where systems interact at speed and without direct human involvement at the moment of agreement? The second question is epistemic: how can knowledge of formation and content be attributed to an operator where the operator may learn of the agreement only after the fact? The third question concerns consent more directly: how can the operator be treated as assenting not only to the fact of agreement, but to the system's construction of the result – its selection of terms – where those terms may not have been known in detail at the moment of formation? The overall framework is designed to explain how a meeting at system level can be translated into legally meaningful consent at the level of the contracting parties. In other words, how can the meeting of the algorithms be equated with the meeting of the minds?

The conclusion reached is that the requirement of consent can be satisfied in this setting, and algorithmic contracts of the type analysed here can therefore be enforceable. The account developed in chapters five to seven can be stated as a single sequence of propositions that links formation, attribution, and consent.

First, the timing of formation is anchored at the point of system-level convergence. In the case type examined here – where both parties contract through interacting algorithmic systems – agreement crystallises when the systems' outputs align in a manner that performs the function of offer and acceptance. The resulting formation event is operationally comparable to contracting practices in which agreement is established at a determinate moment through direct interaction – analogous, in that limited sense, to face-to-face dealing – even though the interaction now occurs between systems rather than between the individuals behind them. What matters for this analysis is not an ideal of 'face-to-face' exchange, but the fact that the interaction is sufficiently responsive to permit a coincidence of interests within a narrow time window. In practice, that responsiveness commonly depends on technical compatibility between systems, including the ability to exchange and process information in a mutually intelligible form.

The external communication function operates at system level: the relevant exchanges occur between systems rather than between the individuals behind them. If the decisions generated by the algorithms are to be binding, then they must be applicable to the individuals operating them at the exact moment of the contract formation: this reveals a key area to consider in the assessment of algorithmic contracts. It is the bridge connecting the internal communication role with the internal decision-making process, and as such it highlights the interdependence between the different roles and functions involved in algorithmic contract formation. In other words, the algorithmic contract cannot be considered to be formed through the convergence of two algorithms unless knowledge of contract formation can be solidly attributed to the operators behind the system.

Having scrutinised the external function of the communicative role, the analysis turns to its internal dimension: the interactions between the operator and the system, together with the internal dimension of the decision-making function. This shift matters because the attribution of system-level communications and outcomes depends on the operator's governance of the system – how contracting authority is conferred, constrained, and monitored. Internally, the decision-making function is structured by the operator's formulation of objectives, parameters, and rules, which define the framework within which the system is authorised to generate contractual outputs.

The 'proxy problem' concerns attribution where contracting is mediated by an algorithmic system: how can the operator be treated as having legally relevant knowledge of the agreement's conclusion and its terms when formation occurs at system level and the operator's awareness may arise only later? This issue has been addressed by drawing on the logic of the postal rule and related doctrines that allocate risk once a communication leaves one party's control and enters the other's designated sphere. The point is not that the law assumes contemporaneous subjective knowledge; rather, it constructs a formation event and assigns responsibility by reference to the parties' chosen mechanisms of communication. Applied to algorithmic contracting, once a contractual communication is received by the party's designated system, it falls within that party's sphere of responsibility. Where the operator has authorised the system to receive and generate contractual communications – and has reasonable means of access to the relevant outputs – knowledge of formation and content can be attributed to the operator as legally relevant knowledge notwithstanding delayed awareness. This approach aligns with objective contract theory: contractual obligation turns on outward manifestation, and here the decisive manifestation is the operator's deployment and authorisation of the system as an instrument for contracting on its behalf.

The timing of formation and the attribution of knowledge that an agreement has been concluded can largely be explained within the objective theory of contract, together with doctrines on receipt and risk allocation.

A fuller account is required, however, for the attribution of knowledge relating to the *content* of the contract – specifically, for the processes by which terms are delineated and then treated as binding on the human operator. In algorithmic contracting, the operator may authorise a system to generate and accept terms within a defined space while being unaware of the particular terms produced at the moment of formation. Algorithmic contracting therefore relocates the legally decisive manifestation of consent to the point of authorisation and system governance, rather than to a contemporaneous act of human agreement at the moment of formation. The analysis must therefore do more than establish that a contract exists: it must explain how terms generated through that authorised process can be attributed to the operator in a manner consistent with the consent requirement.

This completes the inquiry into how system outputs are communicated and how, under rules of attribution, they may constitute the operator's legally relevant knowledge and assent notwithstanding delayed awareness.

From this point, the analysis turns to the internal dimension of the decision-making function and its implications for the system's external operation. Internally, the operator establishes objectives, parameters, constraints, and escalation rules; what lies beyond the operator's control is the particular data the system encounters in its external environment. That dependence on external inputs is one practical dimension of the shift from automation to autonomy, and it underscores the interdependence between decision-making and communication in algorithmic contracting.

The account then comes full circle. External communication proceeds within the internally defined authorisation framework: the system communicates, analyses data, draws conclusions, formulates its offer, and identifies a correlative offer, in a manner shaped by the operator's predefined objectives and constraints. Algorithmic contracts of the type analysed here thus operate as bilateral agreements in which a general offer is delineated or specified by the system by reference to its parameters and prevailing market conditions. These contracts become binding when the systems' outputs meet in a way that performs the function of reciprocal offer and acceptance. The communication process between algorithms is synchronous and instantaneous in the relevant sense: the systems exchange and process communications in near real time, such that the formation event is effectively contemporaneous and leaves no meaningful interval for human intervention at the point of agreement. As a result, assent is concurrent. This interaction is the meeting of the algorithms. However, it is imperative to underline that this phenomenon takes place mainly at the systems level.

Human subjectivity remains central to algorithmic contract formation in two related respects. First, it is reflected in the system's design and operation: where a system is configured to pursue the operator's objectives within defined parameters and constraints, the contractual outputs it generates can be understood as implementing an authorised intention. Second, it is reflected in the operator's deliberate decision to deploy that system as the vehicle through which contracting authority is exercised. That act of authorisation – combined with the system's operation within the authorised space – provides the doctrinal bridge from system-level convergence to attributable assent. In this way, the meeting of the algorithms becomes the meeting of the minds.

In conclusion, the symbiotic relationship inherent in algorithmic contracts can be seen to be complete and solid, but the understanding we have achieved and the identification of the legal grounds for the strength of this relationship would not have been possible without the deconstruction of it into smaller units of analysis. This has revealed the complementary nature of the communication role and the decision-making process and the intricate interplay between them: one might even say that they are the yin and yang of algorithmic contracts. The nature of the communication role is intimately tied to the decision-making process, and, conversely, the decision-making process cannot be completely understood without reference to the nuances of the communication role. The information communicated outwards occurs unbeknownst to the operator, but it emanates from a decision-making process consciously selected and shaped by this same operator. Conversely, the tangibility of this output is contingent on the decision-making function since the absence of external communication and data collection impedes the decision-making process even if the overarching goal was set by the operator. In essence, the interdependence of communication and decision-making summarises the holistic functioning of algorithmic contracts.

## III. Comparative Perspectives: Common Law vs. Civil Law in Algorithmic Contracts

### A. Algorithmic Contract Formation Beyond English Law

As comparative lawyers have long emphasised, contract law remains a particularly natural site for cross-border comparison because it sits at the intersection of economic exchange and the practical demands of international transactions.[5]

English contract law has been used in this study as a stringent reference point for testing whether established formation categories can accommodate algorithmic contracting. The concluding task is to consider the portability of that account beyond common-law doctrine. That inquiry necessarily extends to civil-law systems, not because they lack adaptive capacity, but because the translation problem is framed differently: the same architecture of system-level formation and party-level attribution must be articulated through civil-law vocabularies of declaration, validity, and vitiation. The existing literature remains comparatively thin, which makes the exercise exploratory rather than exhaustive.[6]

There are well-known methodological differences between common-law and civil-law approaches to contract formation and consent; yet, as one comparative account observes, 'there is a difference of approach between common and civil law systems, but the end effect is probably the same'.[7] The analysis therefore proceeds in two stages. It first outlines, at a general level, how the theory developed in chapters five to seven – system-level formation combined with party-level attribution – maps onto common-law and civil-law vocabularies. That general comparison is designed

[5] H Kötz, 'Comparative Contract Law' in M Reimann and R Zimmermann (eds), *The Oxford Handbook of Comparative Law*, 2nd edn (Oxford University Press, 2019) 903–06.

[6] See, eg, B Sáenz de Jubera Higuero, 'Retos jurídicos de la inteligencia artificial en el ámbito del consentimiento contractual: una aproximación general' [2023] *Revista de Derecho Civil* 41, 41–70. D Andrés Malham and A Huerta Fernández, 'Naturaleza de la intervención de la inteligencia artificial en la formación del consentimiento contractual: análisis desde la óptica jurídica venezolana' [2021] *Icade: Revista de la Facultad de Derecho* 1, 1–24.

[7] EM Weitzenboeck, 'Electronic Agents and the Formation of Contracts' (2001) 9(3) *International Journal of Law and Information Technology* 204, 210.

to isolate which elements of the account are genuinely structural and which are artefacts of English doctrinal expression. It then turns to a civil-law instantiation through Spanish contract law. English law remains the primary baseline because it supplies the formation-and-attribution framework developed throughout the study; Spanish law is introduced subsequently as a concrete test of how that framework translates into a codified, validity-oriented idiom, and as a useful reference point for a wider family of systems influenced by similar civil-law traditions.

## B. Translation of the Formation-Attribution Architecture

The theory's organising commitments can be stated without importing additional doctrine. Formation is located at system level, at the point of convergence where outputs perform the function of offer and acceptance. The binding significance of that formation event depends on attribution: system outputs are treated as legally relevant only insofar as they are attributable to an operator by virtue of the operator's authorisation and governance of the system. The resulting 'meeting of the minds' is doctrinal rather than psychological, and must be understood as objective manifestation plus attribution, rather than as contemporaneous subjective awareness of terms. The comparative task is therefore one of translation: the theory identifies the operative event (convergence) and the connecting mechanism (attribution through use) and asks how those elements are expressed and constrained in civil-law terms.

The baseline is most comfortable where civil-law oriented accounts begin from the same descriptive premise: automated interaction can be a contracting setting, even though the decisive moment is marked by the 'lack of intervention by a natural person' and by the 'distancing' of human actors from the formation event.[8] That framing corresponds closely to the theory's premise that the formation event is external and system-mediated, and that doctrinal work must be performed by attribution and consent rather than by insisting upon contemporaneous subjective awareness.

This is the setting in which an instrument-based attribution model does its principal work. Herbosch's analysis makes explicit a comparative anchor: if AI systems are treated as 'legal objects' and 'mere tools', the contracting party remains the human user, and party status is not relocated to the system.[9] On that footing, it becomes coherent to locate the legally relevant declaration in the user's decision to deploy and authorise a contracting instrument within a defined space, and to treat the system's outputs as attributable implementations of that authorised use.

[8] T Rodríguez de las Heras Ballell, 'Human Autonomy and Artificial Intelligence Agency. A New Dilemma for Contract Law: Automated Contracting or Intuitu Homini Contracts' (2025) 11(1) *The Italian Law Journal* 377, 383.

[9] M Herbosch, 'Contracting with Artificial Intelligence: A Comparative Analysis of the Intent to Contract' (2023) 87(4) *RabelsZ* 672, 697. Herbosch uses the term 'user' to refer to the person deploying the AI system; in this study, this corresponds to the 'operator'. See ch 1, section II.B.

Herbosch states, in this connection, that for formation purposes 'only the human user of the AI system is capable of being a party to the contract'.[10] The point is not terminological. Once the system is treated as an instrument rather than a consenting subject, both common-law and civil-law vocabularies can describe the same structure without conceptual distortion: the outward commitment lies in the authorisation-and-governance act, and the system-level outputs matter juridically only through attribution to that act.

The main point of strain is not the attribution architecture as such, but the risk of conceptual slippage in the vocabulary used to describe it. Herbosch identifies the intuitive difficulty where an AI system may enter into contracts 'unforeseen by its user', making it 'obscure' how intent to form a specific contract – or a 'meeting of the minds' – can be present where the user may not even know that a contract is being entered into.[11] That difficulty is predictable because 'meeting of the minds' is easily read as psychological simultaneity. The phrase remains usable only if defined narrowly as the doctrinal conclusion that follows from objective manifestation and attribution, namely, that the party's outward manifestation is constituted by authorisation and governance, and that the system's outputs are attributable manifestations produced within that authorised space. That is also the natural civil-law translation: the inquiry is not whether the system 'had will', but whether the party can be treated as having made (or adopted) a declaration through the authorised instrument.

The theory begins to strain, however, precisely at the points where it depends most heavily on relocating assent to ex ante authorisation and treating system convergence as the operative moment of formation. The first strain concerns the sufficiency of authorisation as consent to outcomes whose particular terms are not known at formation. Herbosch's analysis helps rather than hinders this relocation, by tying intent to objective expectations and by classifying AI systems as tools. His account stresses that the intent requirement can be formulated 'too generally', thereby 'unnecessarily obstructing' contract formation via AI systems.[12] The comparative sensitivity lies in how far the legal system is prepared to treat the party as having consented to a space of dynamically generated terms through that authorisation alone. Civil-law analysis tends to police the boundary through attribution limits and vitiation doctrines rather than by treating contemporaneous subjective awareness as a formation prerequisite.

A second strain arises from doubts about the legal equivalence of system outputs to the kinds of declarations ordinarily treated as contract-forming acts. Rodríguez de las Heras centres the 'attribution of the actions performed by the automated system'.[13] She also notes that diminished user control 'could be a factor for non-attribution of the decision or for assuming/presuming a consent-invalidating error'.[14] This caution

[10] ibid 699.
[11] ibid 672–73.
[12] ibid.
[13] Rodríguez de las Heras (n 8) 395.
[14] ibid 386.

matters for the convergence account because it shows that functional equivalence cannot simply be asserted at the level of system behaviour. Even if outputs can be described operationally as offer and acceptance, civil-law analysis may require a principled basis for treating those outputs as the party's declaration and may withhold attribution where governance and control conditions fail. The authorisation-and-governance proposition is intended to supply exactly that basis, but the comparative lesson is that the translation step must be explicit: the legally relevant declaration is not the system's output taken in isolation, but the operator's decision to deploy and authorise the system to generate outputs with contractual meaning within defined limits, coupled with the conditions that justify attribution.

Finally, the comparative account must take contractual safety valves seriously, because civil-law materials place much of the stabilising work in vitiation and non-attribution, rather than in any requirement of contemporaneous subjective awareness. Fortuna treats mutual misunderstanding as capable of remaining a formation problem: a mistake 'in the communication between the parties' can 'prevent the formation of the agreement'.[15] At the same time, the literature cautions against assuming that 'mistake' will always be an available corrective for machine-generated defects. Fortuna observes that software malfunction is unlikely to qualify as a 'recognisable mistake', and that mistake doctrine 'does not appear to be applicable to a large part of AI systems error'.[16] This limitation is closely connected to a further civil-law intuition about opposability: Frattone notes that misalignment between the human party's will and the consent expressed by the machine can remain 'a purely internal fact' and therefore cannot be invoked against a counterparty who relies on the agreement.[17] The corrective pressure thus shifts to the point at which the defect becomes legally external – where the output affects the outward manifestation that counts as consent – rather than remaining a purely internal mismatch.[18]

In parallel, there is a practical tendency to manage error through ex ante allocation: contractual clauses may characterise cases of error as 'malfunctioning' and distribute risk accordingly.[19] The same tendency is visible in mediated contracting environments, where the platform's framework terms can foreclose avoidance by rendering trades 'irreversible', thereby converting what would otherwise be framed as a defect question into a risk-allocation question.[20] Without treating platform practices as doctrinal substitutes, the comparative implication is straightforward: if enforceability is grounded in attribution to authorised system use, the legitimacy of that attribution depends on an explicit account of the corrective architecture – non-attribution where control conditions fail, vitiation where defects undermine

[15] J Fortuna, 'Contractual Mistake, Smart Contract and Artificial Intelligence from a Comparative Perspective' (2024) 15(2) *Comparative Law Review* 69, 87.

[16] ibid 98–99.

[17] C Frattone, 'Algorithmic mistakes in machine-made contracts: the legal consequences of errors in automated contract formation' (2023) 28 *Uniform Law Review* 407, 423.

[18] ibid.

[19] Rodríguez de las Heras (n 8) 393.

[20] Frattone (n 17) 424.

valid consent, and contractual risk allocation where the parties (or intermediaries) have allocated the risk of machine error in advance.

On this evidence, the theory can be made comparably applicable to civil-law systems by treating its core architecture as a translation framework rather than a common-law artefact. System-level convergence identifies the operational point at which contractual outputs align; civil-law doctrine then asks whether those outputs can be characterised as party agreement through attributable declarations made via authorised tools, and whether validity should be denied or obligations adjusted through non-attribution, vitiation, or risk allocation when governance fails or error undermines meaningful consent. The organising structure – formation at convergence, binding force through attribution grounded in authorisation and governance, and safety valves for defective outputs – can therefore be expressed in civil-law idioms without treating AI as a legal subject, while remaining faithful to the theory's objective definition of 'meeting of the minds' as manifestation plus attribution.

## C. Spanish Law as a Translation Test: Concurrence, Attribution, and Validity Controls

Spanish law is introduced here not to provide an exhaustive comparison of formation doctrine, but to test three translation questions that matter for algorithmic contracting. The first concerns the moment of formation: whether the theory's system-level convergence can be expressed as the point at which consent is manifested through the concurrence of offer and acceptance, notwithstanding that the relevant communications are generated and processed by interacting systems. The second concerns attribution: whether the operator's authorisation and governance of the system can be framed as the legally relevant declaration (or adoption) such that the system's outputs count as attributable manifestations for formation purposes. The third concerns stability and defect: whether the safety-valve structure assumed by the theory can be articulated through Spanish validity and vitiation categories, so that enforceability does not rest on a requirement of contemporaneous subjective awareness of terms.

The general comparative discussion has shown that civil-law analysis is comfortable treating automated interaction as a contracting setting, while insisting that the binding effect must be justified through attribution and policed through validity and vitiation controls. The Spanish sections that follow therefore do not ask whether algorithmic contracts are 'possible' under civil law in the abstract; they ask how, in a codified idiom, the convergence event is legally characterised, how it is attributed to the parties, and how defects are managed when machine-generated outputs misstate or distort what can properly be treated as consent.

Spanish contract law is a useful civil-law instantiation because it articulates formation and validity through a codified vocabulary that is structurally different from the common-law decomposition of agreement, consideration, and intention, while remaining committed to outward manifestation as the basis of contractual obligation. The Civil Code does not proceed by offering an abstract definition of 'contract' for general purposes; instead, it identifies the existence of a contract through agreement to bind and specifies the essential requirements for validity. Article 1254 provides that a contract exists once one or more persons agree to bind themselves, in relation to another or others, to give something or render a service.[21] Article 1261 then sets out the essential requirements: consent of the contracting parties, a certain object which is the subject matter of the contract, and cause of the obligation to be established.[22] The relevance of these provisions for present purposes is not taxonomic. They show that Spanish law is organised around a formation-and-validity structure in which consent is necessary but not sufficient, and in which validity controls operate alongside the formation inquiry.

The first translation question concerns the moment of formation. Spanish law identifies consent through a concurrence test. Article 1262 states that consent is manifested by the concurrence of the offer and the acceptance of the thing and the cause that are to constitute the contract.[23] The provision functions as a rule for determining when consent has been manifested, rather than as a psychological definition of will. That structure is compatible, in principle, with locating formation at system level in the algorithmic setting. If the relevant contractual communications are generated and processed through interacting systems, the convergence account can be restated in Spanish terms as follows: formation occurs at the point at which attributable outputs satisfy the concurrence condition – when the system-mediated offer and the system-mediated acceptance align in relation to the thing and the cause that constitute the contract. The key comparative point is that the translation does not require contemporaneous human awareness of the particular terms at the instant of formation; it requires that the legally relevant manifestations can be identified as offer and acceptance and that they can be attributed to the parties.

The second translation question concerns attribution. The theory's common-law articulation grounds attribution in ex ante authorisation and governance: the operator configures objectives, parameters, constraints, and escalation rules, and thereby authorises the system to generate contractual outputs within a defined space. The Spanish vocabulary can accommodate the same move without treating the system as a consenting subject. The decisive manifestation remains human: the party's legally relevant act is the decision to deploy and authorise a contracting instrument to make and receive communications with contractual meaning. The system's outputs then matter only insofar as they are treated as attributable manifestations produced within that authorised framework. The translation task is therefore not to locate 'will' in the system, but to identify how the party's

[21] Art 1254 Código Civil [CC]. Royal Decree of July 24, 1889 by which the Civil Code is published. 'Gaceta de Madrid' núm. 206, de 25/07/1889.

[22] Art 1261 CC.

[23] Art 1262 CC.

outward act of authorisation and the system's operation within the authorised limits together provide the basis for treating the system's offer and acceptance as the party's manifested consent under Article 1262.

This translation also helps to clarify the relationship between Spanish consent and the common-law requirement of intention to create legal relations. Common law isolates 'intention' as a distinct, objectively assessed condition of enforceability. Spanish law does not present an identical doctrinal element in the same form; instead, the Civil Code ties contractual obligation to agreement to bind (Article 1254) and to manifested consent through offer and acceptance (Article 1262), while policed by validity requirements (Article 1261). The point for present purposes is therefore functional rather than taxonomic. Spanish doctrine can sustain an objective account of contracting without reproducing the common-law category of 'intention to create legal relations' as a separate element. Binding commitment is expressed through agreement to bind and manifested consent, rather than through enquiry into undisclosed mental states. On that basis, the relocation of legally decisive assent to ex ante authorisation and governance can be presented as a civil-law-compatible account of manifested commitment, provided the system output is attributable and falls within the authorised contracting space.

The third translation question concerns stability and defect. Spanish law does not treat formation as a consent-only inquiry; the existence of a valid obligation is conditioned by object and cause (Article 1261). In algorithmic contracting, this matters because defects may arise not only from misalignment between offer and acceptance but also from errors that undermine what may properly be treated as valid consent, or that call into question the satisfaction of other essential requirements. The comparative claim is therefore not that attribution automatically yields enforceability. Rather, attribution explains why system-level outputs can bind in principle, while the validity and vitiation structure supplies the corrective architecture for defective outputs. In this sense, the Spanish framework supports the broader comparative conclusion developed in III.B: enforceability in automated formation must be paired with an explicit account of how the legal system responds when outputs are defective in legally salient ways, without insisting on contemporaneous subjective awareness as the universal condition of binding force.

On this limited basis, the theory developed in chapters five to seven is portable into Spanish law as a matter of conceptual structure. System-level convergence can be expressed through the concurrence criterion for manifested consent; authorisation and governance can be framed as the party's outward act that justifies attributing system outputs to that party; and validity-oriented controls can perform the stabilising work where defects undermine what may properly be treated as consent. The remaining questions are jurisdiction-specific: the conditions under which authorisation is sufficiently bounded to justify attribution, and the circumstances in which defects should be treated as formation failure, vitiation, or risk allocation. Those questions define the proper scope of any Spanish-specific extension of the account.

## IV. Expanding the Impact of this Research Beyond Algorithmic Contracts

The analysis in this work has been developed using a stringent case type within the broader category of algorithmic contracting: transactions in which both parties act through interacting algorithmic systems and the formation event occurs at system level. That focus is deliberate. It isolates the setting in which formation timing and party-level attribution come apart most sharply, and it therefore provides a clear test for whether established formation categories can accommodate AI-mediated contracting without relocating legal personality or consent to the system. The implications of the account are not confined, however, to that bilateral configuration. The same formation-attribution architecture is capable of illuminating neighbouring technologies and contracting contexts in which a system generates communications, selects terms, or executes commitments within an operator-defined space.

Algorithmic contracts sit within a wider family of agent-mediated contracting tools. The 'intelligent agent technology', 'electronic agents' or, simply, the 'contracting agents' envisioned by Ian Kerr are responsive to the same complexities and synergies highlighted above. Lerouge's 'electronic agents' 'search the Internet for some alternatives across a range of prices and valued-added options proposing an adequate transaction, while taking our demand into account. The agent will even conduct the entire negotiation based on designated criteria'.[24] The operational pattern is familiar across that literature: an agent is deployed to identify transactional opportunities, evaluate them against user-defined preferences, and communicate with counterparties in a manner that can culminate in commitment. In the framework developed here, those functions map onto the two roles performed by the contracting system. Externally, the system communicates with its environment and with other systems to locate and coordinate on matching offers and acceptances (or their functional equivalents). Internally, the system implements a decision-making mandate set by the operator through objectives, parameters, constraints, and escalation rules. This framework addresses what Chopra and White termed the 'contracting problem',[25] adapting it to the contemporary capabilities offered by AI-based systems.

The framework developed here complements Sartor's examination of 'cognitive automata' or 'software agents' by focusing specifically on the transfer of knowledge from the system to its operator. In contrast with Sartor's emphasis on the legal importance of these entities when autonomous decision-making is delegated to them, the present study has taken a different approach to this issue. Instead of focusing on the presumed cognitive capacity of the system, the focus is on the

[24] J-F Lerouge, 'The Use of Electronic Agents Questioned Under Contractual Law: Suggested Solutions on a European and American Level' (1999) 18 *John Marshall Journal of Computer & Information Law* 403, 405.

[25] S Chopra and LF White, 'Artificial Agents and the Contracting Problem: A Solution via an Agency Analysis' (2009) 2009 *University of Illinois Journal of Law, Technology & Policy* 363, 363.

presence of the operator's subjectivity, such that, from a technological point of view, the output of the decision-making process conforms to the overarching goal sought by its operator.

This study may also shed new light on the concerns expressed by Gunter Teubner about the unpredictable behaviours of self-learning algorithms, reminiscent of the reservations expressed by Lauren Scholz about so-called black-box algorithms, although these are related to the issues of algorithmic transparency or explainability.

As we have seen in this monograph, explainability is a mathematical concept intended to illuminate the decision-making process of a trained deep neural network, and it appears in discussions of algorithmic decision-making within computer science. Although the relevance of explainability with regard to understanding the decision-making mechanism is clear, it is important to note that the main focus of this concept is on understanding the process rather than solely ensuring that the system achieves its objectives. The fact that explaining certain aspects of machine-learning models is difficult does not mean that they deviate from their intended purpose, and it does not affect the consent requirement in contract formation, where the rationale behind decision-making is only relevant if there is a defect in the consent. Despite the perceived opacity of black-box algorithms, where understanding the decision-making process can be challenging, it is crucial to recognize that this lack of transparency does not alter the fundamental goal for which the AI was programmed. Overall, the way systems pursue high-level goals, including the selection of lower-level instrumental goals, responds to the social and physical environment in which they operate, without deviating from the overall goal.[26]

## V. Limitations and Further Research

The analysis has been deliberately confined to a stringent case type of algorithmic contracting: transactions formed through interacting algorithmic systems on both sides of the exchange, examined primarily through the lens of the agreement requirement and its interaction with attribution. That focus establishes a framework for locating formation at system-level convergence and for translating that event into party-level commitment through authorisation and governance. Several adjacent questions follow from that framework and remain to be developed.

Firstly, consideration has not been analysed in any systematic way. The omission matters because algorithmic contracting relocates the legally decisive manifestation of assent to ex ante authorisation while allowing the content of the bargain to be dynamically generated at system level. A fuller account is therefore required of how reciprocity and exchange are identified and attributed where the system selects

[26] C Novelli, G Bongiovanni and G Sartor, 'A Conceptual Framework for Legal Personality and Its Application to AI' (2022) 13 *Jurisprudence* 194, 197.

terms and executes commitments within an operator-defined space. Existing literature has flagged this issue, particularly in relation to systems whose internal decision-making is opaque, but no sustained treatment has yet integrated consideration into a formation-at-convergence model.

Secondly, a comprehensive treatment of doctrinal defences remains outstanding. If formation and enforceability are grounded in attribution to authorised system use, the stabilising work necessarily shifts to the conditions under which attribution is denied and to the circumstances in which liability is avoided or adjusted. Scholarship has begun to explore mistake,[27] undue influence,[28] and related doctrines in contexts involving autonomous software, including the use of unilateral mistake as a corrective where the system produces erroneous outcomes.[29] These lines of inquiry are not peripheral. They constitute the next doctrinal layer required to complete a formation account that takes defective outputs seriously, particularly where machine-generated error does not map neatly onto classical categories.

Thirdly, consumer contracting has been left aside. The present analysis proceeds at the level of general contract formation, deliberately abstracting from the regulatory asymmetries and protective techniques that characterise consumer law. That choice is methodological. Establishing the compatibility of algorithmic formation with core formation doctrine is a precondition for asking how consumer-protective regimes should respond where automated systems personalise terms, curate choices, and conclude contracts at speed. Future work should therefore examine how consumer law duties – particularly those relating to information, transparency, and unfair terms – interact with the governance conditions that underpin attribution and with the safety-valve architecture required for defective outputs.[30]

## VI. Final Remarks

This work has argued that algorithmic contracts of the case type examined – where both parties contract through interacting systems – can satisfy the formation requirement of agreement within English contract law when formation is located at the point of system-level convergence and the resulting outputs are attributed to the parties through authorisation and governance. By deconstructing the

[27] V Ooi, 'Contracts Formed by Software: An Approach Form the Law of Mistake' (2022) 2 *Journal of Business Law* 97, 97–117.

[28] M Rizzi and N Skead, 'Algorithmic Contracts and the Equitable Doctrine of Undue Influence: Adapting Old Rules to a New Legal Landscape' (2020) 14 *Journal of Equity* 301, 301–26.

[29] M Oliver, 'Contracting by Artificial Intelligence: Open Offers, Unilateral Mistakes, and Why Algorithms Are Not Agents' (2021) 2 *Australian National University Journal of Law and Technology* 45, 83–87.

[30] Future research in this area may also benefit from a comparative analysis of the work conducted by the European Law Institute (ELI) in the field of EU Consumer Law and algorithmic decision-making. For further reference, see C Busch and others, 'EU Consumer Law and Automated Decision-Making (ADM): Is EU Consumer Law Ready for ADM?' (ELI Project on Guiding Principles and Model Rules on Algorithmic Contracts, 2023).

internal and external dimensions of the communication and decision-making roles performed by contracting systems, the analysis has shown how a system-level meeting can be translated into party-level commitment as a matter of objective manifestation and attribution. The remaining task for future scholarship is not to revisit the possibility of algorithmic contracting in the abstract, but to develop the associated doctrines – consideration, defences, and consumer protections – in a manner that preserves the legitimacy of attribution-based enforceability while providing principled correctives where system outputs are defective.

# BIBLIOGRAPHY

## Books

Beckers, A and Teubner, G, *Three Liability Regimes for Artificial Intelligence. Algorithmic Actants, Hybrids, Crowds* (Hart Publishing, 2021).
Blackstone, W, *Commentaries on the Laws of England* (Clarendon Press, 1766).
Bostrom, N, *Superintelligence: Paths, Dangers, Strategies* (Oxford University Press, 2014).
Bucher, T, *If...Then: Algorithmic Power and Politics* (Oxford University Press, 2018).
Burrows, A, *A Restatement of the English Law of Contract*, 2nd edn (Oxford University Press, 2020).
Burrows, A, Cartwright, J and Beatson, J, *Anson's Law of Contract*, 31st edn (Oxford University Press, 2020).
Cartwright, J, *Contract Law*, 3rd edn (Hart Publishing, 2016).
Chopra, S and White, LF, *A Legal Theory for Autonomous Artificial Agents* (University of Michigan Press, 2011).
Copeland, BJ, *The Essential Turing* (Oxford University Press, 2004).
Dalla Massara, T, *Il consenso annichilito. La critica radicale del contratto in Siegmund Schlossmann* (Il Mulino, 2022).
Davies. PS, *JC Smith's The Law of Contract* (Third edn, Oxford University Press 2021).
Engelberger JF, *Robots in Practice* (Kogan Page Ltd, 1980).
Filippi, PD and Wright, A, *Blockchain and the Law: The Rule of Code* (Harvard University Press, 2018).
Fried, C, *Contract as Promise: A Theory of Contractual Obligation*, 2nd edn (Oxford University Press, 2015).
Furmston, MP, *Cheshire, Fifoot and Furmston's Law of Contract*, 17th edn (Oxford University Press, 2017).
Goodfellow, I, Bengio, Y and Courville, A, *Deep Learning* (MIT Press, 2016).
Haugeland, J, *Artificial Intelligence: The Very Idea* (MIT Press, 1985).
McKendrick. E, *Contract Law: Text, Cases and Materials* (Oxford University Press, 2022).
Michie, D and Johnston, R, *The Creative Computer: Machine Intelligence and Human Knowledge* (Viking, 1984).
Mitchell, TM, *Machine Learning* (McGraw-Hill, 1997).
Mukanata, T, *Fundamentals of the New Artificial Intelligence: Neural, Evolutionary, Fuzzy and More*, 2nd edn (Computer Sciences; Springer 2008).
Nicholas, B, *An introduction to Roman law* (Oxford University Press, 2008).
Russell, S and Norvig, P, *Artificial Intelligence: A Modern Approach, Global Edition*, 4th edn (Pearson Education, Limited, 2021).
Shanahan, M, *The Technological Singularity* (The MIT Press, 2015).
Segrave, K, *Vending Machines: An American Social History*, 1st edn (McFarland & Co, 2002).
Schlossmann, S, *Der Vertrag* (Breitkopf und Härtel, 1876).
Schwab, K, *The Fourth Industrial Revolution*, 1st edn (Crown Business, 2017).
Sutton, RS and Barto, AG, *Reinforcement Learning: An Introduction*, 2nd edn (MIT Press, 2018).
Taylor, R and Taylor, D, *Contract Law Directions*, 8th edn (Oxford University Press, 2023).
Todd, P, *E-Commerce Law*, 1st edn (Routledge-Cavendish, 2005).
Turner, J, *Robot Rules: Regulating Artificial Intelligence* (Palgrave Macmillan 2019).

## Contributions to Edited Books

Abdullah, A and Yihan G, 'Making Smart Contracts a Reality' in JG Allen and P Hunn (eds), *Smart Legal Contracts* (Oxford University Press, 2022).
Bayern, SJ, 'The Nature and Timing of Contract Formation' in LA Di Matteo and M Hogg (eds), *Comparative Contract Law* (Oxford University Press, 2016).
_____ 'Algorithms, Agreements, and Agency' in W Barfield (ed), *The Cambridge Handbook of the Law of Algorithms* (Cambridge University Press, 2020).
Brownsword, R, 'Smart Transactional Technologies, Legal Disruption, and the Case of Network Contracts' in LA DiMatteo, M Cannarsa and C Poncibò (eds), *The Cambridge Handbook of Smart Contracts, Blockchain Technology and Digital Platforms* (Cambridge University Press, 2020).
Cserne, P, 'Paternalism and Contract Law' in K Grill and J Hanna (eds), *The Routledge Handbook of the Philosophy of Paternalism* (First edn, Routledge 2018).
Di Matteo, LA, 'Artificial Intelligence: The Promise of Disruption' in LA Di Matteo, C Poncibò and M Cannarsa (eds), *The Cambridge Handbook of Artificial Intelligence: Global Perspectives on Law and Ethics* (Cambridge University Press, 2022).
Durovic, M and Janssen, A, 'Formation of Smart Contracts under Contract Law' in LA DiMatteo, M Cannarsa and C Poncibò (eds), *The Cambridge Handbook of Smart Contracts, Blockchain Technology and Digital Platforms* (Cambridge Law Handbooks, Cambridge University Press, 2019).
Ebers, M, 'Artificial Intelligence, Contracting and Contract Law: An Introduction' in M Ebers, C Poncibò and M Zou (eds), *Contracting and Contract Law in the Age of Artificial Intelligence* (Hart Publishing, 2022).
Garside, A and Blycha, N, 'A Model for the Integration of Machine Capabilities into Contracts' in JG Allen, and P Hunn (eds), *Smart Legal Contracts: Computable Law in Theory and Practice* (Oxford University Press, 2022).
Kalligeropoulos, D and Vasileiadou, S, 'The Homeric Automata and Their Implementation' in SA Paipetis, (ed), *Science and Technology in Homeric Epics* (History of Mechanism and Machine Science, Springer Netherlands, 2008).
Kang, M and Halliburton, B, 'The Android of Albertus Magnus: A Legend of Artificial Being' in S Cave, K Dihal and S Dillon (eds), *AI Narratives: A History of Imaginative Thinking about Intelligent Machines* (Oxford University Press, 2020).
Katz, A and MacDonald, M, 'Autonomous Intelligent Agents and the Roman Law of Slavery' in L Edwards, S Burkhard and E Harbinja (eds), *Future Law: Emerging Technology, Regulation and Ethics* (Edinburgh University Press, 2022).
König, PD and others, 'Essence of AI: What Is AI?' in LA DiMatteo, C Poncibò and M Cannarsa (eds), *The Cambridge Handbook of Artificial Intelligence: Global Perspectives on Law and Ethics* (Cambridge University Press, 2022).
Kötz, H, 'Comparative Contract Law' in M Reimann and R Zimmermann (eds), *The Oxford Handbook of Comparative Law*, 2nd edn (Oxford University Press, 2019).
LaGrandeur, K, 'Artificial Slaves in the Renaissance and the Dangers of Independent Innovation' in S Cave, K Dihal and S Dillon (eds), *AI Narratives: A History of Imaginative Thinking about Intelligent Machines* (Oxford University Press, 2020).
Linarelli, J, 'A Philosophy of Contract Law for Artificial Intelligence: Shared Intentionality' in M Ebers, C Poncibò and M Zou (eds), *Contracting and Contract Law in the Age of Artificial Intelligence* (Hart Publishing, 2022).
Lipshaw, JM, 'Lawyering Somewhere between Computation and the Will to Act' in LA Di Matteo and others (eds), *The Cambridge Handbook of Lawyering in the Digital Age* (Cambridge University Press, 2021).
Liu, N, 'The "Contracting Problem" Revisited: Explaining the Formation of Algorithmic Contracts under the Common Law' in Z Slakoper and I Tot (eds), *Digital Technologies and the Law of Obligations* (Routledge, 2022).

March-Russell, P, 'Machines Like Us? Modernism and the Question of the Robot' in S Cave, K Dihal and S Dillon (eds), *AI Narratives: A History of Imaginative Thinking about Intelligent Machines* (Oxford University Press, 2020).
Martinelli, S and Rossi Chauvenet, C, 'From Document to Data: Revolution of Contract through Legal Technologies' in M Ebers, C Poncibò and M Zou (eds), *Contracting and Contract Law in the Age of Artificial Intelligence* (Hart Publishing, 2022).
Merli, R, Massa, I and Lucchetti, MC, 'High Frequency Trading: Technology, Regulation and Ethical Issues' in A Chochół, and J Szakiel (eds), *Achievements and Challenges of Commodity Science in the Age of Globalization* (Polish Society of Commodity Science, 2014).
Mik, E, 'The Resilience of Contract Law in Light of Technological Change' in M Furmston (ed), *The Future of the Law of Contract* (Routledge, 2020).
_____ 'AI as a Legal Person?' in JA Lee, RM Hilty and KC Liu (eds), *Artificial Intelligence and Intellectual Property* (Oxford University Press, 2021).
_____ 'AI in Negotiating and Entering into Contracts' in LA Di Matteo, C Poncibò and M Cannarsa (eds), *The Cambridge Handbook of Artificial Intelligence* (Cambridge University Press, 2022).
_____ 'Deconstructing Smart Contracts' in N Kim and E Stacy-Ann (eds), T*he Cambridge Handbook of Emerging Issues at the Intersection of Commercial Law and Technology* (Cambridge University Press, 2025)
Muller, VC, 'Philosophy of Ai: A Structured Overview' in NA Smuha (ed), *Cambridge Handbook on the Law, Ethics and Policy of Artificial Intelligence* (Cambridge University Press, 2024).
Murphy, S, 'Heron of Alexandria's on Automation-Making' in G Hollister-Short, and F James (eds), *History of Technology* (Bloomsbury Academic, 1996).
Murray, AD, 'Entering into Contracts Electronically: The Real W.W.W.' in L Edwards and C Waelde (eds), *Law and the Internet: a Framework for Electronic Commerce* (Hart Publishing, 2000).
Nolan, D, 'Offer and Acceptance in the Electronic Age' in A Burrows and E Peel (eds), *Contract Formation and Parties* (Oxford University Press, 2010).
Park, J, 'Making the Automaton Speak: Hearing Artificial Voices in the Eighteenth Century' in S Cave, K Dihal and S Dillon (eds), *AI Narratives: A History of Imaginative Thinking about Intelligent Machines* (Oxford University Press, 2020).
Paterson, JM and Bant, E, 'Automated Mistakes: Vitiated Consent and State of Mind Culpability in Algorithmic Contracting' in E Bant (ed), *The Culpable Corporate Mind*, 1st edn (Hart Publishing, 2023).
Poncibò, C, 'Remedies for Artificial Intelligence' in M Ebers, C Poncibò and M Zou (eds), *Contracting and Contract Law in the Age of Artificial Intelligence* (Hart Publishing, 2022).
Portinale, L, 'Mapping artificial intelligence: Perspectives from Computer Sciences' in M Ebers, C Poncibò and M Zou (eds), *Contracting and Contract Law in the Age of Artificial Intelligence* (Hart Publishing, 2022).
Raheni, TD and Thirumoorthi, P, 'Stochastic Artificial Intelligence: Review Article' in T Sands (ed), *Deterministic Artificial Intelligence* (Intechopen Ltd, 2020).
Sartor, G, 'Contracts Without Agreement, or Agreement by Artefacts?' in Academy of Sciences in Göttingen (ed), *Digitalisierung. Privatheit und öffentlicher Raum (Digitalization. Privacy and public space)* (Universitätsverlag Göttingen, 2020).
Sirena, P and Patti, FP, 'Smart Contracts and Automation of Private Relationships' in HW Micklitz and others (eds), *Constitutional Challenges in the Algorithmic Society* (Cambridge University Press, 2020).
Scholz, LH, 'Algorithms and Contract Law' in W Barfield (ed), *The Cambridge Handbook of The Law of Algorithms* (Cambridge University Press, 2020).
Twigg-Flesner, C, 'Online Intermediary Platforms and English Contract Law' in PS Davies and T Cheng-Han (eds), *Intermediaries in Commercial Law* (Hart Publishing, 2022).
Verbeek, P, 'Subject to Technology: On Autonomic Computing and Human Autonomy' in M Hildebrandt and A Rouvroy (eds), *Law, Human Agency and Autonomic Computing: The Philosophy of Law Meets the Philosophy of Technology* (Taylor & Francis Group, 2011).

Waddams, S, 'Contract Law and the Challenges of Computer Technology' in R Brownsword, E Scotford and K Yeung (eds) *The Oxford Handbook of Law, Regulation and Technology* (Oxford Handbooks, Oxford University Press, 2017).
Ward, M, 'Victorian Fictions of Computational Creativity' in S Cave, K Dihal and S Dillon (eds), *AI Narratives: A History of Imaginative Thinking about Intelligent Machines* (Oxford University Press, 2020).
Wellstead, A, Heikkila, T and Wood, M, 'Fourth Industrial revolution and Algorithms: New Challenges for Policy Design' in BG Peters and G Fontaine (eds), *Research Handbook of Policy Design* (Edward Elgar Publishing, 2022).
Werthmann, B, 'Legal Drafting and Automation' in LA Di Matteo and others (eds), *The Cambridge Handbook of Lawyering in the Digital Age* (Cambridge University Press, 2021).
Wilkinson, S and Giuffre, J, 'Six Levels of Contract Automation: The Evolution of "Smart Legal Contracts"' in JG Allen and P Hunn (eds), *Smart Legal Contracts: Computable Law in Theory and Practice* (Oxford University Press, 2022).
Yeung, K and Lodge, M, 'Algorithmic Regulation: An Introduction' in K Yeung and M Lodge (eds) *Algorithmic Regulation* (Oxford University Press, 2019).
Zou, M, 'When AI Meets Smart Contracts: The Regulation of Hyper-Autonomous Contracting Systems?' in M Ebers, C Poncibò and M Zou (eds), *Contracting and Contract Law in the Age of Artificial Intelligence* (Hart Publishing, 2022).

## Journals

Agnikhotram, S and Kouroutakis, A, 'Doctrinal Challenges for the Legality of Smart Contracts: Lex Cryptographia or a New, "Smart" Way to Contract?' (2019) XIX(2) *Journal of High Technology Law* 300.
Albers, G, 'Tommaso Dalla Massara: Il consenso annichilito, La critica radicale del contratto in Siegmund Schlossmann' (2023) 19 *European Review of Contract Law* 90.
Allen, T and Widdison, R, 'Can Computers Make Contracts?' (1996) 9(1) *Harvard Journal of Law & Technology* 25.
Alvisi, C, 'Drive and Agency in the Age of Algorithmic-Based Decision Making' (2022) 8(2) *Italian Law Journal* 895.
Andrade, F and others, 'Contracting Agents: Legal Personality and Representation' (2007) 15(4) *Artificial Intelligence and Law* 357.
Andrés, Malham D and Huerta, Fernández A, 'Naturaleza de la intervención de la inteligencia artificial en la formación del consentimiento contractual: análisis desde la óptica jurídica venezolana' [2021] *Icade: Revista de la Facultad de Derecho* 1, 1–24.
Andriychuk, O, 'The New EU and UK Regimes for Regulating Competition in Digital Markets: We Finally See What's on the Plate—but Do We Know How to Eat It?' (2024) 12 *Journal of Antitrust Enforcement* 195.
Balkin, JM, '2016 Sidley Austin Distinguished Lecture on Big Data Law and Robotics: The Three Laws of Robotics in the Age of Big Data' (2017) 78(5) *Ohio State Law Journal* 1217.
Barnett, RE, 'A Consent Theory of Contract' (1986) 86(2) *Columbia Law Review* 269.
Bathaee, Y, 'The Artificial Intelligence Black Box and the Failure of Intent and Causation' (2018) 31(2) *Harvard Journal of Law & Technology* 889.
Bayern, SJ, 'Offer and Acceptance in Modern Contract Law: A Needless Concept' (2015) 103(1) *California Law Review* 67.
Bellia, AJ, 'Contracting with Electronic Agents' (2001) 50 *Emory Law Journal* 1047.
Bodo, B and others, 'Tackling the Algorithmic Control Crisis: The Technical, Legal, and Ethical Challenges of Research into Algorithmic Agents' (2017) 19(1) *Yale Journal of Law & Technology* 133.

Boom, WHv and Ogus, A, 'Introducing, Defining and Balancing "Autonomy v. Paternalism"' (2010) 1 *Erasmus Law Review* 1.
Borch, C, 'High-frequency Trading, Algorithmic Finance and the Flash Crash: Reflections on Eventalization' (2016) 45(3-4) *Economy and Society* 350.
Borch, C and Lange, A, 'High-frequency Trader Subjectivity: Emotional Attachment and Discipline in an Era of Algorithms' (2017) 15(2) *Socio-Economic Review* 283.
Bringsjord, S, Bello, P and Ferrucci, D, 'Creativity, the Turing Test, and the (better) Lovelace Test' (2001) 11 *Minds and Machines* 3.
Brownsword, R and Howells, G, 'When Surfers Start to Shop: Internet Commerce and Contract Law' (1999) 19(3) *Legal Studies* (Society of Legal Scholars) 287.
Busch, D, 'MiFID II: Regulating High Frequency Trading, Other Forms of Algorithmic Trading and Direct Electronic Market Access' (2016) 10(2) *Law and Financial Markets Review* 72.
Campolo, A and Crawford, K, 'Enchanted Determinism: Power without Responsibility in Artificial Intelligence' (2020) 6 *Engaging Science, Technology, and Society* 1.
Cannarsa, M, 'Interpretation of Contracts and Smart Contracts: Smart Interpretation or Interpretation of Smart Contracts?' (2018) 26(6) *European Review of Private Law* 773.
Caria, RD, 'The Legal Meaning of Smart Contracts' (2018) 26(6) *European Review of Private Law* 731.
Carneiro, D and others, 'Online Dispute Resolution: An Artificial Intelligence Perspective' (2014) 41 *Artificial Intelligence Review* 211.
Casey, AJ and Niblett, A, 'The Death of Rules and Standards' (2017a) 92(4) *Indiana Law Journal* 1401.
_____ 'Self-Driving Contracts' (2017b) 43(1) *The Journal of Corporation Law* 1.
Cheong, T, 'A Promising Idea: Reconceptualising the Formation of Unilateral Contracts' (2014) 3 *Oxford University Undergraduate Law Journal* 1.
Chopra, S and White, LF, 'Artificial Agents and the Contracting Problem: A Solution Via an Agency Analysis' (2009) 2 *University of Illinois Journal of Law, Technology & Policy* 363.
Christensen, S, 'Formation of Contracts by Email - Is it Just the Same as the Post?' (2001) 1(1) *Queensland University of Technology Law Review.*
Cohen, J, 'Non-Deterministic Algorithms' (1979) 11(2) *Computing Surveys* 79.
Collier, J, 'What is Autonomy?' (2002) 12 *International Journal of Computing Anticipatory Systems* 212.
Cuccuru, P, 'Beyond Bitcoin: An Early Overview on Smart Contracts' (2017) 25(3) *International Journal of Law and Information Technology* 179.
Davis, KE, 'Contracts as Technology' (1950) 88 *New York University Law Review* 83.
De Elizalde, F, 'Algorithms and Law' (2022) 37(4) *Prometheus* 385.
De Moor, A, 'Contract and Agreement in English and French Law Review Article' (1986) 6(2) *Oxford Journal of Legal Studies* 275.
Defossez, D, 'Acceptance Sent Through Email; is the Postal Rule Applicable?' (2019) 11(1) *Law, State and Telecommunications Review* 23.
Dodd, JC and Hernandez, JA, 'Contracting in Cyberspace' (1998) 1 *Computer Law Review and Technology Journal.*
Easterbrook, FH, 'Cyberspace and the Law of the Horse' (1996) 1 *University of Chicago Legal Forum* 207.
Eenmaa-Dimitrieva, H and Schmidt-Kessen, MJ, 'Creating Markets in No-Trust Environments: The Law and Economics of Smart Contracts' (2019) 35(1) *Computer Law and Security Report* 69.
Eifert, M, Metzger A, Schweitzer, H and Wagner, G, 'Taming the Giants: The DMA/DSA Package' (2021) 58 *Common Market Law Review* 987.
Eiselen, S, 'The Electronic Data Interchange Agreement' (1995) 7 S *African Mercantile Law Journal* 1.
Elia, C, 'Automation of Non-Disclosure Agreements: A Roadmap for a Legal Department to Gain Advantage Using AI (Artificial Intelligence)' (2019) 12(49) *International In-House Counsel Journal* 1.
Farrell, S, Machin, H and Hinchiffle, R, 'Lost and Found in Smart Contracts Translation - Considerations in Transitioning to Automation in Legal Architecture' (2017) 25 *Journal of International Banking Law & Regulation* 1.

Fasciano, P, 'Internet Electronic Mail: A Last Bastion for the Mailbox Rule' (1997) 25(3) *Hofstra Law Review* 971.
Fortuna, J, 'Contractual Mistake, Smart Contract and Artificial Intelligence from a Comparative Perspective' (2024) 15(2) *Comparative Law Review* 69, 87.
Frattone, C, 'Algorithmic Mistakes in Machine-Made Contracts: The Legal Consequences of Errors in Automated Contract Formation' (2023) 28 *Uniform Law Review* 407.
Gal, MS, 'Algorithmic Challenges to Autonomous Choice' (2018) 1(25) *Michigan Technology Law Review* 59.
Gambino, AM and Stazi, A, 'Contract Automation from Telematic Agreements to Smart Contracts Essays' (2021) 7(1) *Italian Law Journal* 97.
Ganesh, MI, 'The Ironies of Autonomy' (2020) 7 *Humanities and Social Sciences Communications* 1
Gilmore, G, 'From Tort to Contract: Industrialization and the Law' (1977) 86(4) *Yale Law Journal* 788.
Goodrich, P, 'Habermas and the Postal Rule' (1996) 17(4-5) *Cardozo Law Review* 1457.
Grundmann, S and Hacker, P, 'Digital Technology as a Challenge to European Contract Law' (2017) 13(3) *European Review of Contract Law* 255.
Haber, S and Stornetta, WS, 'How to Time-Stamp a Digital Document' (1991) 3(2) *Journal of Cryptology* 99.
Haenlein, M and Kaplan, A, 'A Brief History of Artificial Intelligence: On the Past, Present, and Future of Artificial Intelligence' (2019) 61(4) *California Management Review* 5.
Halaburda, H, 'Economic and Business Dimensions: Blockchain Revolution without the Blockchain?' (2018) 61(7) *Communications of the ACM* 27.
Herbosch, M, 'Contracting with Artificial Intelligence: A Comparative Analysis of the Intent to Contract' (2023) 87(4) *RabelsZ* 672.
Hill, SWB, 'Flogging a Dead Horse: The Postal Acceptance Rule and Email' (2001) 17(2) *Journal of Contract Law* 151.
Howells, G, 'Protecting Consumer Protection Values in the Fourth Industrial Revolution' (2020) 43(1) *Journal of Consumer Policy* 145.
Johnson, DG and Verdicchio, M, 'AI Anxiety' (2017) 68(9) *Journal of the Association for Information Science and Technology* 2267.
Kaplan, A and Haenlein, M, 'Siri, Siri, in my Hand: Who's the Fairest in the Land? On the Interpretations, Illustrations, and Implications of Artificial Intelligence' (2019) 62(1) *Business Horizons* 15.
Karnow, CEA, 'The Encrypted Self: Fleshing Out the Rights of Electronic Personalities' (1994) 13(1) *John Marshall Journal of Computer & Information Law* 1.
Katz, DM, 'Quantitative Legal Prediction -or- How I Learned to Stop Worrying and Start Preparing for the Data-Driven Future of the Legal Services Industry' (2013) 62(4) *Emory Law Journal* 909.
Kerr, IR, 'Ensuring the Success of Contract Formation in Agent-Mediated Electronic Commerce' (2001) 1(1) *Electronic Commerce Research* 183.
Kidd, DL, Jr and Daughtrey, WH, Jr, 'Adapting Contract Law to Accommodate Electronic Contracts' (2000) 26(2) *Rutgers Computer & Technology Law Journal* 215.
Legg, S and Hutter, M, 'Universal Intelligence: A Definition of Machine Intelligence' (2007) 17 *Mind and Machines* 391.
Lerouge, JF, 'The Use of Electronic Agents Questioned Under Contractual Law: Suggested Solutions on a European and American Level' (1999) 18(2) *John Marshall Journal of Computer & Information Law* 403.
Lessig, L, 'The Law of the Horse: What Cyberlaw Might Teach' (1999) 113(2) *Harvard Law Review* 501.
Levy, KEC, 'Book-Smart, Not Street-Smart: Blockchain-Based Smart Contracts and The Social Workings of Law' (2017) 3 *Engaging Science, Technology, and Society* 1.
Linarelli, J, 'Artificial General Intelligence and Contract' (2019) 24(2) *Revue de droit uniforme* 330.
Lippi, M and others, 'Consumer Protection Requires Artificial Intelligence' (2019) 1(4) *Nature Machine Intelligence* 168.

Loke, A, 'Mistakes in Algorithmic Trading of Cryptocurrencies' (2020) 83(6) *The Modern Law Review* 1343.

Lopucki, LM, 'Algorithmic Entities' (2018) 95(4) *Washington University Law Review* 887.

Low, KFK and Mik, E, 'Lost in Transmission: Unilateral Mistakes in Automated Contracts' (2020) 136 *Law Quarterly Review* 563.

Macdonald, E, 'When is a Contract Formed by the Browse-Wrap Process?' (2011) 19(4) *International Journal of Law and Information Technology* 285.

_____ 'Dispatching the Dispatch Rule? The Postal Rule, e-Mail, Revocation and Implied Terms' (2013) 19(2) *European Journal of Current Legal Issues.*

Malik, P, Pathania, M and Rathaur, VK, 'Overview of Artificial Intelligence in Medicine' (2019) 8(7) *Journal of Family Medicine and Primary Care* 2328.

Martinelli, A, Mina, A and Moggi, M, 'The Enabling Technologies of Industry 4.0: Examining the Seeds of the Fourth Industrial Revolution' (2021) 30(1) *Industrial and Corporate Change* 161.

McCarthy, J and others, 'A Proposal for the Dartmouth Summer Research Project on Artificial Intelligence: August 31, 1955' (2006) 27(4) *Haenlein* 12.

McKendrick, E, 'English Contract Law: A Rich Past, an Uncertain Future?' (1997) 50(1) *Current Legal Problems* 25.

McLauchlan, D, 'Contract Formation and Subjective Intention' (2017) 34(1) *Journal of Contract Law* 41.

Medvedeva, M, Wieling, M and Vols, M, 'Rethinking the Field of Automatic Prediction of Court Decisions' (2023) 31 *Artificial Intelligence and Law* 195.

Mik, E, 'The Effectiveness of Acceptances Communicated by Electronic Means, or – Does the Postal Acceptance Rule Apply to Email?' (2009) 26(1) *Journal of Contract Law* 68.

_____ 'The Unimportance of Being "Electronic" or Popular Misconceptions about "Internet Contracting"' (2011) 19(4) *International Journal of Law and Information Technology* 324.

_____ 'Smart Contracts: Terminology, Technical Limitations and Real World Complexity' (2017) 9(2) *Law, Innovation and Technology* 269.

_____ 'From Automation to Autonomy' (2020) 26 *Modern Law Review* 205, 205.

_____ 'Contracts in Code?' (2021) 13(2) *Law, Innovation and Technology* 478

_____ 'Much Ado About Artificial Intelligence or: The Automation of Contract Formation' (2023) 30(4) *International Journal of Law and Information Technology* 484.

Moll, I, 'The Myth of the Fourth Industrial Revolution' (2021) 68(167) *Theoria* 1.

Mollers, TMJ, 'Working with Legal Principles – Demonstrated Using Private Autonomy and Freedom of Contract as Examples' (2018) 14(2) *European Review of Contract Law* 101.

Newell, A and Simon, H, 'The Logic Theory Machine--A Complex Information Processing System' (1956) 2(3) *IRE Transactions on Information Theory* 61.

Novelli, C, Bongiovanni, G and Sartor, G, 'A Conceptual Framework for Legal Personality and its Application to AI' (2022) 13(2) *Jurisprudence* 194.

Nussbaum, A, 'Comparative Aspects of the Anglo-American Offer-and-Acceptance Doctrine' (1936) 36(6) *Columbia Law Review* 920.

O'Shields, R, 'Smart Contracts: Legal Agreements for the Blockchain' (2017) 21(1) *North Carolina Banking Institute* 177.

Oliver, M, 'Contracting by Artificial Intelligence: Open Offers, Unilateral Mistakes, and Why Algorithms are not Agents' (2021) 2(1) *Australian National University Journal of Law and Technology* 43.

Ooi, V, 'Contracts Formed by Software: An Approach form the Law of Mistake' (2022) 2 *Journal of Business Law* 97.

Owsia, P, 'The Notion and Function of Offer and Acceptance Under French and English Law' (1992) 66(4) *Tulane Law Review* 871.

Pacini, C, Andrews, C and Hillison, W, 'To Agree or not to Agree: Legal Issues in Online Contracting' (2002) 45(1) *Business Horizons* 43.

Perillo, JM, 'The Origins of the Objective Theory of Contract Formation and Interpretation' (2001) 69(2) *Fordham Law Review* 427.
Poncibò, C, 'Artificial Intelligence as a Communication Tool in Contract Law' (2023) 31(2/3) *European Review of Private Law* 239.
Rahwan, I and others, 'Machine Behaviour' (2019) 568(7753) *Nature* 477.
Rai, K and Alla, A, 'From Phones to Emails: The Curious Case of Instantaneous Communication and Law on Contract Formation' (2021) 25(4) *Journal of Northeastern University* 1841.
Raskin, M, 'The Law and Legality of Smart Contracts' (2017) 1(2) *Georgetown Law Technology Review* 305.
Rawls, A, 'Contract Formation in an Internet Age' (2009) 10 *Columbia Science and Technology Law Review* 200.
Reyes, CL, 'A Unified Theory of Code-Connected Contracts' (2021) 46(4) *Journal of Corporation Law* 981.
Rizzi, M and Skead, N, 'Algorithmic Contracts and the Equitable Doctrine of Undue Influence: Adapting Old Rules to a New Legal Landscape' (2020) 14(3) *Journal of Equity* 301.
Robertson, M, 'Is Assent Still a Prerequisite for Contract Formation in Today's E-conomy?' (2003) 78(1) *Washington Law Review* 265.
Rodríguez de las Heras Ballell, T, 'Human Autonomy and Artificial Intelligence Agency. A New Dilemma for Contract Law: Automated Contracting or Intuitu Homini Contracts' (2025) 11(1) *The Italian Law Journal* 377.
Sáenz de Jubera Higuero, B, 'Retos jurídicos de la inteligencia artificial en el ámbito del consentimiento contractual: una aproximación general' [2023] *Revista de Derecho Civil* 41, 41–70.
Sage, N, 'Reconciling Contract Law's Objective and Subjective Standards ' (2023) 86(6) *Modern Law Review* 1422.
Sales, L, 'Algorithms, Artificial Intelligence and the Law' (2021) 105(1) *Judicature* 23.
Sartor, G, 'Cognitive Automata and the Law: Electronic Contracting and the Intentionality of Software Agents' (2009) 17(4) *Artificial Intelligence and Law* 253.
Savelyev, A, 'Contract Law 2.0: "Smart" Contracts As the Beginning of the End of Classic Contract Law' (2017) 26(2) *Information & Communication Technology Law* 116.
Savirimuthu, J, 'Online Contract Formation: Taking Technological Infrastructure Seriously' (2005) 2(1) *University of Ottawa Law and Technology Journal* 105.
Schaeffer, J and Plaat, A, 'Kasparov versus Deep Blue: The Rematch' (1997) 20 *International Computer Games Association Journal* 95.
Scholz, LH, 'Algorithmic Contracts' (2017) 20 *Stanford Technology Law Review* 128.
Schuster, E, 'Cloud Crypto Land' (2021) 84(5) *Modern Law Review* 974.
Searle, JR, 'Minds, Brains and Programs' (1980) 3 *Behavioral and Brain Sciences* 417.
Shakerin, S, 'Engineering Art' (2001) 123(7) *Stephens* 66.
Sklaroff, JM, 'Smart Contracts and the Cost of Inflexibility' (2017) 166(1) *University of Pennsylvania Law Review* 263.
Smith SA, 'Future Freedom and Freedom of Contract' (1996) 59(2) *Modern Law Review* 167.
Solan, LM, 'Contract as Agreement' (2007) 83(1) *Notre Dame Law Review* 353.
Solum, LB, 'Legal Personhood for Artificial Intelligences' (1992) 70(4) *North Carolina Law Review* 1231.
Stephens, E, 'The Mechanical Turk: A Short History of "Artificial Artificial Intelligence"' (2023) 37(1) *Cultural Studies* 65.
Stoljar, SJ, 'The False Distinction between Bilateral and Unilateral Contracts' (1955) 64(4) *Yale Law Journal* 515.
Surden, H, 'Computable Contracts' (2012) 46 *U.C. Davis Law Review* 629.
_____ 'Machine Learning and Law' (2014) 89(1) *Washington Law Review* 87.
Tan Ming En, J, 'Non-Deterministic Artificial Intelligence Systems and the Future of the Law on Unilateral Mistakes in Singapore' (2022) 34(1) *Singapore Academy of Law Journal* 91.

Teubner, G, 'Digitale Rechtssubjekte? Zum privatrechtlichen Status autonomer Softwareagenten/ Digital Personhood? The Status of Autonomous Software Agents in Private Law' (2018) 2018 *Ancilla Iuris* 35.
Treleaven, P, Barnett, J and Koshiyama, A, 'Algorithms: Law and Regulation' (2019) 52(2) *Computer* 32.
Turing, AM, 'On Computable Numbers, with an Application to the Entscheidungsproblem' (1937) 42(2) *Proceedings of the London Mathematical Society* 230.
_____ 'Computing Machinery and Intelligence' (1950) 59 *Mind* 433.
Turner, M, Traynor, M and Smith, H, 'E-Commerce Directive – UK Implementation: Electronic Commerce (EC Directive) Regulations 2002 – Worth the Wait?' (2002) 18(6) *Computer Law & Security Review* 396.
Weitzenboeck, EM, 'Electronic Agents and the Formation of Contracts' (2001) 9(3) *International Journal of Law and Information Technology* 204.
Weizenbaum, J, 'ELIZA – a Computer Program for the Study of Natural Language Communication Between Man and Machine' (1966) 9(1) *Communications of the ACM* 36.
Wendehorst, C, 'Discussion Draft: Principles for AI in Contracting (Version 2.1)' (2024) 13(1) *Journal of European Consumer and Market Law* 43.
Werbach, K and Cornell, N, 'Contracts Ex Machina' (2017) 67 *Duke Law Journal* 313.
Werner, J, 'E-commerce.co.uk – Local Rules in a Global Net' (2000) 6 *International Journal of Communications, Law and Policy* 1.
Wessman, MB, 'Should We Fire the Gatekeeper? An Examination of the Doctrine of Consideration' (1993) 48 *University of Miami Law Review* 45.
Williston, S, 'Mutual Assent in the Formation of Contracts' (1920) 14(2) *Illinois Law Review* 85
Winfield, PH, 'Some Aspects of Offer and Acceptance' (1939) 55(4) *Law Quarterly Review* 499
Xu, M, David, JM and Kim, SH, 'The Fourth Industrial Revolution: Opportunities and Challenges' (2018) 9(2) *International Journal of Financial Research* 90.

## Online Journals

Buterin, V, 'Ethereum White Paper. A next generation Smart Contract & decentralized application platform' (2013) burnersxxx.files.wordpress.com/2015/01/pdfs-ethereumwhitepaper.pdf.
Cheng, MM and Hackett, RD, 'A critical review of algorithms in HRM: Definition, theory, and practice' (2021) 31(1) *Human Resource Management Review* 100698 www.sciencedirect.com/science/article/abs/pii/S1053482219302682.
Clack, CD, Bakshi, VA and Braine, L, 'Smart Contract Templates: Foundations, Design Landscape and Research Directions' (2016) arXiv arxiv.org/abs/1608.00771.
Dellermann, D and others, 'The Future of Human-AI Collaboration: a Taxonomy of Design Knowledge for Hybrid Intelligence Systems' (2021) arXiv arxiv.org/abs/2105.03354.
Hussain, AA and Al-Turjman, F, 'Artificial Intelligence and Blockchain: A Review' (2021) 32(9) *Transactions on Emerging Telecommunications Technologies* doi.org/10.1002/ett.4268.
Kutyniok, G, 'The Mathematics of Artificial Intelligence' (2022) arXiv (Cornell University) 1 arxiv.org/abs/2203.08890/.
Mariani, MM and others, 'Artificial intelligence in innovation research: A systematic review, conceptual framework, and future research directions' (2023) 122 *Technovation* 102623 www.sciencedirect.com/science/article/pii/S0166497222001705.
Milossi, M, Alexandropoulou, E and Psannis, KE, 'AI Ethics: Algorithmic Determinism or Self-Determination? The GDPR Approach' (2021) 9 *IEEE Journals & Magazine* 58455 ieeexplore.ieee.org/document/9400809.
Schmidt-Kessen, MJ, Eenmaa, H and Mitre, M, 'Machines that make and keep promises - Lessons for contract automation from algorithmic trading on financial markets' (2022) 46 *Computer Law & Security Review* 105717 www.sciencedirect.com/science/article/pii/S0267364922000553.

Stone, R, 'Forming Contracts without Offer and Acceptance, Lord Denning and the Harmonisation of English Contract Law' (2012)(4) *Web Journal of Current Legal Issues* www.bailii.org/uk/other/journals/WebJCLI/2012/issue4/stone4.html.
Szabo, N, 'Smart Contracts' (1994) Essays on Smart Contracts, Commercial Controls and Security www.fon.hum.uva.nl/rob/Courses/InformationInSpeech/CDROM/Literature/LOTwinterschool2006/szabo.best.vwh.net/smart.contracts.html.
_____ 'Smart Contracts: Building Blocks for Digital Markets' (1996) www.fon.hum.uva.nl/rob/Courses/InformationInSpeech/CDROM/Literature/LOTwinterschool2006/szabo.best.vwh.net/smart_contracts_2.html.
_____ 'Formalizing and Securing Relationships on Public Networks' (1997) 2(9) firstmonday.org/ojs/index.php/fm/article/view/548.
Tamò-Larrieux, A, 'Decision-making by machines: Is the 'Law of Everything' enough?' (2021) 41 *Computer Law & Security Review* 105541 www.sciencedirect.com/science/article/abs/pii/S0267364921000145.

## Research Papers

Chohan, U, 'What Is a Ricardian Contract?' (2017) papers.ssrn.com/abstract=3085682 accessed 2 May 2024.
Linarelli, J, 'Artificial Intelligence and Contracts Formation: Back to Contract as Bargain?' (2023) Emerging Issues at the Intersection of Commercial Law and Technologies ssrn.com/abstract=4363410 accessed 2 May 2024.

## Conference Proceedings

Cervone, L, Palmirani, M and Vitali F, 'The Intelligible Contract' (53rd Hawaii International Conference on System Sciences 2020 Jan) 1780 hdl.handle.net/10125/63959.
Cooper, FA, Frankle, J and De Sa, C, 'Non-determinism and the Lawlessness of Machine Learning Code' (Proceedings of the 2022 Symposium on Computer Science and Law ACM, Washington DC, Nov 1, 2022) dl.acm.org/doi/proceedings/10.1145/3511265.
Gallese, C, 'The AI Act Proposal: a New Right to Technical Interpretability?' (2023 1st ISLC Online International Conference, Milan 20–22 Feb 2023) arxiv.org/pdf/2303.17558.
Grigg, I, 'The Ricardian contract' (Proceedings. First IEEE International Workshop on Electronic Contracting, 2004) 25.
Gugerty, L, 'Newell and Simon's Logic Theorist: Historical Background and Impact on Cognitive Modeling' (2006) 50(9) Proceedings of the Human Factors and Ergonomics Society Annual Meeting 880.
Korf, RE, 'Does deep blue use AI?' (Deep Blue Versus Kasparov: The Significance for Artificial Intelligence AAAI Press, 1997) 1.
Newell, A, Simon, H and Shaw, JC, 'Report on a General Problem-Solving Program' (International Conference on Information Processing June 1959) exhibits.stanford.edu/feigenbaum/catalog/sy501xd1313.
Williams, M, 'Autonomy: Life and Being' (International Conference on Knowledge Science, Engineering and Management, Belfast, 2010) 137 link.springer.com/book/10.1007/978-3-642-15280-1.

## Reports

Busch C et al, *EU Consumer Law and Automated Decision-Making (ADM): Is EU Consumer Law Ready for ADM?* (ELI Project on Guiding Principles and Model Rules on Algorithmic Contracts, 2023).
Delipetrev, B, Tsinarakli, C and Kostić, U, *AI Watch. Historical Evolution of Artificial Intelligence* (Publications Office of the European Union, 2020).
Law Commission, *Smart Legal Contracts: Advice to Government* (Law Com No. 401, 2021).

## Online Articles, Book Reviews, Websites, Blogs & Speeches (Other Secondary Sources)

'AI-Principles Overview – OECD.AI' oecd.ai/en/principles accessed 2 May 2024.
'Digital contract rules – European Commission' commission.europa.eu/business-economy-euro/doing-business-eu/contract-rules/digital-contracts/digital-contract-rules_en accessed 2 May 2024.
'Gartner Hype Cycle Research Methodology' www.gartner.com/en/research/methodologies/gartner-hype-cycle accessed 2 May 2024.
'High Frequency Trading (HFT) Definition' www.nasdaq.com/glossary/h/high-frequency-trading accessed 2 May 2024.
Barlow, JP, 'A Declaration of the Independence of Cyberspace' (1996) www.eff.org/es/cyberspace-independence accessed 2 May 2024.
Brown, S, 'Machine Learning, Explained ' (MIT Management Sloan School, 21 April 2021) mitsloan.mit.edu/ideas-made-to-matter/machine-learning-explained accessed 2 May 2024.
Browne, R, 'An AI just negotiated a contract for the first time ever — and no human was involved' www.cnbc.com/2023/11/07/ai-negotiates-legal-contract-without-humans-involved-for-first-time.html accessed 2 May 2024.
Buterin, V, 'On Public and Private Blockchains' (2015) blog.ethereum.org/2015/08/07/on-public-and-private-blockchains/ accessed 2 May 2024.
Criddle, C and Ring, S, 'Allen & Overy rolls out AI contract negotiation tool in challenge to legal industry' *Financial Times* (Dec 21, 2023) www.ft.com/content/f1aff4d0-b2c5-4266-aa0a-604ef14894bb accessed 2 May 2024
Del Mol, L, 'Turing Machines' (2018) plato.stanford.edu/entries/turing-machine/ accessed 2 May 2024.
Grigg, I, 'On the Intersection of Ricardian and Smart Contracts' (February 2015) iang.org/papers/intersection_ricardian_smart.html accessed 27 August 2025.
Lewis, PH, 'Attention shoppers: Internet is open' *The New York Times* (12 August 1994) www.proquest.com/docview/429852687?sourcetype=Newspapers accessed 2 May 2024.
McCarthy, J, 'What is Artificial Intelligence?' (2007) www-formal.stanford.edu/jmc/whatisai.pdf accessed 2 May 2024.
Mols, B, 'In Black Box Algorithms We Trust (or Do We?)' cacm.acm.org/news/in-black-box-algorithms-we-trust-or-do-we/ accessed 2 May 2024.
Nakamoto, S, 'Bitcoin: A Peer-to-Peer Electronic Cash System' (2008) bitcoin.org/bitcoin.pdf accessed 2 May 2024.
Lord Sales, Law and the Digital World (*The UK Supreme Court,* 16 April) www.supremecourt.uk/speeches/cour-de-cassation-seminar.html accessed 2 May 2024.
Tafula, M, 'A Brief History of E-commerce' michaeltefula.medium.com/a-brief-history-of-e-commerce-c4692a3b2cd9 accessed 2 May 2024.

# INDEX

www.ingramcontent.com/pod-product-compliance
Ingram Content Group UK Ltd.
Pitfield, Milton Keynes, MK11 3LW, UK
UKHW020814290926
15470UKWH00003B/1155

9 781509 992720